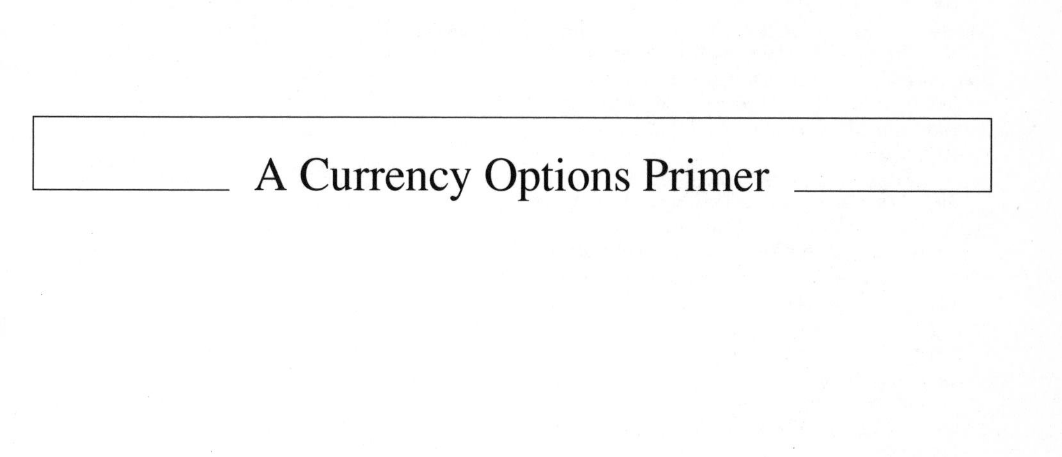
A Currency Options Primer

Wiley Finance Series

A Currency Options Primer
Shani Shamah

Risk Measures in the 21st Century
Giorgio Szegö (Editor)

Modelling Prices in Competitive Electricity Markets
Derek Bunn (Editor)

Inflation-Indexed Securities: Bonds, Swaps and Other Derivatives, 2nd Edition
Mark Deacon, Andrew Derry and Dariush Mirfendereski

European Fixed Income Markets: Money, Bond and Interest Rates
Jonathan Batten, Thomas Fetherston and Peter Szilagyi (Editors)

Global Securitisation and CDOs
John Deacon

Applied Quantitative Methods for Trading and Investment
Christian L. Dunis, Jason Laws and Patrick Naïm (Editors)

Country Risk Assessment: A Guide to Global Investment Strategy
Michel Henry Bouchet, Ephraim Clark and Bertrand Groslambert

Credit Derivatives Pricing Models: Models, Pricing and Implementation
Philipp J. Schönbucher

Hedge Funds: A resource for investors
Simone Borla

A Foreign Exchange Primer
Shani Shamah

The Simple Rules: Revisiting the art of financial risk management
Erik Banks

Option Theory
Peter James

Risk-adjusted Lending Conditions
Werner Rosenberger

Measuring Market Risk
Kevin Dowd

An Introduction to Market Risk Management
Kevin Dowd

Behavioural Finance
James Montier

Asset Management: Equities Demystified
Shanta Acharya

An Introduction to Capital Markets: Products, Strategies, Participants
Andrew M. Chisholm

Hedge Funds: Myths and Limits
Francois-Serge Lhabitant

The Manager's Concise Guide to Risk
Jihad S. Nader

Securities Operations: A guide to trade and position management
Michael Simmons

Modeling, Measuring and Hedging Operational Risk
Marcelo Cruz

Monte Carlo Methods in Finance
Peter Jäckel

Building and Using Dynamic Interest Rate Models
Ken Kortanek and Vladimir Medvedev

Structured Equity Derivatives: The Definitive Guide to Exotic Options and Structured Notes
Harry Kat

Advanced Modelling in Finance Using Excel and VBA
Mary Jackson and Mike Staunton

Operational Risk: Measurement and Modelling
Jack King

Interest Rate Modelling
Jessica James and Nick Webber

A Currency Options Primer

Shani Shamah

John Wiley & Sons, Ltd

Published 2004 John Wiley & Sons Ltd, The Atrium, Southern Gate, Chichester, West Sussex PO19 8SQ, England

Telephone (+44) 1243 779777

Email (for orders and customer service enquiries): cs-books@wiley.co.uk
Visit our Home Page on www.wileyeurope.com or www.wiley.com

Other Wiley Editorial Offices

John Wiley & Sons Inc., 111 River Street, Hoboken, NJ 07030, USA

Jossey-Bass, 989 Market Street, San Francisco, CA 94103-1741, USA

Wiley-VCH Verlag GmbH, Boschstr. 12, D-69469 Weinheim, Germany

John Wiley & Sons Australia Ltd, 33 Park Road, Milton, Queensland 4064, Australia

John Wiley & Sons (Asia) Pte Ltd, 2 Clementi Loop #02-01, Jin Xing Distripark, Singapore 129809

John Wiley & Sons Canada Ltd, 22 Worcester Road, Etobicoke, Ontario, Canada M9W 1L1

Wiley also publishes its books in a variety of electronic formats. Some content that appears in print may not be available in electronic books.

Library of Congress Cataloging-in-Publication Data

Shamah, Shani.
A currency options primer / Shani Shamah.
p. cm. – (Wiley finance series)
Includes bibliographical references and index.
ISBN 0-470-87036-2 (cloth : alk. paper)
1. Options (Finance). 2. Foreign exchange. I. Title. II. Series.
HG6024.A3 S47 2004
332.4′5–dc22

2003023104

British Library Cataloguing in Publication Data

A catalogue record for this book is available from the British Library

ISBN 0-470-87036-2

Typeset in 10/12pt Times by TechBooks, New Delhi, India
Printed and bound in Great Britain by Antony Rowe Ltd, Chippenham, Wiltshire
This book is printed on acid-free paper responsibly manufactured from sustainable forestry in which at least two trees are planted for each one used for paper production.

Contents

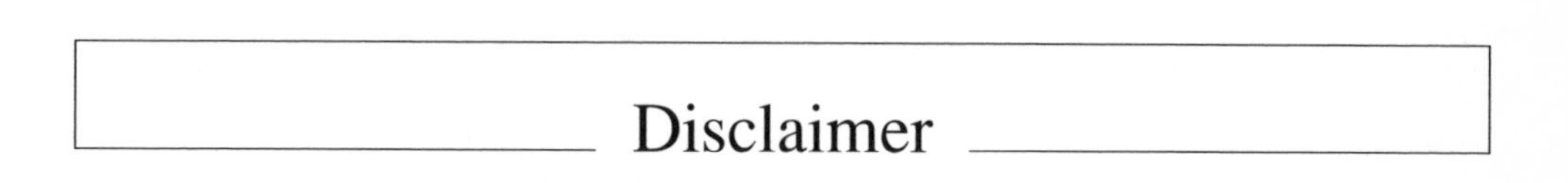

Disclaimer

This publication is for information purposes only and may contain information, advice, recommendations and/or opinions, which may be used as the basis for trading.

This publication should not be construed as solicitation nor as offering advice for the purposes of the purchase or sale of any financial product. The information and opinions contained within this publication were considered to be valid when published.

The author has attempted to be as accurate as possible with the information presented here, she does not guarantee the accuracy or completeness of the information and makes no warranties of merchantability or fitness for a particular purpose. In no event shall she be liable for direct, indirect or incidental, special or consequential damages resulting from the information here regardless of whether such damages were foreseen or unforeseen. Any opinions expressed herein are given in good faith, but are subject to change without notice.

Please note: All rates and figures used in the examples are for illustrative purposes only and do not reflect current market rates.

COPYRIGHT

1 Introduction

Since the breakdown of the Bretton Woods agreement in the early 1970s, currencies of the major industrial nations have fluctuated widely in response to trade imbalances, interest rates, commodity prices, war and political uncertainty. In recent years, the pressure of governments maintaining currency parity has led to the breakdown of quite a few exchange rate mechanisms and has, thus, reinforced the need for companies, in particular, to take active foreign exchange hedging decisions in order to prevent the erosion of profit margins.

1.1 THE FORWARD FOREIGN EXCHANGE MARKET

The forward foreign exchange market developed to assist companies protect themselves from some of the uncertainty of exchange rate movements, but foreign exchange forwards are truly appropriate for known exposures. Using them to cover contingent, variable or translation exposures could force a company to accept losses on unnecessary currency transactions. Not only that, but rival companies that leave their exposure unhedged may suddenly acquire a competitive advantage. This has, therefore, partially led to the expansion in the currency options market, which has been even more spectacular than the tremendous growth seen in the entire foreign exchange market over the past decade or so.

1.2 THE CURRENCY OPTIONS MARKET

The currency options market shares its origins with the new markets in derivative products and was developed to cope with the rise in volatility in the financial markets worldwide. In the foreign exchange markets, the dramatic rise (1983 to 1985) and the subsequent fall (1985 to 1987) in the dollar caused major problems for central banks, corporate treasurers, and international investors alike. Windfall foreign exchange losses became enormous for the treasurer who failed to hedge, or who hedged too soon, or who borrowed money in the wrong currency. The investor in the international bond market soon discovered that the risk on their bond position could appear insignificant relative to their currency exposure. Therefore, currency options were developed, not as another interesting off-balance sheet trading vehicle but as an alternative risk management tool to the spot and forward foreign exchange markets. Therefore, they are a product of currency market volatility and owe their existence to the demands of foreign exchange users for alternative hedging and exposure management techniques.

Today, the currency options market is traded in its listed form mainly in Philadelphia and Chicago. There is also a liquid interbank market or over-the-counter market (OTC), which exists in all the world's financial centres. The importance of options is that they have bought an extra dimension, i.e. volatility, to the financial markets. By using options, it is possible to take a view not only on the direction of a price change, but also on the volatility of that price.

1.3 THE ALTERNATIVES TO CURRENCY OPTIONS

Considering over-the-counter currency options versus foreign exchange forwards:

Currency options	Foreign exchange forwards
Right but not an obligation to buy/sell a currency	Obligation to buy/sell a currency
Premium payable	No premium payable
Wide range of strike prices	Only one forward rate for a particular date
Retains unlimited profit potential while limiting downside risk	Eliminates the upside potential as well as the downside risk
Flexible delivery date of currency (can buy an option longer than needed)	Fixed delivery date of currency

And considering over-the-counter currency options versus open positions:

Currency options	Foreign exchange positions
Right but not an obligation to buy/sell a currency	No obligation to buy/sell a currency
Premium payable	No premium payable
Retains unlimited profit potential while limiting downside risk	Profit and loss potential unlimited
Flexible delivery date of currency	Indefinite delivery date of currency

1.4 THE USERS

The users of the market are widespread and varied, from commercial and investment banks which take strategic currency positions or which may offset some of their over-the-counter options exposure in the listed market, to corporate treasurers and international investment managers wishing to hedge their currency risk or to increase their returns on overseas assets, to private individuals looking to hedge an offshore exposure such as the purchase or sale of a house, to those wishing to speculate in the foreign exchange market.

1.5 WHOSE DOMAIN?

As with the foreign exchange market, activity in the currency options market remains predominately the domain of the large professional players, for example major international banks, but with liquidity and the availability of margin trading, this 24-hour market is accessible to any person with the relevant knowledge. However, a very disciplined approach to trading must be followed, as both profit opportunities and potential loss are equal and opposite.

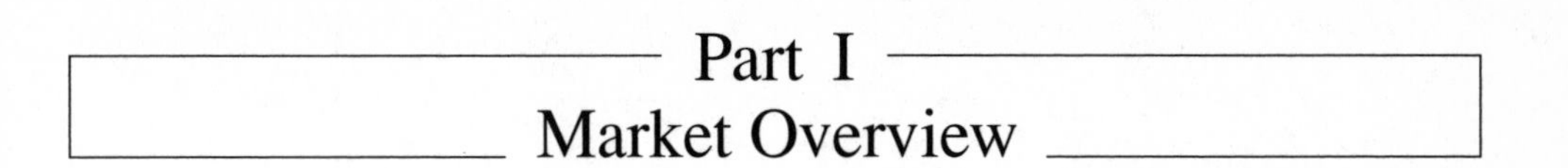

Part I
Market Overview

2
The Foreign Exchange Market

The foreign exchange market is the medium through which foreign exchange is transacted.

The foreign exchange market is a global network of buyers and sellers of currencies.

Foreign exchange or FX or Forex is all claims to foreign currency payable abroad, whether consisting of funds held in foreign currency with banks abroad, or bills or cheques payable abroad, i.e. the exchange of one currency for another.

A foreign exchange transaction is a contract to exchange one currency for another currency at an agreed rate on an agreed date.

2.1 TWENTY-FOUR-HOUR GLOBAL MARKET

It is by far the largest market in the world, with an estimated $1.6 trillion average daily turnover. What distinguishes it from the commodity or equity markets is that it has no fixed base. In other words, the foreign exchange market exists at the end of a phone, the Internet or other means of instant communications and is not located in a building nor is it limited by fixed trading hours. The foreign exchange market is truly a 24-hour global trading system. It knows no barriers and trading activity in general moves with the sun from one major financial centre to the next. The foreign exchange market is an over-the-counter market where buyers and sellers conduct business.

2.2 VALUE TERMS

Throughout history, man has traded with fellow man, sometimes to obtain desired raw materials by barter, sometimes to sell finished products for money, and sometimes to buy and sell commodities or other goods for no other reason than that there should be a profit from the transactions involved. Prehistoric "bartering" of goods and the use of cowrie shells or similar objects of value as payment eventually gave way to the use of coins struck in precious metals approximately 4000 years ago. Even in those far-off days, there was international trade and payments were settled in such coinage as was acceptable to both parties. Early Greek coins were almost universally accepted in the then known world. These coinages were soon given values in terms of their models, and a price for any raw material or finished goods could be quoted in value terms of either Greek originals or other nations' copies.

The first forward foreign exchange transactions can be traced back to the moneychangers in Lombardy in the 1500s. Foreign exchange, as we know it today, has its roots in the gold standard, which was introduced in 1880. It was a system of fixed exchange rates in relation to gold and the absence of any exchange controls.

2.3 COFFEE HOUSES

Banking and financial markets closer to those of today were started in the coffee houses of European financial centres, such as the City of London. In the seventeenth century these coffee houses became the meeting places of merchants looking to trade their finished goods and of the men who bought and sold solely for profit. It is the City of London's domination of these early markets that saw it maturing through the powerful late Victorian era and it was strong enough to survive two world wars and the depression of the 1930s.

2.4 SPOT AND FORWARD MARKET

Today, foreign exchange is an integral part of our daily lives. Without foreign exchange, international trade would not be possible. For example, a Swiss watch maker will incur expenses in Swiss francs. When the company wants to sell the watches, they want to receive Swiss francs to meet those expenses. However, if they sell to an English merchant, the Englishman will want to pay in sterling, his home currency. In between, a transaction has to occur that converts one currency into the other. That transaction is undertaken in the foreign exchange market. However, foreign exchange does not involve only trade. Trade these days is only a small part of the foreign exchange market, movements of international capital seeking the most profitable home for the shortest term dominate.

The main participants in the foreign exchange market are:

- Commercial banks;
- Commercial organisations;
- Brokers;
- The International Monetary Market (IMM);
- Speculators;
- Central Banks;
- Funds;
- Money managers; and
- Investors.

Most transact in foreign currency not only for immediate delivery but also for settlement at specific times in the future. By using the forward markets, the participant can determine today the currency equivalent of future foreign currency flows by transferring the risk of currency fluctuations (hedging or covering foreign currency exposure). The market participants on the other side of any trade must either have exactly opposite hedging needs or be willing to take a speculative position. The most common method for a participant to transact in either the spot or forward foreign currency is to deal directly with a bank, although today Internet trading is making impressive inroads.

A spot transaction is where delivery of the currencies is two business days from the trade date (except the Canadian dollar, which is one day).

A forward transaction is any transaction that settles on a date beyond spot.

These banks usually have large foreign exchange sales and trading departments that not only handle the requests from their clients but also take positions to make trading profits and balance foreign currency positions arsing from other bank business. Typical transactions in the bank market range from $1 million to $500 million, although banks will handle smaller sizes as requested by their clients at slightly less favourable terms.

2.5 ALTERNATIVE MARKETS

Besides the bank spot and forward markets, other markets have been developed that are gaining acceptance. Foreign currency futures contracts provide an alternative to the forward market and have been designed for major currencies. The advantages of these contracts are smaller contract sizes and have a high degree of liquidity for small transactions. The disadvantages include the inflexibility of standardised contract sizes, maturities, and higher costs on large transactions. Options on both currency futures and on spot currency are also available. Another technique used today to provide long-dated forward cover of foreign currency exposure, especially against the currency flow of foreign currency debt, is a foreign currency swap.

A currency future obligates its owner to purchase a specified asset at a specified exercise price on the contract maturity date.

A foreign currency swap is where two currencies are exchanged for an agreed period of time and re-exchanged at maturity at the same exchange rate.

2.6 CURRENCY OPTIONS

The essential characteristics of a currency option for its owner are those of risk limitation and unlimited profit potential. It is similar to an insurance policy, whereby instead of a householder paying a premium for insuring the house against fire risk, a company pays a premium to insure itself against adverse foreign exchange risk movement. This premium is paid upfront and is the company's maximum cost. Exchange of currencies in the future may take place at the strike price or, if it is more beneficial, at the prevailing exchange rate.

An option gives the owner the right but not the obligation to buy or sell a specified quantity of a currency at a specified rate on or before a specified date.

Options can be obtained directly from banks, known as *over-the-counter* (OTC) options, or via brokers from an exchange (exchange traded options). The essential characteristics of over-the-counter options are their flexibility. The buyer can choose the currencies, time period, strike price and the contract size, in order to match the particular exposure requirements at the time. Against this, exchange traded options have standardised time periods and strike prices and only a certain number of currencies are traded, thus limiting choice. This standardisation of option contracts promotes tradability, but this is at the expense of flexibility.

The main users of options are organisations whose business involves foreign exchange risk and may be a suitable means of removing that foreign exchange risk instead of using forward foreign exchange. Against this, in general, the exchange traded options markets will be accessed by the professional market makers and currency risk managers. The over-the-counter option market has as its market makers banks, who sometimes use the exchanges to offset risk.

Options can be and are used in many different circumstances, but essentially in times of uncertainty. For example, a British company wanting to make an acquisition in Japan is faced with a possible uncertainty in the timing of a foreign exchange cash flow. The British company does not know exactly when the acquisition will take place as there are so many factors to be put in place, but it does know that at some stage the company will have to buy Japanese yen and sell sterling. The foreign exchange risk is obviously key to a successful acquisition. By using a currency option, the treasurer would know exactly the maximum cost of the acquisition but would also have the potential for greater profit if the Japanese yen weakened.

Another example would be in a tender-to-contract situation, where a company is uncertain as to whether there will be an exposure at all. By using options, the company will know with certainty the worst rate at which it can exchange one currency for another should the company win the contract. If the exchange rate moves in its favour, the company can deal at the better prevailing rate. If, however, the company loses the contract, it will either have lost the premium, which is a known cost paid upfront, or it may have the potential for gain if the prevailing exchange rate is better than the rate agreed under the option.

Thus, normal foreign exchange transaction risk obviously gives rise to uncertainty. Using options as an insurance policy can result in peace of mind for the user. The cost, the premium, is known and paid upfront. The treasurer then knows what the worst rate would be and can budget accordingly knowing that there may be a windfall gain. Translation risk is always a difficult problem for a company. If an unrealised exposure is hedged using an option, the maximum cost is known upfront. If it is hedged using a foreign exchange forward, then there is potential for a realised loss when the foreword contract is rolled.

2.7 CONCLUDING REMARKS

In summary, activity in the foreign exchange market remains predominately the domain of the large professional players, for example major international banks such as Citibank, JP Morgan, HSBC, and Deutsche Bank. However, with liquidity and the advent of Internet trading, plus the availability of margin trading, this 24-hour market is accessible to any person with the relevant knowledge and experience.

Since currency options started trading in the early 1980s, their use by corporations and financial institutions has been growing. The importance of options is that they have brought an extra dimension, namely volatility, to the financial markets. By using options, one can take a view not only on the direction of a price change but also on the volatility of that price. Nevertheless, a very disciplined approach to trading must be followed, as options are not the type of financial product to be managed on the back of a cigarette packet.

3
A Brief History of the Market

Foreign exchange is the medium through which international debt is both valued and settled. It is also a means of evaluating one country's worth in terms of another's and, depending upon circumstances, can therefore exist as a store of value.

9000 to 6000 BC saw cattle (cows, sheep, camels) being used as the first and oldest form of money.

3.1 THE BARTER SYSTEM

Throughout history, man has traded with fellow man for various reasons. Sometimes to obtain desired raw materials by barter, sometimes to sell finished products for money and sometimes to buy and sell commodities or other goods for no other reason than to try to profit from the transaction involved. For example, a farmer might need grain to make bread while another farmer might have a need for meat. They would, therefore, have the opportunity to agree terms, whereby one farmer could exchange his grain for the cow on offer from the other farmer. The barter system, in fact, provided a means for people to obtain the goods they needed as long as they themselves had goods or services that other people were in need of.

This system worked quite well and even today, barter, as a system of exchange, remains in use throughout the world and sometimes in quite a sophisticated way. For example, during the cold war when the Russian rouble was not an exchangeable currency, the only way that Russia could obtain a much-needed commodity, such as wheat, was to arrange to obtain it from another country in exchange for a different commodity. Due to bad harvests in Russia, wheat was in short supply, while America had a surplus. America also had a shortage of oil, which was in excess in Russia. Thus Russia delivered oil to America in exchange for wheat.

Although the barter system worked quiet well, it was not perfect. For instance it lacked:

Convertibility – what is the value of a cow? In other words, what could a cow convert into?

Portability – how easy is it to carry around a cow?

Divisibility – If a cow is deemed to be worth three pigs, how much of a cow would one pig be worth?

It was the introduction of paper money, which had the three characteristics lacking in the barter system, which has allowed the development of international commerce as we know it today.

3.2 THE INTRODUCTION OF COINAGE

Approximately 4000 years ago, prehistoric bartering of goods or similar objects of value as payment eventually gave way to the use of coins struck in precious metals. An important concept of early money was that it was fully backed by a reserve of gold and was convertible to gold (or silver) at the holder's request.

1200 BC was the year cowries (shells) were viewed as money.

Even in those days, there was international trade and payments were settled in such coinage as was acceptable to both parties. Early Greek coins were almost universally accepted in the then known world. In fact, many Athenian designs were frequently mimicked, proving that coinage's popularity in design as well as acceptability.

1000 BC saw the first metal money and coins appeared in China. They were made out of base metals, often containing holes so that they could be put together like a chain.

AD 800 was when the first paper bank notes appeared in China and, as a result, currency exchange started between some countries.

3.3 THE EXPANDING BRITISH EMPIRE

Skipping through time, banking and financial markets closer to those we know today started in the coffee houses of European financial centres. In the seventeenth century these coffee houses became the meeting places of merchants looking to trade their finished products and of the entrepreneurs of the day. Soon after the Battle of Waterloo, during the nineteenth century, foreign trade from the expanding British Empire, and the finance required to fuel the industrial revolution, increased the size and frequency of international monetary transfers. For various reasons, a substitute for large-scale transfer of coins or bullion had to be found (the "Dick Turpin" era) and the bill of exchange for commercial purposes and its personal account equivalent, the cheque, were both born. At this time, London was building itself a reputation as the world's capital for trade and finance, and the City became a natural centre for the negotiation of all such instruments, including foreign-drawn bills of exchange.

3.4 THE GOLD STANDARD

The nineteenth century was when gold was officially made the standard value in England. The value of paper money was tied directly to gold reserves in America.

Foreign exchange, as we know it today, has its roots in the gold standard, which was introduced in 1880. The main features were a system of fixed exchange rates in relation to gold and the absence of any exchange controls. Under the gold standard, a country with a balance of payments deficit had to surrender gold, thus reducing the volume of currency in the country, leading to deflation. The opposite occurred when a country had a balance of payments surplus.

Thus the gold standard ensured the soundness of each country's paper money and ultimately controlled inflation as well. For example, when holders of paper money in America found the value of their dollar holdings falling in terms of gold, they could exchange dollars for gold. This had the effect of reducing the amount of dollars in circulation. Inevitably, as the supply of dollars fell, its value stabilised and then rose. Thus, the exchange of dollars for gold reserves was reversed. As long as the discipline of linking each currency's value to the value of gold was maintained, the simple laws of supply and demand would dictate both currency valuation and the economics of the country.

The gold standard of exchange sounds ideal:

- Inflation was low;
- Currency values were linked to a universally recognised store of value;
- Interest rates were low meaning inflation was virtually non-existent.

The gold standard really survived until the outbreak of World War I. Hence, foreign exchange, as we know it today, really started after this period. Currencies were convertible into either gold or silver, but the main currencies for trading purposes were the British pound and, to a lesser extent, the American dollar. The amounts were relatively small by today's standards, and the trading centres tended to exist in isolation.

The early twentieth century saw the end of the gold standard.

3.5 THE BRETTON WOODS SYSTEM

Convertibility ended with the Great Depression. The major powers left the gold standard and fostered protectionism. As the political climate deteriorated and the world headed for war, the foreign exchange markets all but ceased to exist. With the end of World War II, reconstruction for Europe and the Far East had as its base the Bretton Woods system. In 1944, the post-war system of international monetary exchange was established at Bretton Woods in New Hampshire, USA. The intent was to create a gold-based value of the American dollar and the British pound and link other major currencies to the dollar. This system allowed for small fluctuations in a 1% band.

In 1944 the Bretton Woods agreement devised a system of convertible currencies, fixed rates and free trade.

3.6 THE INTERNATIONAL MONETARY FUND AND THE WORLD BANK

The conference, in fact, rejected Keynes' suggestion for a new world reserve currency in favour of a system built on the dollar. To help in accomplishing its objectives, the Bretton Woods conference saw to the creation of the International Monetary Fund (IMF) and the World Bank. The function of the IMF was to lend foreign currency to members who required assistance, funded by each member according to size and resources. Gold was pegged at $35 an ounce. Other currencies were pegged to the dollar and under this system inflation would be precluded among the member nations.

In the years following the Bretton Woods agreement, recovery soon got under way, trade expanded again and foreign exchange dealings, while primitive by today's standards, returned. While the amount of gold held in the American central reserves remained constant, the supply of the dollar currency grew. In fact, this increased supply of dollars in Europe funded post-war reconstruction of Europe.

During the 1950s, as the Western economies grew, the supply of dollars also grew and contributed to the reconstruction of post-war Europe. It seemed that the Bretton Woods accord had achieved its purpose. However, events in the 1960s once again bought turmoil to the currency markets and threatened to unravel the agreement.

3.7 THE DOLLAR RULES OK

By 1960, the dollar was supreme and the American economy was thought immune to adverse international developments. The growing balance of payments deficits in America did not appear to alarm the authorities. The first cracks started to appear in November 1967. The British pound was devalued as a result of high inflation, low productivity and a worsening balance of payments. Not even massive selling by the Bank of England could avert the inevitable. President Johnson was trying to finance "the great society" and fight the Vietnam War at the same time. This inevitably caused a drain on the gold reserves and led to capital controls.

In 1967, succumbing to the pressure of the diverging economic policies of the members of the IMF, Britain devalued the pound from $2.80 to $2.40. This increased demand for the dollar and further increased the pressure on the dollar price of gold, which remained at $35 an ounce. Under this system free market forces were not able to find an equilibrium value.

3.8 SPECIAL DRAWING RIGHTS

In 1968 the IMF created special drawing rights (SDR), which made international foreign exchange possible.

By now markets were becoming increasingly unstable, reflecting confused economic and political concerns. In May 1968, France underwent severe civil disorder and saw some of the worst street rioting in recent history. In 1969, France unilaterally devalued the franc and Germany was obliged to revalue the Deutschemark. This resulted in a two-tier system of gold convertibility. Central banks agreed to trade gold at $35 an ounce with each other and not intercede in the open marketplace where normal pressures of supply and demand would dictate the prices.

In 1969, special drawing rights (SDR) were approved as a form of reserve that central banks could exchange as a surrogate for gold.

As an artificial asset kept on the books of the IMF, SDRs were to be used as a surrogate for real gold reserves. Although the word asset was not used, it was in fact an attempt by the IMF to create an additional form of paper gold to be traded between central banks. Later, the SDR was defined as a basket of currencies, although the composition of that basket has been changed several times since then.

During 1971 the Bretton Woods agreement was dissolved.

3.9 A DOLLAR PROBLEM

As the American balance of payments worsened, money continued to flow into Germany. In April 1971, the German Central Bank intervened to buy dollars and sell Deutschemarks to support the flagging dollar. In the following weeks, despite massive action, market forces overwhelmed the central bank and the Deutschemark was allowed to revalue upwards against the dollar. In May 1971, Germany revalued again and others quickly followed suit.

The collapse of the Bretton Woods system finally came when the American authorities acknowledged that there was a "dollar" problem. President Nixon closed "the gold window" on 15 August 1971, thereby ending dollar convertibility into gold. He also declared a tax on all imports, but only for a short time, and signalled to the market that a devaluation of the dollar versus the major European currencies and the Japanese yen was due. This resulted in:

- Widening of the official intervention bands to 2.25% versus the dollar and 1.125 versus other currencies in the EEC;
- The official price of gold was now $38 an ounce.

3.10 THE SMITHSONIAN AGREEMENT

A final attempt was made to repair the Bretton Woods agreement during late 1971 at a meeting at the Smithsonian Institute. The result was aptly known as the Smithsonian agreement. A widening of the official intervention bands for currency values of the Bretton Woods agreement from 1 to 2.25% was imposed, as well as a realignment of values and an increase in the official price of gold to $38 an ounce.

3.11 THE SNAKE

With the Smithsonian agreement the dollar was devalued. Despite the fanfare surrounding the new agreement, Germany nevertheless acted to impose its own controls to keep the Deutschemark down. In concert with its Common Market colleagues, Germany fostered the creation of the first European monetary system, known as the "snake".

This system referred to the narrow fluctuation of the EEC currencies bound by the wider band of the non-EEC currencies. This short-lived system began in April 1972. Even this mechanism was not the panacea all had hoped for and Britain left the snake, having spent millions in support of the pound.

3.12 THE DIRTY FLOAT

All the while, the dollar was still under pressure as money flowed into Germany, the rest of Europe and Japan. The final straw was the imposition of restrictions by the Italian government to support the Italian lira. It ultimately caused the demise of the Smithsonian agreement and led to a 10% devaluation of the dollar in February 1973. Currencies now floated freely with occasional central bank intervention. This was the era of the "dirty float". 1973 and 1974 saw a change in the dollar's fortunes. The four-fold increase in oil prices following the Yom

Kippur War in the Middle East created tremendous demand for dollars, and, since oil was dollar priced, the dollar soared and those used to selling dollars were severely tried. The collapse of the Herstatt and Franklin Banks followed as a direct result of this shift in the dollar's fortunes. The dollar was again under pressure during the mid-1970s, reflecting still worsening balance of payments figures. Treasury secretary Michael Blumenthal, in trying to foster export growth, constantly talked the dollar down. Europe and Japan were glad to see a lower dollar, since their oil payments were correspondingly cheaper.

In 1979 the European Monetary System (EMS) and European Rate Mechanism (ERM) were established.

3.13 THE EUROPEAN MONETARY SYSTEM

The European Monetary System (EMS), established in 1979, is where the member currencies were permitted to move within broad limits against each other and a central point. It represented a further attempt at European economic coordination. A grid was established, linking the values of each currency to each other. This attempt to "fix" exchange rates met with near extinction during 1992–1993, when built-up economic pressures forced devaluations of a number of weak European currencies.

EEC band of currency fluctuations:

- 2.25% among strong currencies within EEC;
- 6.00% among weak currencies within EEC;
- Unlimited with other countries and the dollar.

The maximum divergence from these values would be allowed, varying from 2.25% for the strong currencies to 6% for the weaker members. Divergence beyond these boundaries required the central banks of each country to intervene in the foreign exchange markets, selling the strong currency and buying the weak to maintain their relative values.

3.14 THE EXCHANGE RATE MECHANISM

In 1979, central banks agreed to another tool to intervene in the market called the Exchange Rate Mechanism (ERM). This allowed changing short-term interest rates thus punishing speculators by raising rates in the weaker currencies to discourage short selling. Members of the ERM were:

Austrian schilling
Belgium franc
Danish krone
Dutch guilder
French franc
German mark
Irish punt
Portuguese escudo
Spanish peseta

3.15 THE EUROPEAN CURRENCY UNIT

The European Currency Unit (ECU) was also introduced as a forerunner to creating a single European currency. The ECU was a currency based on the weighted average of the currencies of the common market. The ECU also served to provide a measure of relative value for each currency in the EMS.

An active market in ECU-denominated bonds developed, as well as a liquid spot and forward ECU foreign exchange market. The primary activity in these markets was to supply liquidity through speculative trading and arbitrage of the component elements of the ECU unit. All such trading activity serves to stabilise the currency and interest markets and is therefore valuable.

Throughout the 1980s, the EMS suffered occasional periods of stress in the system, with speculative runs on the weak currencies of the system resulting in frequent realignments. The German Bundesbank's conservative anti-inflationary policies were out of step with the more inflation-prone, loose money policies of Italy, France, Spain, Portugal and the Scandinavian countries. Devaluation of those currencies versus the Deutschemark was often associated with large speculative positions, which were taken by banks, hedge funds and other market participants, almost always at the expense of currency holders of the weaker countries.

3.16 THE MAASTRICHT TREATY

The quest for currency stability in Europe continued with the signing of the Maastricht Treaty in 1991. This treaty proposed that a single European Central Bank be established, much as the Federal Reserve was established in 1913 to act on behalf of American interests. After the European currencies were fixed, they were moved into a single currency, which has led to the actual replacement of many European currencies with the euro.

3.17 THE TREATY OF ROME

The Euro has actually been in the making since 1958 with the Treaty of Rome, with a declaration of a common European market as a European objective with the aim of increasing economic prosperity and contributing to "an ever closer union among the people of Europe". The Single European Act and the Treaty on European Union have built on this, introducing Economic and Monetary Union (EMU) and laying the foundations for a single currency.

1991 saw the European Council approve the Treaty of the European Union. Fifteen countries signed for the European currency – the euro.

In 1992, the EMS came under the most intense pressure in its short history. In September, Britain was forced out of the ERM after less than two years as a member. Germany's tight monetary policy proved incompatible with most of the other members of the EMS, leading to devaluations or total departures from the system.

Over the summer of 1992 through to 1993, speculators proved many times that the market in foreign exchange was far more potent a force in driving exchange rates than central banks. One of the most famous examples of speculation driving economic policy occurred when George Soros was reputed to have earned one billion dollars selling British pounds and buying dollars and Deutschemarks by "betting" against the ability of the central banks to withstand market forces.

In August 1993, the ERM intervention points were widened to 15% for most currencies, an admission by the central banks to the markets of their inability to dictate exchange rates. Speculators made fortunes in foreign exchange trading betting against central banks capacity to manage foreign exchange rates in contradiction of the divergent economies and policies of the EMS members.

Periods of volatility are always associated with speculation, as the market attempts to find an equilibrium value for each currency that reflects all of the information in the marketplace. It is, in fact, the speculators that provide most of the capital in efforts to revalue or devalue a currency, rather than central banks' current reserves. For example, when the dollar reached its all-time lows against the yen in 1995, the resulting loss of competitiveness of Japanese products globally caused a severe recession in Japan, leading to several bank failures, a real estate sell-off globally and drastic changes in economic and interest rate policies.

3.18 ECONOMIC REFORM

Similarly in early 1998, strength in the yen against all the major currencies was associated with high volatility and much speculative activity. The marketplace reacted to the political pressure imposed by America in attempting to reduce the trade imbalance between America and Japan by strengthening the yen. With the American Federal Reserve Bank intervening in the foreign exchange market to sell dollars and buy yen, coupled with treats of a trade war and import tariffs, the yen was significantly revalued upwards. However, in the second half of 1998, the financial crisis in Asia, coupled with the opinion that the yen was severely overvalued, caused the yen to tumble against the dollar and other major currencies. Speculation in the marketplace, once again, had caused economic reform.

3.19 A COMMON MONETARY POLICY

The next stage of EMU began on 1 January 1999, when the exchange rates of the participating currencies were irrevocably set. Euro area member states began implementing a common monetary policy and the euro was introduced as legal tender. The 11 currencies of the participating member states became subdivisions of the euro with Greece becoming the twelfth member on 1 January 2001.

The composition of the European Central Bank occurred in 1998. Eleven countries signed for the euro: Austria, Belgium, Finland, France, Germany, Ireland, Italy, Luxembourg, Netherlands, Portugal and Spain. January 1999 was the conversion weekend. The equity markets of 11 European nations have been united into one monetary unit – the euro.

On 1 January 2001, Greece became the twelfth country to join the European Union.

3.20 THE SINGLE CURRENCY

In January 2002 the euro currency became the legal tender in all the twelve participating countries.

In January 2002, euro notes and coins were actually being circulated in the different countries and by the end of the first quarter, national notes and coins no longer existed. This change had an impact on everyone, from manufacturers, importers and exporters with trade flows to hedge, central banks with reserve asset and debt management concerns, to financial institutions and pension funds with international portfolios. In fact, even though this event was specific to Europe, the impact affected the world's currency market community from American to Japan. The single currency in Europe formed one corner of the new triangular world of the dollar, the yen and the euro.

The fixing rates – legacy currencies rates against the euro are shown below:

Austrian schilling:	Ats	13.7603
Belgian franc:	Bef	40.3399
Finnish mark:	Fim	5.94573
French franc:	Frf	6.55957
German mark:	Dem	1.95583
Greek drachma:	Grd	340.75
Irish punt:	Iep	0.787564
Italian lira:	Itl	1936.27
Luxembourg franc:	Luf	40.3399
Dutch guilder:	Nlg	2.20371
Portuguese escudo:	Pte	200.482
Spanish peseta:	Esp	166.386

The conversion of national legacy currencies meant that organisations had to have the ability to accept both forms of transaction. It has been quite complicated because, for instance, to convert sterling to francs you had to have a conversion via the euro. This is because the national legacy currency no longer existed in its own right but was a denomination of the euro, fixed by the conversion rate. The European currencies have always fluctuated against the dollar, even as the debate about the euro raged. This can be shown by:

Birth of European Monetary System – it was the economic crisis of the 1970s that led to the first plans for a single currency. The system of fixed exchange rates pegged to the dollar was abandoned. European leaders agreed to create a "currency snake", tying together European currencies. However, the system immediately came under pressure from the dollar, causing problems for some of the weaker European currencies.

Plaza accord – during the 1980s, the dollar strengthened dramatically. American interest rates were high, which was caused by a dispute between the Reagan administration and the American Federal Reserve Bank over the size of the budget deficit. In 1986, the world's leading industrial countries agreed to act and lower the value of the dollar. The successful deal was struck at New York's Plaza Hotel.

Kuwait crisis – on 2 August 1990 Iraq invaded Kuwait. On the same day, the UN Security Council passed a resolution condemning the invasion.

Maastricht Treaty – in 1991, the 15 members of the European Union, meeting in the Dutch town of Maastricht, agreed to set up a single currency as part of a drive towards economic and monetary union. There were strict criteria for joining, including targets for inflation, interest rates and budget deficits. A European Central Bank was established to set interest rates. Britain and Denmark, however, opted out of these plans.

ERM crisis – the exchange rate mechanism was established in 1979 and was used to keep the value of European currencies stable. However, fears that voters might reject the Maastricht Treaty led currency speculators to target the weaker currencies. In September 1992, Britain and a few of the other EU countries were forced to devalue. Only the French franc was successfully defended against the speculators.

Asian crisis – the turbulence in the Asian currency markets began in July 1997 in Thailand and quickly spread throughout the Asian economies, eventually reaching Russia and Brazil. Foreign lenders withdrew their funds amid fears of a global financial meltdown and the dollar strengthened. Many EU countries were struggling to cut their budget deficits to meet the criteria for euro membership.

Euro launch – the euro, of course, was launched on 1 January 1999 as an electronic currency used by banks, foreign exchange dealers and stock markets. The new European Central Bank set interest rates across the euro zone. However, uncertainty about its policy and public disagreements among member governments weakened the value of the euro on the foreign exchange markets.

Central bank intervention – after just 20 months, the euro had lost nearly 30% in value against the dollar. The European Central Bank and other central banks finally joined forces to boost its value. The move helped put a floor under the euro, but it has still not recovered its value. A weak euro has helped European exports, but it has also undermined the credibility of the currency and has fuelled inflationary pressures.

Terrorist attack on New York and Washington – this attack in New York severely tested the currency markets. Money flowed out of the dollar into safe havens like the Swiss franc and, for the first time, into the euro. The central banks tried to calm the markets and interest rates were cut across the globe. Many observers believe it may have marked the coming of age of the euro as an international currency.

Euro becomes cash currency – on 1 January 2002, the euro became a reality for approximately 300 million citizens of the 12 countries in the euro zone. The arrival of the euro as a cash currency may foster closer integration and greater price competition within the euro zone. It may also help boost its international role, as doubts grow over the strength of the dollar, especially as American economy continues to slow.

3.21 CURRENCY OPTIONS

It can be argued that options were alive and kicking in the ancient world because an applied mathematician called Thales (624–547 BC) may have been one of the first people to trade options. According to Aristotle:

> ".... according to the story, he knew by his skills in the star's while it was yet winter that there would be a great harvest of olives in the coming years, so, having little money, he gave deposits for the use of all the olive presses, which he hired at a low price because no one bid against him. When the harvest time came, and many wanted them all at once and of a sudden, he let them out at any rate which he pleased, and made a quantity of money.... "

It is likely, however, that options and futures contracts were used in Africa up to 1000 years before the birth of Thales.

In about 1600, tulip mania swept Holland with very high prices being paid for tulips and tulip bulbs. Growers bought put options (right to sell) and sold futures contracts in order to make sure they would receive good prices for their bulbs. Tulip retailers, on the other hand, bought call options (right to buy) and futures to protect themselves against sudden price rises by their suppliers.

However, the market was not regulated and dramatically crashed during the early part of 1637 after months of frenzied trading and outrageously high prices. More than 100 years ago, options on shares were traded on the London Stock Exchange. These were contracts between the buyer and seller, with no obligations on the part of the exchange itself. Similar instruments began to be used in other financial centres, most notably New York, and were developed and refined over the years.

During 1973, two important events occurred which were to mould the options market: first, the opening of the world's first formalised options market, the Chicago Board Options Exchange. For the first time, the exchange itself became party to the contracts rather than just the venue where the contracts were negotiated. Second, a paper published by Fischer Black and Myron Scholes provided the first reasonable mathematical model for the pricing of options. Since this period, interest in options has exploded, with an enormous variety of options being traded, not only via exchanges, but also via the over-the-counter market as well.

In 1982, the Philadelphia Stock Exchange (PHLX) pioneered options on currencies and since then they are generally credited with being the instigators of the dramatic growth in the product worldwide. They were designed not as a substitute for forward foreign exchange, or futures, but as an additional and versatile financial vehicle that can offer opportunities and advantages to those seeking either protection or investment profit from changes in exchange rates. Thus, the PHLX contracts gave banks the opportunity to hedge their option books and the product gained in popularity as banks started to market options as an effective hedging tool. At the same time, banks started to quote each other and the secondary over-the-counter (OTC) market was born.

In 1985, standard terms and conditions for London OTC options were devised and they soon became internationally accepted giving further growth to the market. The two markets, exchange-listed and OTC, developed together through the next few years, but the flexibility of the OTC option, with its almost unlimited range of strikes, currencies, cross-currencies and maturities, eventually left the exchanges behind.

Since then, the OTC market has achieved new levels of volume and liquidity with billions of dollars in options being traded by participants who have recognised the potential of options for managing foreign exchange risk and for gaining access to the foreign exchange market.

Today, perhaps the most significant development for the market has been the increased willingness of both financial institutions and potential corporate treasurers and investors to use options. As the banks have better understood the complex risks of managing an options portfolio, a greater variety of options covering a broader range of currencies have been made available. Various structures, each with several names, have been developed to get over investors' unwillingness to pay the upfront premium. These can hide the premium to maturity, reduce the premium by giving up some of the benefit or negate it altogether. Nearly all of these early structures were just combinations of call and put options (and sometimes spot and forward foreign exchange) in varying amounts and/or different strikes.

Nowadays, there are true option derivatives available, which extend the choice of option products considerably, depending on the risk profile of the user. Once again, many of these "exotic" options have been devised to reduce the premium cost by giving up a portion of the protection provided by a plain vanilla option. End users of options now do more than simply purchase options as insurance and many of the larger institutions actively manage their foreign exchange exposure by selling options to gain the premium income. In addition to this familiarity, there has been an increase in transaction size. Options provide the purchaser with a guaranteed exchange rate on the amount of the contract regardless of market conditions. For many participants, an option represents the most efficient way to manage exposure. Finally, the transaction cost of entering into a contract has been reduced dramatically in the last decade. Bid/offer spreads are now in the same range as the spot market and there is rarely a liquidity concern. Several years ago, these costs would have been prohibitive.

3.22 CONCLUDING REMARKS

Over the past 30 years or so, nations in the West have variously experienced currency devaluations, revaluations, the abandonment of the dollar/gold convertibility, oil crises, crises of confidence, exchange controls, snakes in tunnels, basket currencies, recycling pressure and the subsequent Third World debtor nations' crisis. However, on the whole we live in a world of freely floating exchange rates. There is a far better understanding of monetary economics on the part of the world's governments, much reduced dependence on artificial trade barriers or exchange controls and a freedom and speed of international communication, which creates a single global foreign exchange market.

While this tremendous growth has been occurring in the foreign exchange market, the expansion in the currency options market has been even more spectacular. It has been reported that, according to a market survey, average daily turnover in the foreign exchange market rose by 116% between 1986 and 1989. At the same time, currency options gained in market share from less than 1% in 1986 to over 6%. More recent studies have shown that options have accounted for up to 48% of daily foreign exchange transactions in some financial centres. This international growth in OTC options and its development into a very specialised market has resulted in many changes from the original terms and conditions set in 1985.

It will be difficult to predict how the currency options markets will shake out in the next few years, but two points are certain:

1. London will remain the largest currency option centre, outperforming in volume both New York and Tokyo.
2. Risk management will continue to be a key issue for corporates, speculators and financial institutions alike, where options will continue to be evaluated as an alternative to the standard foreign exchange products on offer.

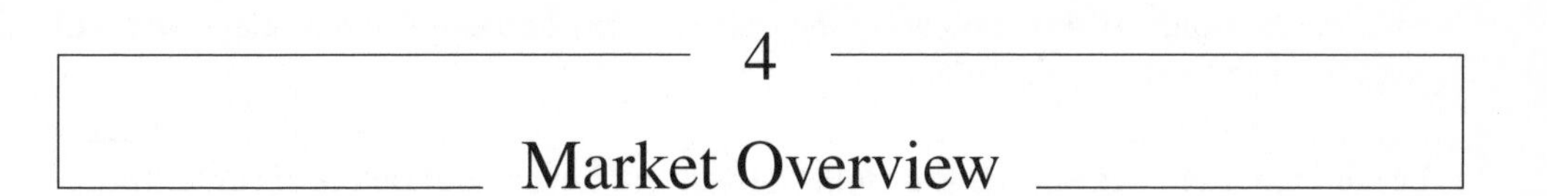

4
Market Overview

4.1 GLOBAL MARKET

Simply defined, foreign exchange is the buying of one currency and selling of another, always achieved in pairs. For example, the European euro against the American dollar (eur/usd) or the dollar against the Japanese yen (usd/jpy). It is a global, over-the-counter market, which is unregulated and is in operation 24 hours a day, virtually seven days a week. There are dealing centres in all the major capitals of the free world, from sunrise in Sydney, Tokyo and the rest of the Far East financial centres, through daytime trading activities in London and the European centres, across the Atlantic to New York and Chicago and on westwards to sunset in Los Angeles and Hawaii.

Individual buyers and sellers will generally deal verbally over the telephone, or act through brokers, or electronically. This means that rates change from dealer to dealer rather than being controlled by a central market. For example, investors do not call around to get the best price on a specific stock because the price is quoted on the stock exchange, but they do call around to different dealers to get the best exchange rate on a specific currency. They may also refer to various widely available bank/broker screens for indicative pricing.

The foreign exchange market has an average daily turnover of approximately $1.6 trillion and is the largest in the world.

4.2 NO PHYSICAL TRADING FLOOR

The market is decentralised with no physical trading floor. However, there are two exceptions to the lack of a physical marketplace. First, foreign currency futures are traded on a few regulated markets, of the better known are the IMM in Chicago, SIMEX in Singapore and LIFFE in London. Second, there are daily "fixings" in some countries where major currency dealers meet to "fix" the exchange rate of their local currency against currencies of their major trading partners, at a predetermined moment in the day. Immediately after the fixing, the rates continue to fluctuate and trade freely. An example is the dollar against the Israeli shekel. These fixings actually happen less and less and are really only symbolic meetings.

Currency futures obligates its owner to purchase a specified asset at a specified exercise price on the contract maturity date.

4.3 A "PERFECT" MARKET

By dint of these modern communications and information systems being dynamically available in all centres to all market participants, and the international applicability of the products traded, the foreign exchange market is probably the nearest of any of the global financial markets to being considered a "perfect" market.

The foreign exchange market is a global network of buyers and sellers of currencies.

The United Kingdom is, in effect, the geographic centre with America a distant second and Japan coming in third. Approximately 84% of the world's foreign exchange business is executed in these three major dealing centres. Of course, there are also many smaller centres in different parts of the world. For example, Zurich, Frankfurt and Singapore. Perhaps the most important reason for London to be in such a prominent position is the fact of its location among disparate time zones. London markets, at one time of the day or another, are open with European markets, several Asian and Middle East markets and major North American markets. Also, this leading position arises from the large volume of international business, which is generated in London.

4.4 THE MAIN INSTRUMENTS

The main instruments for foreign exchange trading include both traditional products such as spot, forwards and swaps, and more exotic products such as currency options and currency swaps. The beauty of the foreign exchange market is its ability to accommodate new products, for instance currency options come in all shapes and sizes, all tailor made to serve a specific purpose.

The products used today are described as:

Spot – a single outright transaction involving the exchange of two currencies at a rate agreed on the date of the contract for value or delivery (cash settlement) within two business days.

Forward – a transaction involving the exchange of two currencies at a rate agreed on the date of the contract for value or delivery at some time in the future (more than two business days).

Swap – a transaction which involves the actual exchange of two currencies (principal amount only) on a specific date, at a rate agreed at the time of conclusion of the contract (the short leg) and a reverse exchange of the same two currencies at a date further in the future, at a rate agreed at the time of the contract (the long leg).

Currency swap – a contract, which commits two counterparties, to exchange streams of interest payments in different currencies for an agreed period of time and to exchange principal amounts in different currencies at a pre-agreed exchange rate at maturity.

Currency option – a contract, which gives the owner the right, but not the obligation, to buy or sell a currency with another currency at a specific rate during a specific period.

Foreign exchange futures – this is a forward contract for standardised currency amounts and for standard value dates. Buyers and sellers of futures are required to post initial margin or security deposits for each contract and have to pay brokerage commissions.

4.5 COMPARISON OF OPTIONS WITH SPOT AND FORWARDS

The most convenient way of explaining the difference between these three products is via an example. Assume an American company is importing goods from Britain and has to pay £1 million in 90 days' time. The company treasurer, depending upon their foreign exchange rate forecasts, can cover this impending position by leaving open this position, by covering through the forward market or by taking out a three-month sterling call (right to buy sterling) option.

Consider the following rates:

Sterling/dollar	1.7000	to	1.7005
3 months	125	to	120

Three-month sterling call/dollar put option (right to buy sterling and sell dollars):

Strike price	1.700
Premium	2.5 cents

Evaluating the alternatives at the outset, the treasurer could cover the position by:

1. Leaving the position open and the eventual exchange rate will, of course, be unknown;
2. Buying sterling forward at an outright rate of 1.6885 (1.7005 – 0.0120); or
3. Buying a sterling call option where the net price/worst exchange rate would be 1.7250 (1.7000 + premium of 0.0250).

Considering only costs, the option proves to be the least attractive. By buying sterling forward, the exchange rate would be 1.6885, which is better than that achieved when buying sterling spot at 1.7005. However, looking at costs alone does not represent the full picture. Each alternative has to be viewed in the light of where exchange rates in three months' time could possibly be.

As shown in Figure 4.1, it can be seen that:

- By leaving the position open, the company gains if sterling weakens to say £/\$ 1.60 and will lose if sterling strengthens to say £/\$ 1.80.
- By locking themselves in at £/\$ 1.6885, by using a forward exchange contract, if sterling weakens and the exchange rate falls below £/\$ 1.6885 to say £/\$ 1.6000, there is an opportunity loss as the company still has to pay \$1 688 500 (£1 000 000 × 1.6885) for the

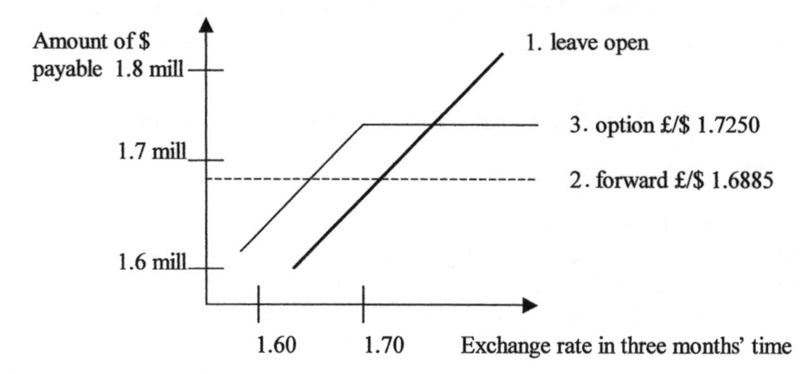

Figure 4.1

sterling instead of $1 600 000. Conversely, if sterling strengthens there will be an opportunity gain.

- By buying the option, when sterling weakens and falls below £/$ 1.7000, the option is not exercised and the treasurer simply buys sterling at the current spot rate. If, for example, sterling weakened to a rate of £/$ 1.6000, the treasurer would only pay $1 600 000 for the equivalent £1 000 000. However, the premium of $25 000 has already been paid, so the effective exchange rate is £/$ 1.6250. If sterling strengthened to £/$ 1.8000, the option would be exercised and the treasurer would be able to buy sterling at £/$ 1.7000 (strike price of the option). Including the premium cost of 2.5 cents, the net price would be £/$ 1.7250.

The option contract gives the owner certainty, whereby in this case, an exchange rate of £/$ 1.7250 and the opportunity to obtain the best prevailing exchange rate. In this case, if sterling weakens, the option holder can let the option lapse and can then proceed to buy sterling at the lower market prevailing rate.

Thus, it can be seen that the advantages of using an option in this way are:

1. Limited risk;
2. Unlimited profit potential; and
3. Possibility to take advantage of a favourable price change.

Against these advantages, the disadvantages are:

1. More expensive than forward cover; and
2. The premium has to be paid upfront.

However, specialised option products can be constructed to overcome these disadvantages.

4.6 THE DOLLAR'S ROLE

Approximately 80% of foreign exchange transactions have a dollar leg, amounting to over $1 trillion per day. The dollar plays such a large role in the markets because:

1. It is used as an investment currency throughout the world;
2. It is a reserve currency held by many central banks;
3. It is a transaction currency in many international commodity markets; and
4. Monetary bodies use it as an intervention currency for operations in their own currencies.

4.7 WIDELY TRADED CURRENCY PAIRS

The most widely traded currency pairs are:

- The American dollar against the Japanese yen (usd/jpy);
- The European euro against the American dollar (eur/usd);
- The British pound against the American dollar (gbp/usd); and
- The American dollar against the Swiss franc (usd/sfr).

In general, eur/usd is by far the most traded currency pair and has captured approximately 30% of the global turnover. It is followed by usd/jpy with 20% and gbp/usd with 11%. Of course, most national currencies are represented in the foreign exchange market in one form or another.

Most currencies operate under a floating exchange rate mechanism against one another. The rates can rise or fall depending largely on economic, political and military situations in a given country.

4.8 CONCLUDING REMARKS

Thus, the foreign exchange market consists of a global network, where currencies are bought and sold 24 hours a day. What began as a way of facilitating trade across country borders has grown into one of the most liquid, hectic and volatile financial markets in the world – where the players have the potential of generating huge profits or losses.

5 Major Participants

Participants in the foreign exchange market are many and varied and the individual involvement of each participant can vary dramatically. Surveys over recent years tend to indicate that participants can broadly be divided into three main groups: banks, brokers and clients. Commercial banks are by far the most active, while brokers act as intermediaries. Clients can be classed as anything from multinational corporations to individual investors to speculators. Who then are the active participants in this global market?

5.1 GOVERNMENTS

Governments sometimes have requirements for foreign currency. This may be for paying staff salaries and local bills of an embassy abroad, or for a foreign currency credit line, most often in dollars, to a third world national government for industrial or agricultural development. In its turn, the third world nation's government will periodically have to pay interest due on any foreign loans with the capital sum eventually having to be repaid. It is more than likely the government would approach the market via its own central bank or a commercial bank.

Foreign exchange rates are of particular concern to governments because changes in foreign exchange rates affect the value of products and financial instruments. As a result, unexpected or large changes can affect the health of a nation's markets and financial systems. Exchange rate changes also impact a nation's international investment flow, as well as export and import prices. These factors, in turn, can influence inflation and economic growth.

For example, suppose the price of the Japanese yen moves from 120 yen per dollar to 110 yen per dollar over the course of a few weeks. In market jargon, the yen is "strengthening", or becoming more expensive against the dollar. If the new exchange rate persists, it will lead to several related effects:

- Japanese exports to America will become more expensive. Over time, this might cause export volumes to America to decline, which, in turn, might lead to job losses in Japan;
- The higher American import prices might be an inflationary influence in America; and
- American exports to Japan will become less expensive, which might lead to an increase in American exports and a boost to American employment.

5.2 BANKS

Central banks are the traditional moderators of excess. The Bank of England, the European Central Bank, the Swiss National Bank, the bank of Japan and, to a lesser extent, the Federal Reserve Bank will enter the market to correct what are felt to be unnecessarily large movements, often in conjunction with one another. By their actions, however, they can sometimes create the excesses they are specifically trying to prevent.

Monetary authorities occasionally intervene in the foreign exchange market to counter disorderly market conditions.

For example, two recent instances of intervention involved the sale of dollars for yen in June 1998 and for euros in September 2000.

Intervention, in general, does not shift the balance of supply and demand immediately. Instead, intervention affects the present and future behaviour of investors. In this regard, intervention is used as a device to signal a desired exchange rate movement.

The second group of banks can best be described as aggressive managers of their reserves. Some of the Middle Eastern and Far Eastern central banks fall into this category. They are major speculative risk takers and their activities often disturb market equilibrium. Along side this activity, the central banks have clients in their own right and they will have commercial transactions to undertake. In certain countries, central banks are involved in local fixing sessions between commercial banks, often acting as an adjudicator to the correct fixing of the daily rates, or to ensure the supply and demand for foreign currency is balanced at a rate in line with its current monetary policy.

Trading banks deal with each other in the "interbank market", where they are obliged to make a "two-way price", i.e. to quote a bid and an offer (a buy and a sell price). This category is perhaps the largest and includes international, commercial and trade banks. The bulk of today's trading activity is concentrated between 100 to 200 banks worldwide, out of a possible 2000 dealer participants. These banks also deal with their clients, some of the more important of which also qualify for two-way prices. In the vast majority of cases, however, most corporations will only be quoted according to their particular requirement. These banks rely on the knowledge of the market and their expertise in assessing trends in order to take advantage of them for speculative gain.

Commercial banks (clearing banks in the UK) operate as international banks in the foreign exchange market, as do many retail banks in other major dealing centres. Many banks in the UK have specialised regional branches to cater for all their client's foreign business, including foreign exchange. All this retail business will eventually be channelled through to the bank's City of London foreign exchange dealing room for consolidation with other foreign currency positions either for market cover or continued monitoring by the specialist dealing-room personnel.

The situation in America is slightly different, where legislation prohibits banks in certain states from maintaining branch networks, but all banks have their affiliates or preferred agents in the main dealing centres of New York, Chicago and Los Angeles.

Other commercial banks have large amounts of foreign exchange business to transact on behalf of their clients and although they will have their own dealing rooms, for one reason or another have not developed their operations to become involved in the interbank foreign exchange markets.

Regional or correspondent banks do not make a market or carry positions and in fact turn to the larger money centre banks to offset their risk. Such relationships have been built up over many years of reciprocal service, and in many instances are mutual, whereby the correspondent bank abroad acts as the clearing agent in its own currency for the other bank involved.

Investment and merchant banks' strength lies in their corporate finance and capital markets activities, which have been developed over many years' servicing the financial needs of large corporations, rather than retail clients. With the multi-currency sophistication of the capital markets and the wide international spread of corporations and other market participants, they are frequently required to transact foreign exchange business, which they effect either by dealing direct or through the brokers' market.

5.3 BROKERING HOUSES

Brokering houses exist primarily to bring buyer and seller together at a mutually agreed price. The broker is not allowed to take a position in a currency and must act purely as a liaison. For this service, they receive a commission from both sides of the transaction, which will vary according to currency handled and from centre to centre. However, the use of live brokers has decreased in recent years, due mostly to the rise of the various interbank electronic brokerage systems.

5.4 INTERNATIONAL MONETARY MARKET

International Monetary Market (IMM) in Chicago trades currencies for contract amounts, which are relatively small in size and for only four specific maturities a year. Originally designed for the small investor, the IMM has grown apace since the early 1970s, and the major banks whose original attitude was somewhat jaundiced, now find that it pays to keep in touch with developments on the IMM, which is often a market leader.

5.5 MONEY MANAGERS

Money managers tend to be large New York commission houses and are frequently very aggressive players in the foreign exchange market. They act on behalf of their clients and often deal for their own account. Neither are they limited to one time zone, dealing around the world through their agents as each centre becomes functional.

5.6 CORPORATIONS

Corporations are, in the final analysis, the real end users of the foreign exchange market. With the exception only of the central banks that alter liquidity by means of their intervention, it is the corporate player by and large who affects supply and demand. When the other major players enter the market to buy and sell currencies, they do so not because they have a need, but in the hope of a quick and profitable return. The corporate, however, by coming to the market to offset currency exposure permanently changes the liquidity of the currency being dealt.

5.7 RETAIL CLIENTS

Alongside these corporates, there is a none-too-significant volume from retail clients. This category includes many smaller companies, hedge funds, companies specialising in investment services linked to foreign currency funds or equities, fixed income brokers, the financing of aid programme by registered worldwide charities and private individuals. With the rise in popularity in online equity investing and a corresponding rise in online fixed income investing, it was only a matter of time before the average retail investor began to see opportunities in the foreign exchange market. Retail investors have been able to trade foreign exchange using highly leveraged margin accounts. The amount of trading, both in total volume and individual trade amounts, remains low and is certainly dwarfed by both the corporate and interbank market.

5.8 OTHERS

Other financial institutions involved in the foreign exchange market include:

- Stockbrokers;
- Commodity firms;
- Insurance companies;
- Charities and private institutions;
- Private individuals.

5.9 SPECULATORS

All the above tend to have some sort of underlying exposure that has to be covered. Speculators, however, have no underlying exposure to hedge, rather they attempt to fulfil the adage "buy low, sell high" by attempting to trade for trading profit alone. Foreign exchange is an ideal speculative tool, offering volatility, liquidity and easy margin or leverage. This activity is vital to the stability of the markets. Without speculation, hedgers would find the market too illiquid to accommodate their needs.

While speculators seek excess profits as a reward for their activities, the process of speculating itself drives the markets towards lower volatility and price stability. No modern commodity, equity, or debt market could operate without the speculators. It is estimated that up to 90% of the daily volume of trading activity in the foreign exchange markets is a result of speculator's activity, with the balance primarily made up of commercial hedging transactions.

5.10 TRADE AND FINANCIAL FLOWS

The foreign exchange market provides the liquidity for all these market participants to convert their trade and financial flows from the currency of one money centre to that of another. These participants buy and sell foreign exchange directly or indirectly from the interbank market, which is made up of professional foreign exchange traders who operate in every financial centre of the world.

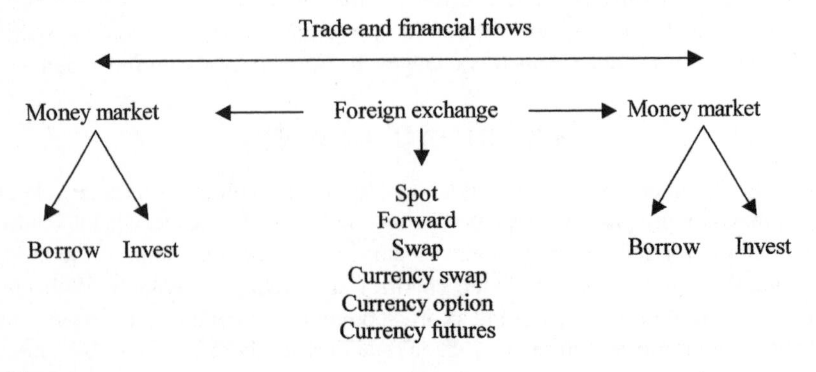

Figure 5.1

These flows and the products available to facilitate these conversions are shown in Figure 5.1. These products – the majority of which have been developed for the clients of the foreign exchange market rather than for professional traders – are also used to hedge or protect the values of cash flows, as these can be affected by the potential changes in the relationships of the currencies involved. The funds borrowed or invested in the money markets may also need to be hedged for the same reasons.

6
Roles Played

To make a market means to be willing and ready to buy and sell currencies.

6.1 MARKET MAKERS

Market makers are those market participants that both buy and sell currencies. As market makers, dealers (or traders) generally, according to market practice, quote a two-way price to another market maker, but not to most corporations.

The terms dealer and trader are used interchangeably when referring to market makers.

For market makers, reciprocity is standard practice. They constantly make prices to one another. Market makers are primarily major banks, for example Barclays, HSBC, JP Morgan Chase, Morgan Stanley, Deutsche Bank, Union Bank of Switzerland and Citibank.

6.2 PRICE TAKERS

Price takers are those market participants seeking either to buy or sell currencies. They are usually corporations and fund managers (investors). For price takers, there is no reciprocity inasmuch as they won't quote prices back to the other market participants.

6.3 A NUMBER OF ROLES

The major participants in the market play a number of roles depending on their need for foreign exchange and the purpose of their activities:

International money centre banks are market makers and deal with other market participants.

Regional banks deal with market makers to meet their own foreign exchange needs and those of their clients.

Central banks are in the market to handle foreign exchange transactions for their governments, for certain state-owned entities and for other central banks. They also pay or receive currencies not usually held in reserves and stabilise markets through intervention.

Investment banks, like money centre banks, can be market makers and deal with other market participants.

Corporations are generally price takers and usually enter into a foreign exchange transaction for a specific purpose, such as to convert trade or capital flows or to hedge a currency position.

*Brokers*are the intermediaries or middlemen in the market, and as such do not take positions on their own behalf. They act as a mechanism for matching deals between market makers. Brokers provide market makers with a bid and/or offer quote left with them by other market makers. Brokers are bound by confidentiality not to reveal the name of one client to another until after the deal is done.

Investors are usually managers of large investment funds and are a major force in moving exchange rates. They may engage in the market for hedging, investment and/or speculation.

Regulatory authorities, while not actually participants in the market, impact the market from time to time. Regulatory authorities include government and international bodies. Most of the market is self-regulated, with guidelines of conduct being established by groups such as the Bank for International Settlements (the BIS) and the International Monetary Fund (IMF). National governments can and do impose controls on foreign exchange by legislation or market intervention through the central banks.

Speculators seek excess profits as a reward for their activities.

6.4 A NUMBER OF ROLES – OPTIONS

Institutional investors and corporate treasurers can use options to:

- Limit risk against adverse currency fluctuations while maintaining the ability to profit from favourable changes in exchange rates;
- Lock in maximum cost or minimum revenues on a foreign exchange transaction with an uncertain completion date;
- Hedge foreign stock and bond holdings; and
- Potentially earn additional profits from foreign business transactions or investments.

Individual investors can use options to:

- Profit from directional views of the underlying currency;
- Potentially earn profits from foreign investments;
- Hedge foreign stock and bond holdings.

6.5 CONCLUDING REMARKS

In summary, all of the above activities can be undertaken by a variety of market participants. For example, banks may most of the time be market makers, but for some of the time, they can be hedgers or speculators as well.

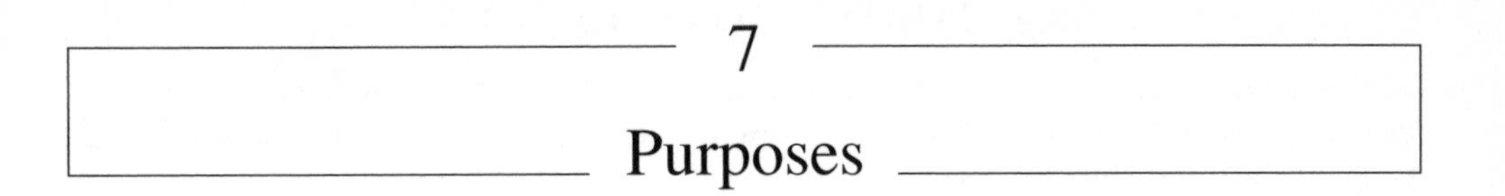

7 Purposes

The participants in the foreign exchange markets effect transactions for various purposes, principally arising from the need to cover or hedge other financial or commercial operations, although in practice it is sometimes difficult to draw a clear line between these categories. For example, covering and hedging operations may well contain elements of speculation. Whatever the nature of the transaction, they are initiated by the banks' clients or by banks themselves for their own account.

The following are examples of those types of transaction, undertaken by all categories of market participants, which are commonplace in the foreign exchange market today.

7.1 COMMERCIAL TRANSACTIONS

For commercial transactions, manufacturing companies buying in raw materials from abroad and exporting finished products undertake both purchases and sales of foreign exchange, always dependent upon the companies' domicile and the currency used for invoicing. Importers of goods, whether acting as principals or intermediaries, will undertake purchases of foreign currency. Contractors involved in overseas projects will be market participants as both buyers and sellers of foreign currency. Also, international insurance, shipping, air transport and travel companies have need of frequent involvement in the market, as do any other individuals or companies offering services overseas.

7.2 FUNDING

Banks and multinational corporations seek specific wholesale funding for their commercial loan or other foreign investment portfolios, alongside day-to-day funding requirements of their net currency cash flows.

7.3 HEDGING

The hedging of any open currency exposure is frequently better handled through off-balance sheet products, like currency options, which ultimately will have an effect on the foreign exchange market. Also, companies involved in direct commercial investment overseas, the purchase and maintenance of plant and materials, or those financing operations of foreign-based subsidiaries, will be frequent participants in the market, as well as property companies or individuals involved in the purchase and sale of property overseas. They may seek foreign currency financing or may convert local currency funding via the foreign exchange market.

7.4 PORTFOLIO INVESTMENT

Added to this group are banks and other entities involved in portfolio investment overseas, or dealing in foreign securities, and will, for position establishment and profit realisation purposes, be both buyers and sellers of foreign currencies.

7.5 PERSONAL

On the personal transaction front, tourists, immigrants and emigrants making outward and inward remittances in foreign currency make up the bulk of the volume, if not the value, of retail foreign exchange business transacted in the market. Royalties, commissions, patents and copyrights from abroad will also be transacted in the market.

7.6 MARKET MAKING

Market making transactions by international banks is also a purpose for being involved in the foreign exchange market, and taking this role a stage further, the trading banks will seek to position themselves against anticipated currency movements. Positions can be set up defensively in the light of the banks' known immediate (or future) requirements, or opportunistically, with dealers looking for a short-term gain. Today, there are many intra-day traders who will close all long and short cash positions at the end of the trading day.

As mentioned already, many organisations are at risk to the financial impact of the market due to changes in foreign exchange rates. In particular, there are three types of foreign exchange exposure:

Foreign exchange exposure is the risk of financial impact due to changes in foreign exchange rates.

7.7 TRANSACTION EXPOSURE

Transaction exposure principally impacts a company's profit and loss and cash flow. It results from transacting business in a currency or currencies different from the company's home base currency. Companies face transaction exposures when they import or export goods and services denominated in foreign currencies, or when they borrow or invest in foreign currencies.

For example, when a small Irish vitamin company, a subsidiary of a large Dublin-based food conglomerate, imports cod liver oil from Sweden, it is invoiced in Swedish krona. Payment is due on delivery of the oil in three months, but in the next two weeks the food manufacturer has to fix the pricing levels and send a profit and loss forecast for the next six months to the treasurer of the parent company. The company has a transaction exposure because they have a risk that the Swedish krona will strengthen against the euro by the time the payment is due, making the cost of goods in euros greater than the company anticipated and possibly eroding their profit margins.

Of course, this exposure could be eliminated or mitigated through the use of foreign exchange products, such as a forward contract, which could lock in a specific exchange rate now for settlement at the time the payment is due.

7.8 TRANSLATION EXPOSURE

Translation exposure principally impacts a company's balance sheet and results from the translation of foreign assets and liabilities into the company's home currency for accounting purposes. This occurs when the financial statements of a company's foreign subsidiaries are consolidated into the parent's statements and translated into the parent's reporting base currency. (Transaction and translation exposure do overlap with each other at times).

For example, a Swiss food company has an American subsidiary in the sweet business. The subsidiary company had an asset value of Swiss francs 52.5 million (or $35 million) at the beginning of the year, when the exchange rate was sfr1.50 per $1. There was no change in the asset value of the subsidiary during the year due to operational reasons. In that time, however, the Swiss franc strengthened to sfr1.43 per $1. The asset value of the sweet company on the Swiss company's balance sheet has dropped to sfr 50 050 000 ($35 million at 1.43), a loss of sfr 2 450 000 (52 500 000 minus 50 050 000), simply from the translation of the Swiss company's long-term investment in the American sweet company from dollars to Swiss francs.

Again, this exposure can be eliminated or mitigated through the use of foreign exchange products such as a forward contract or a currency option.

7.9 ECONOMIC EXPOSURE

Economic exposure relates to a company's exposure to foreign markets and suppliers. It can also be referred to as competitive, strategic or operational exposure and is more difficult to identify. In fact, identification of economic exposure involves in-depth forecasting to determine how sensitive the company's business is to changes in exchange rates. It recognises that the value of a company is impacted by changes in the exchange rate on both its current and future products and markets. For instance, a company has foreign exchange exposure arising from payables and receivables not yet booked but which will most likely occur. These exposures cannot receive hedge accounting treatment and are a problem for companies.

An example often cited in discussing economic exposure is that of a major American film manufacturer whose largest competitor in most of its markets is a large Japanese film manufacturer. The American company has an active exchange rate risk-management programme, which recognises that when the value of the yen rises against the dollar, say from an exchange rate of 150 to 140, the American film becomes more competitive with the Japanese film in Japanese markets and the Japanese film becomes less competitive with the American film in American markets. When the yen weakens against the dollar, say from an exchange rate of 140 to 150, it has the opposite competitive impact.

Again, products available in the foreign exchange market can address economic exposure.

7.10 CONCLUDING REMARKS

Today, there are products available in the foreign exchange market, which can address all types of foreign exchange exposures and purposes. As mentioned in an earlier chapter, there are six basic foreign exchange products:

- Spot transactions;
- Forward contracts;
- Foreign exchange swaps;
- Currency swaps;
- Currency options; and
- Foreign exchange futures contracts.

8
Applications of Currency Options

The users of the option market are widespread and varied, but the main users are organisations whose business involves foreign exchange risk. Options may be a suitable means of removing that risk and are an alternative to forward foreign exchange transactions. In general, the exchange traded options markets will be accessed by the professional market makers and currency risk managers, where the standardisation of options contracts promotes tradability, but this is at the expense of flexibility.

In spite of the fact that options are becoming more and more popular with corporate clients, funds and private individuals, there is still some client resistance to using options as a means to managing currency exposures. Some clients consider options to be expensive and/or speculative. When you buy an option, the most you can lose is the premium (price paid for the option). In some cases, options can help minimise downside risk, while allowing participation in the upside potential. One of the reasons a client may choose to use an option, instead of a forward to manage their downside risk, is this opportunity to participate in the upside profit potential which is given up with a forward contract. Clients who buy currency options enjoy protection from any unfavourable exchange rate movements.

Companies use currency options to hedge contingent/economic exposures, hedge an existing currency exposure, and possibly profit from currency fluctuations, while funds may use options to enhance yield.

Sometimes a strategy may involve more than one option and some option strategies employ multiple and complex combinations. Certain combinations can yield a low or no-cost option strategy by trading off the premium spent on buying an option with the premium earned by selling an option.

Hence, in buying a currency option, it may help the purchaser by:

- Limiting downside currency fluctuation risk while retaining upside potential;
- Providing unlimited potential for gain;
- Providing a hedge for a contingent risk; and
- Enable planning with more certainty.

Selling currency options may assist the writer (seller) by:

- Providing immediate income from the premium received; and
- Providing flexibility when used with other tools as part of an exchange rate strategy.

For a hedger, in terms of exchange rate risk management, currency options can be used to guarantee a budget rate for a transaction. By buying a call (the right to buy) the maximum cost can be fixed for a purchase and by purchasing a put (the right to sell) the minimum size of a receipt can be fixed. The purchase of the option involves paying a premium but gives the buyer the full protection against unfavourable moves while retaining full potential to profit should rates subsequently move beneficially. This contrasts with a forward contract, which locks the hedger into a fixed exchange rate, where no premium is payable but no benefit can be taken from subsequent favourable moves.

In the case of trading, to assume risk in order to make a profit, traders use options to benefit from both directional views and/or changes in volatility. (This allows profit to be made from expecting volatility either to increase or decrease over a period of time.) For example, in order to take a directional view, an options trader might feel strongly that the dollar will strengthen against the Swiss franc in the next three months from its current level of $/sfr 1.66. The trader buys a dollar call (right to buy), Swiss franc put (right to sell) option with a strike price of 1.6835, with expiry in three months' time.

The trader has two choices:

- To hold the option to expiry and if the spot rate has risen to, for example, $/sfr 1.73, the trader would exercise his right to buy dollars and sell Swiss francs at 1.6835, and hence, make money. If the spot rate is below $/sfr 1.6835 at expiry, then the maximum loss is limited to the premium paid for the option.
- Alternatively, if the spot rate rises, say one month after the trader has purchased the option, the trader could choose to sell the option back. By doing this, the trader will recoup both the time value and intrinsic value of the option.

9 Users of Currency Options

There is one very important factor to remember regarding currency options, in that for the buyer of an option, the maximum risk is limited to the premium paid, while for the option seller, the maximum profit is limited to the premium received and the seller is potentially exposed to unlimited losses. Additionally, because of the credit risk involved when writing options, typically there are fewer restrictions upon those wishing to buy options than those who wish to sell.

Writing options on exchanges tends to be simpler as the credit risks are controlled by a margin system. The margin is a small percentage of the value of the contract, which must be deposited to cover losses up to a certain limit. The margin is usually adjusted on each trading day and occasionally more frequently to take account of market movements. However, the greater flexibility available in the OTC market allows some of the credit difficulties to be pursued and overcome. Participants in the foreign exchange currency options market include:

- Banks – who provide a service for their clients, to manage their own foreign exchange risk, and in order to take a directional and/or volatility view.
- Supranationals and sovereigns – all issuers of debt in foreign currencies will have exchange rate exposure, which must be managed.
- Multinational companies – multinationals and their subsidiaries will have funds and cross-border transactions in several currencies and so will be subject to foreign exchange risk.
- Importers and exporters – any company that imports or exports goods to a foreign country will have exposure to fluctuations in exchange rates.
- Investors in foreign currency securities – investors in foreign securities will be exposed to fluctuations in the currency in which the securities are denominated.
- High net worth individuals – such individuals may use exchange-traded currency options for speculation on exchange rates because of the gearing they offer.

9.1 VARIETY OF REASONS

Currency options can be used for a wide variety of reasons.

To cover fx exposure:	On existing exposure;
	On contingent exposure;
	Against a budget rate;
	As disaster insurance.
To speculate	On the direction of spot;
	On a volatile or quiet market;
	On the timing of spot movements;
	On changing interest rate differentials.

To lock in profit	
As an investment	In a speculative asset; To alleviate loan costs; To improve deposit yields.
As a funding tool	To generate a cash flow (short option); To transfer cash to another entity.
As a tax management tool	To transfer profit and loss over time.

9.1.1 Example 1

A British-based company that exports consumer goods to several countries. Currently, the company have contracted to supply 10 million dollars' worth of goods to America and expect to receive payment in three months' time, in dollars. The company believes that the dollar will appreciate against the British pound over this three-month period.

The company has several alternative strategies:

1. Leave the future cash flow unhedged, as they believe that the exchange rate will move in their favour.
2. Enter into a forward contract to sell dollars and buy sterling in three months' time.
3. Purchase a three-month sterling call option (the right to buy sterling and sell dollars).

Possible results:

1. If the exchange rate does move in the company's favour, then the company will receive a windfall profit on their long dollar position. However, this strategy is very dangerous because if the exchange rate moves contrary to their expectations, their sterling profits will be reduced and could become a loss as their costs are fixed in sterling.
2. If the company enters into a forward contract, the company is locking in an exchange rate for the supply deal. This gives the company protection against a dollar depreciation but does not allow them to take any profit from a dollar appreciation, which is contrary to their expectations for the exchange rate.
3. If the company purchases a sterling call option, this will require the company to pay out a premium upfront. However, it will guarantee the company a minimum exchange rate for the supply contract. It allows the company to indulge their expectations that the dollar will appreciate from current levels as, should this expected appreciation occur, they are free to abandon the option and transact in the market at the more favourable exchange rate.

If the company decides to purchase a currency option, it could buy a three-month option, European style sterling call/dollar put option, with a strike price of £/$ 1.75 (that is, the right to buy sterling and sell dollars at a rate of £/$ 1.75). Assume the cost of the option is 1.74% of the sterling amount, i.e. £99 428.57 ($10 000 000 divided by 1.75 equals £5 714 285.71 × 1.74%).

Outcome at maturity:

Spot rate	Option exercised/not exercised	Sterling amount from deal (less premium)
1.8500	Exercised	£5 614 857.14
1.8000	Exercised	£5 614 857.14
1.7000	Not exercised – buy spot	£5 782 924.37
1.6500	Not exercised – buy spot	£5 961 177.49

9.1.2 Example 2

A British-based company exports a large quantity of its products to America, earning a significant proportion of its turnover in dollars. As the profit and cost bases are in England, all profit forecast from America must be converted into sterling. If the dollar were to strengthen (i.e. the dollar/pound exchange rate falls), then the company would realise a greater profit than the original forecast. Conversely, should the dollar weaken, the profits would be lower than anticipated and could even slow a loss (as the cost base is fixed in pounds).

The company treasurer wishes to protect the company against a dollar depreciation, so the company purchases a sterling call option. Using a current spot of $/£ 1.57, the treasurer purchases a European style sterling call/dollar put option (the right to buy sterling and sell dollars) expiring in six months' time, with a strike price of $/£ 1.59.

Consequently, at expiry should the spot exchange rate lie above the strike price of $/£ 1.59, then the treasurer will exercise the right to buy sterling. Should the exchange rate be below $/£ 1.59, then the treasurer will allow the option to lapse and purchase the sterling in the spot market at the more favourable rate of exchange.

That is:

Spot rate below $/£ 1.59	Spot rate above $/£ 1.59
Option lapses	Exercise option

Thus the treasurer has been guaranteed a minimum level of profit, while retaining full potential to take benefit of any favourable exchange rate moves.

9.1.3 Example 3

Traders use options to benefit from both directional views and/or changes in volatility, i.e. to assume risk in order to make a profit.

Taking a directional view – an options trader feels strongly that the dollar will strengthen against the Swiss franc in the next three months from its current level of $/sfr 1.66. The trader purchases a dollar call/Swiss franc put option (right to buy dollars and sell francs), with a strike price of $/sfr 1.6835 (the at-the-money-forward strike price) with expiry in three months' time.

The trader has two choices:

1. Either the trader can hold the option to expiry and if the spot rate has risen to, for example, $/sfr 1.73, the trader would exercise the right to buy dollars at $/sfr 1.6835 and would make money. If the spot rate is below $/sfr 1.6835 at expiry, then the maximum loss is limited to the premium paid for the option:
2. Alternatively, if the spot rate rises, say one month after the trader has purchased the option, the trader could choose to sell the option back then. By doing this, the trader will recoup both the time value and intrinsic value of the option.

Taking a volatility view – an option trader can also use options to take a view on the volatility of the currency pair. This allows profit to be made from expecting volatility either to increase or decrease over a period of time.

9.2 HEDGING vs SPECULATION

In viewing whether an option should be viewed as a hedge or as a speculative instrument, a hedger's main concern is the value of the option at maturity. For this reason, any fluctuation of the option's intrinsic value during its life is important but any change in its time value is largely irrelevant. Also, as the option is itself a hedge, no further hedging is required and therefore there are no extra costs.

Intrinsic value is the advantage to the holder of the option of the strike rate over the forward outright rate.

The option premium for a hedger represents:

$$\text{Option premium} = \text{intrinsic value} + \text{time value}$$

For example, if the forward outright rate of the dollar against Swiss francs is $/sfr 1.6000, then for a dollar call (right to buy), Swiss franc put (right to sell) option, with a strike of $/sfr 1.5700, the intrinsic value of the option would be 0.0300 dollar against Swiss francs. For a dollar put (right to sell), Swiss franc call (right to buy) option, with a strike of $/sfr 1.5700, then the intrinsic value of the option is 0.0000 dollar against Swiss francs.

Time value is a mathematical function of implied volatility, time to maturity, interest rate differentials, spot and the strike of an option.

Time value represents the additional value of an option due to the opportunity for the intrinsic value of the option to increase. It is calculated using an option pricing model.

For a trader/speculator, the option premium represents the expected net present value of the cost of delta hedging the option.

A trader's main concern is the value of the option whenever it is marked to market. In other words, the option premium represents the expected net present value of the cost of delta hedging the option. For this reason, any fluctuation in the intrinsic value of the option is important but also any change in the time value will be significant. If the trader, at any time, decided to hedge or partially hedge the option, extra transaction costs may be incurred, which might affect the overall return.

Glossary of Foreign Exchange Terms

Below are some commonly used expressions which market makers employ. Like most esoteric enterprises, the foreign exchange market likes to surround itself with jargon and technical shorthand. Hopefully, this glossary will dispel some of the mythology.

At a discount A currency which is less expensive to purchase forward than for spot delivery. Its interest rates are higher than the latter's

At a premium A currency which is more expensive to purchase forward than for spot delivery. Its interest rates are lower than the latter's

Bid, wanted, firm, strong The currency in question is appreciating, or in demand, and buyers of the currency predominate

Broken date, odd date A value date, which is not the regular forward date and implies an odd number of days

Cash Same as value today, where funds are settled on the same day the contract is struck

End/end If the spot value of the near end of a swap falls on the last business day of the month, the forward date must also be the last business day of the month, for example 28 February to 31 March, not 28 March

Firm A market maker making a commitment to a price

Forward/forward A swap price where both value dates are beyond spot

For indication Quotations which are not firm and are intended as an indication of unwillingness or inability to trade

Long, overbought Excess of purchases over sales

"Mine" The trader buys the currency and amount specified at the time of asking for a quote

Offered weak The currency in question is depreciating and sellers of the currency predominate

Overnight A swap price for today against tomorrow

Par Where spot is the same as the forward price, indicating that interest rates in the respective currencies are identical

Pip The last decimal place of a quotation

Short dates Usually swap prices for days up to one week

Short, oversold Excess of sales over purchases

Spot date Cash settlement two working days from the trade date. The exception to the rule is the Canadian dollar, which is one working day from the trade date

Spot next or spot a day A swap price for spot against the following day

Spot rate The price at which one currency can be bought or sold, expressed in terms of the other currency, for delivery on the spot date

Spread The difference between the buying and selling price of a foreign exchange quotation

Square Purchases and sales are equal, i.e. no position, or no further interest in dealing

Swap pips, points Used to calculate the forward price and are determined by interest rate differentials

Tom/next A swap price for tomorrow against the next day, which is spot

Value date, settlement date The date agreed upon by both parties on which the two payments involved are settled

Value tomorrow Except in Canada, settlement is one day ahead of spot value

"Yours" The trader sells the currency and amount specified at the time of asking for a quote

"Your risk" Where the response is not immediately forthcoming from a market user when a market maker has quoted a price, the market maker may, at its discretion, indicate the price is no longer firm by stating that the market user is now at risk of the price changing against him/her

Part II
Currency Options – The Essentials

10

Definitions and Terminology

A foreign exchange spot or forward transaction creates a symmetrical exposure, so that one party contracts to deliver to another a specified amount of one currency on a specified value date and receive a specified amount of another currency in exchange. A currency option trade, however, is an asymmetrical transaction, in that the buyer of the option has the right, and the option writer (seller) the obligation, to make or take delivery of a specified amount of currency in exchange for another on (or up to) a particular date.

An option is a contract between the buyer (or holder) of the option and the seller (or writer) of the option. This contract describes the rights of the option holder and the obligations of the option writer.

An example of an option is a call option, which represents the right of its holder to buy a specified asset at a specified price on or before a specified date. The call option also represents the obligation of its writer to sell, if called upon, a specified asset at a specified price on or before a specified date. Thus, with options, unlike futures, the buyer has the right, not the obligation, to transact with the seller.

The specified asset involved in the option contract is referred to as the underlying asset on which the option is written. The specified price at which the asset may be bought is called the exercise price, strike price, or contract price. Purchasing the asset through the option contract is referred to as exercising the option and the specified date on or before which the option may be exercised is called the expiration date or the maturity date.

Therefore, a foreign exchange option is a contract, which gives the buyer/holder the right but not the obligation to enter into a specific foreign exchange contract at a future date. The buyer, therefore, knows the worst foreign exchange rate that they will face but retains the flexibility to do better than the option strike rate. The writer/seller of a foreign exchange option receives a fee for guaranteeing an exchange rate at which they will deal. This fee is the *premium*.

The exchange rate on the underlying contract is referred to as the *strike rate* or *exercise rate*. *European* options enable the buyer to exercise the option at any time during the life of the option but settlement always takes place on the *settlement date*. For an *American* option, exercise may take place at any time during the life of the option but settlement may take place two days after the option is exercised.

A foreign exchange option will simultaneously be a *call option* on one currency (the right to buy that currency) and a *put option* on another currency (the right to sell that currency).

There is an active option market between the major currencies and their crosses of the world and other minor currencies may be possible provided there is a liquid forward foreign exchange market for the period required with no restrictions. Options periods are typically from one day up to five years. Currently, options beyond one year are generally only available for the more liquid currency pairs. Most foreign exchange options have an underlying principle in the range from 3 million dollars to 100 million dollars. However, today with many "smaller" participants being involved in the market, it is quite possible to obtain options for much smaller amounts.

10.1 CALL OPTION

Essentially, the buyer of a currency call option has the right to buy (take delivery of) a predetermined amount of one currency in exchange for a predetermined amount of another currency up to a predetermined date and at a predetermined exchange rate. The writer/seller of a currency call option has the obligation to sell (deliver) a predetermined amount of one currency in exchange for a predetermined amount of another currency up to a predetermined date and at a predetermined exchange rate.

A holder of a call option has the right but not the obligation to buy an asset.

For example, take a call option of Swiss francs against the dollar, expiring in three months' time, for 10 million francs, struck at an exchange rate of 1.6700 francs per dollar ($/sfr 1.6700). The specified exchange rate in an option contract is known as the *exercise or strike price*. The buyer of the call option has the right to receive 10 million francs from the call option writer and deliver to that writer 5 988 023.95 dollars (10 000 000 francs divided by 1.67 francs per dollar). The writer of this call option, therefore, has the obligation to deliver 10 000 000 francs to the call option buyer in exchange for 5 988 023.95 dollars, at any time up to and including the three-month expiry date.

10.2 PUT OPTION

The buyer of a currency put option has the right to sell (deliver) a predetermined amount of one currency in exchange for a predetermined amount of another currency up to a predetermined date and at a predetermined exchange rate. The writer of a currency put option has the obligation to buy (take delivery of) a predetermined amount of one currency in exchange for a predetermined amount of another currency in exchange for a predetermined amount of another currency up to a predetermined date and at a predetermined exchange rate.

	CALL	PUT
BUYER	The right (but not the obligation) to **buy**	The right (but not the obligation) to **sell**
SELLER	The potential obligation to **sell**	The potential obligation to **buy**

Figure 10.1

A holder of a put option has the right but not the obligation to sell an asset.

For example, consider a put option on Swiss francs against the dollar, expiring in three months' time, for 6 million Swiss francs struck at an exchange rate of 1.5000 francs per dollar ($/sfr 1.500). The buyer of the put option has the right to deliver 6 million Swiss francs to the put option writer in exchange for 4 million dollars (6 000 000 francs divided by 1.50 francs per dollar) from the option writer. This right expires in three months' time. The writer of this put option, thus, has the obligation to receive 6 million francs from the option holder in exchange for 4 million dollars, at any time, up to and including the three-month expiry date.

10.3 PARTIES AND THE RISKS INVOLVED

As can be seen, there are two parties involved in any currency option transaction – the option buyer and the option writer (seller). The following grid outlines a risk profile for each.

	Financial risk	**Profit potential**	**Credit risk**
Option buyer	Limited to premium paid	Unlimited	Credit worthiness of option seller
Option writer (seller)	Unlimited	Limited to premium earned	Settlement risk if option is exercised

The option buyer has the right to demand fulfilment of the option contract and the owner can exercise the option. The option buyer pays a premium for that right. The option seller (writer) grants the right and receives a premium for accepting the obligation to fulfil the option contract, if the buyer demands.

10.4 CURRENCY OPTION RISK/REWARD PERCEPTION

Also, the above table can be expanded on and can be expressed in the following manner:

	Buy option Limited risk??	**Sell option** Unlimited risk??
Hedger	**Insurance** Hedging a position against a possible risk – "I am happy not to exercise the option"	**Profit taking** Making the most of an existing position – "I don't mind being exercised"
Speculator	**Lottery** Betting on a strong directional market movement – "I must exercise or lose all my money"	**Wizardry** Making money out of thin air – based on a market view – "I must absolutely not be exercised"

10.5 CURRENCY OR DOLLAR CALL OR PUT OPTION?

Because a foreign exchange transaction is, by definition, an exchange of one currency for another, the purchase of one currency is also the sale of another currency. Therefore, the right to buy one currency is also the right to sell another currency. For example, the owner of a Swiss franc call option has the right to buy Swiss francs and also has the right to sell dollars. The writer of a Japanese yen put option is also the writer of a dollar call option. Hence, the terms call and put option in foreign exchange are interchangeable.

This can be a source of some confusion in the market. For example, for a call option struck at a dollar/Japanese rate of 130.00, is it the right to buy dollars or the right to buy Japanese yen? Indeed, there is no definitive answer and much depends on the viewpoint of the user and whether the dollar is seen as the base currency or the foreign currency is viewed as the base currency. For the sake of clarity, it is common practice to use both terms, calls and puts. For example, a trader may well ask for a price for a Swiss franc call/dollar put at a strike of 1.6700 in order to avoid this confusion.

10.6 STRIKE PRICE AND STRIKE SELECTION

The preset price is called the strike price or the exercise price, which is the predetermined rate of exchange at which exercise takes place. The strike is usually chosen at a level close to the current foreign exchange spot of forward rate but may be at any reasonable level. The premium (price) of an option is very sensitive to the relationship of the strike to the current spot foreign exchange rate. However, in general, both buyers and sellers of options will select a strike based on several factors, including their forecast or expectations of the value of the underlying currency during the lifetime of the option and the option's payoff (profit/loss) profile.

The strike price is the exchange rate at which the option may be exercised.

For example, a market participant with a bullish view for the dollar against the Swiss franc may choose to purchase the dollar in the forward foreign exchange market because there is a belief that the value of the dollar will appreciate against the Swiss franc. A long position in the underlying (dollar) represents the most bullish view of the underlying. However, a long dollar forward foreign exchange position has a payoff profile of unlimited gains if the dollar increases in value and unlimited losses if the dollar decreases in value. If the market participant wishes to eliminate the potential loss while keeping the potential gains, this participant may purchase a dollar call/Swiss franc put instead of purchasing the dollars in the forward foreign exchange market. Thus, a long dollar call represents a bullish view of the dollar but with protection. The cost of the protection is the upfront premium, thus there is a trade-off between the premium payment and the payoff profile.

The market participant now needs to select a strike rate. Should it be in-, at- or out-of-the-money?. In order to make this decision, the market participant will need to consider the upfront premium payment, the breakeven point (the point where the gains begin), and the leverage of the given risk. If the market participant has limited funds to spend on the premium, then an out-of-the-money strike, which is relatively inexpensive, reflecting less protection and higher leverage will be chosen. Thus, the purchaser is willing to accept less protection because of a strong view that the dollar value will increase. The breakeven point will not be as favourable as a strike that is further in-the-money because it will represent the premium and the difference between the forward rate and the strike. This may, perhaps, be better understood by considering the following table:

	Foreign exchange forward	**In-the-money**	**At-the-money**	**Out-of-the-money**
Upfront premium	None	High	Medium	Low
Protection	None	High	Medium	Low
Breakeven rank	1st	2nd	3rd	4th
Participation in underlying (delta)	100%	High	50%	Low
Leverage	None	Low	Medium	High

10.7 EXERCISING OPTIONS

When an option is exercised, the physical exchange of the two currencies is effected. In our example above, the holder of the Japanese yen put option will deliver the yen to the writer and receive dollars, at the predetermined exchange rate. Likewise, the holder of a Swiss franc call option will deliver dollars to the writer and will expect to receive Swiss francs, again at the specified exchange rate. The actual exercise procedure varies according to whether the contract is traded in an organised options exchange or in the over-the-counter market.

The exchanges have specific delivery mechanisms, which may vary considerably according to the type of client or to the operational procedures of the exchange broker concerned. However, in the over-the-counter market, exercise occurs in exactly the same manner as if a spot trade had taken place. This flexibility means that exercise happens every business day at either 3pm London time or 3pm Tokyo time. New York has traditionally used 10am New York time, which does coincide with 3pm London, except for when there is a time discrepancy once or twice a year, when both centres change their clocks on different days.

For example, consider a Swiss franc call option for 17 million francs against the dollar at a strike price of 1.7000 francs per dollar ($/sfr 1.7000). Once the holder of the option exercises the option, the holder will receive 17 francs and pay 10 million dollars (17 francs divided by 1.7000 francs per dollar) for spot value, which is in two working days.

It is normal practice in the over-the-counter market to avoid any confusion regarding exercise days and settlement days by quoting both expiry and value date simultaneously. Thus, "to buy a Swiss franc 1.70 call/dollar put on 17 million francs will expire on 12 February, with value on 14 February".

10.8 AMERICAN AND EUROPEAN STYLE OPTIONS

Options can be priced as an *European style* option or as an *American style* option. The holder of a "European-style" option has the right to exercise the option only on the expiration date, while the writer of this option may be assigned only on the expiration date of the option. On the other hand, the holder of an "American style" option has the right to exercise the option on any day until expiry, while the writer of an American style option may be assigned on any day until expiry.

European style option – an option where the purchaser has the right to exercise only at expiration.

American style option – an option a purchaser may exercise for early value at any time over the life of the option up to and including its expiration date.

For example, if an option expires on 28th March, with an American style option, the holder could exercise the option on 5th March and expect delivery of the currencies involved to take effect two business days later. With a European style option, exercise can only occur on 28th March, with delivery then two business days later. It must be remembered that there is a difference in price between the two styles of option, but only sometimes. The difference in price occurs because there is a difference in the interest rates each currency attracts. With American options, the intrinsic value is priced against the spot or the forward outright price, whichever is the most advantageous. This is because the American option can be exercised for spot value at any time during the life of the option.

If the call currency (right to buy) of the option has a higher interest rate than the put currency (right to sell), there will be an advantage in calculating the intrinsic value against spot rather than against the forward outright rate. Therefore, the risk that the writer of the American option has is that at some point in time, if the option is so far in-the-money that there is negligible time value remaining, the holder may exercise early. This would mean the writer would incur the differential interest cost of borrowing the higher interest rate currency and lending the lower interest rate currency. If this happens, the option is said to be at logical exercise.

As the American style option is more flexible, shouldn't it be more expensive all the time? Actually, the American option is not really more flexible than the European option. True, it can be exercised early and therefore the intrinsic value can be realised immediately but unless the option is at logical exercise, the holder would be better to sell the option back and receive the premium. Remember, the premium represents the intrinsic value of an option plus time value. This is true for both American and European options and in both cases, if the option is not at logical exercise, and the aim is to realise maximum profit, it would be better to sell than to exercise the option.

Examples of cases when it would be better to pay the extra premium and buy a more expensive American style option are:

- In buying an option where the call currency has the higher interest rate and it is expected that the interest rate differential will widen significantly;
- In buying an option where the interest rates are close to each other and it is expected that the call interest rate will move above the put interest rate;
- In buying an out-of-the-money option with interest rates as in both above and it is expected that the option will move significantly into the money, then the American style option is more highly leveraged and will produce higher profits.

10.9 IN-, AT-, OR OUT-OF-THE-MONEY

An *in-the-money* option is an option that has intrinsic value, that is the extent to which it is in the money. For a call option, the strike is below the spot rate and for a put option, the strike is above the spot rate. For example, if the sterling spot rate against the dollar is at £/$ 1.8000, a $1.7500 call on sterling (right to buy sterling and sell dollars) is in-the-money, as is a $1.8500 put on sterling (right to sell sterling and buy dollars). The more an option is in-the-money, the higher the intrinsic value and the more expensive it becomes. As an option becomes more in-the-money, its delta increases and it behaves more like the underlying in profit and loss terms. Hence deep in-the-money options will have a delta of close to one.

An in-the-money option describes an option whose strike price is more advantageous than the current market price of the underlying.

Also, the option has time value, which is a mathematical function of implied volatility, time to maturity, interest rate differentials, spot and the strike of an option. It represents the additional value of an option due to the opportunity for the intrinsic value of the option to increase. However, it is difficult to quantify, as it is very subjective. It is a wasting asset, so time value declines as expiration approaches and at a more rapid rate.

An option is said to be *out-of-the-money* when it has no intrinsic value. For a call option the strike is above the spot rate and for a put option, the strike is below the spot rate. Again, as before, using a spot rate of £/$ 1.8000 per pound, a $1.8500 sterling call (right to buy sterling and sell dollars) and a $1.7500 sterling put (right to sell sterling and buy dollars) option are both out-of-the-money.

An out-of-the-money option describes an option whose underlying is above the strike price in the case of a call, or below it in the case of a put.

The more the option is out-of-the-money, the cheaper it is, since the chances of the option being exercised become slimmer. Also, its delta declines and the option becomes less sensitive to movements in the underlying.

An option that is *at-the-money* is one whose strike price is set at the same level as the prevailing market price of the spot or underlying forward contract. For example, with a pound against the dollar spot rate at £/$ 1.8000, a $1.8000 sterling call option is said to be at-the-money spot.

Thus, when considering whether an option is in-, at- or out-of-the-money, it should be remembered that it is the distance between the strike and the market forward foreign exchange price of the underlying when the option contract is negotiated or it is the distance between the strike and the market spot foreign exchange rate of the underlying at expiration because the market forward foreign exchange price is the expected future value of the market spot foreign exchange rate.

In summary, it should be noted that intrinsic value is simply the difference between the spot price and the strike price.

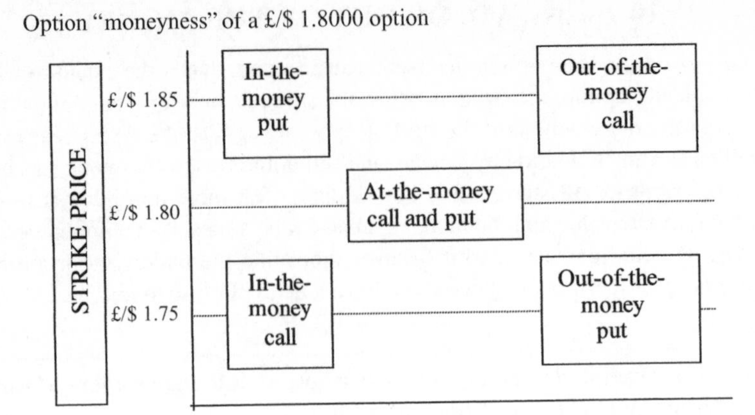

Figure 10.2

For call options this implies:

In-the-money = Spot price is above option strike (exercise) price
Out-of-the-money = Spot price is below option strike (exercise) price
At-the-money = Spot price and option strike (exercise) price are the same

And for put options this implies:

In-the-money = Spot price is below option strike (exercise) price
Out-of-the-money = Spot price is above option strike (exercise) price
At-the-money = Spot price and option strike (exercise) price are the same

Also, it should be noted that intrinsic value versus time value can be explained as:

	In-the-money	**Out-of-the-money**	**At-the-money**
Put/Call	Time value decreases as the option gets deeper in-the-money, while intrinsic value increases	Time value decreases as the option gets deeper out-of-the-money, while intrinsic value is zero	Time value is at a maximum when an option is at-the-money, while intrinsic value is zero

A cause of some confusion in the market, which is more semantic than real, occurs when the forward or futures price differs from the spot. For example, if sterling against the dollar spot is £/$ 1.8000 and the March forward/futures price is £/$ 1.7500, the $1.80 sterling call for March could be said to be at-the-money against the spot but out-of-the-money against the forward/futures price. Alternatively, the $1.75 sterling call for March is in-the-money against the spot rate but at-the-money against the forward/futures price. Thus, traders usually resolve these problems by using the terms "at-the-money spot" to refer to the $1.80 call and "at-the-money forward" to refer to the $1.75 call, in this particular example. Hence, with a Black–Scholes model, the delta of a European style at-the-money forward option will always be 0.5. However, because forwards commonly trade at a premium or discount to the spot, the delta may not be equal to 0.5.

10.10 THE PREMIUM

The premium is the price paid for the option. With a currency option, this can be expressed in different ways and is usually paid with spot value (two business days) from the initial deal date. This is, the premium is usually paid upfront.

An option buyer pays a premium, the price of the option, for the opportunity to benefit from a favourable exchange rate movement. The potential loss is limited to the option premium, and there is unlimited profit potential. On the other hand, the option seller receives a premium as payment to assume the risk of an adverse exchange rate movement. The seller's potential profit is limited to the option premium and there is unlimited risk of loss.

	Maximum profit	**Maximum loss**
Short call	Premium received	Unlimited*
Short put	Premium received	Unlimited**
Long call	Unlimited*	Premium paid
Long put	Unlimited**	Premium paid

* Since the order of magnitude of the profit/loss potential is so much greater than the premium, it is unnecessary to subtract the option premium from it. For a long call, the maximum profit would be reduced by the premium paid. For a short call, the maximum loss would be reduced by the premium.
** Since the price or value of the underlying asset cannot fall below zero, the maximum profit of a long put is actually the strike price minus the premium paid. Similarly, the maximum loss of a short put is actually the strike price minus the premium received.

The option buyer pays a premium to the seller for the right to benefit if the underlying moves in a favourable direction, but risks only the premium if the underlying moves in an unfavourable direction. Thus, from a profit/loss standpoint, a long call option can be described as being equivalent to a long position in the underlying with insurance against the value of the underlying decreasing. Also, again from a profit/loss standpoint, a long put option can be described as being equivalent to a short position in the underlying with insurance against the value of the underlying increasing.

One unfortunate source of confusion in the currency options market is in the method of quoting the option premium itself. This is not a problem encountered in other option markets as for equities or with gold options. For example, the premium is normally expressed in the same terms as used in the underlying instrument, like $5 per share or $3 per ounce. However, with currency options, as with the foreign exchange market itself, there are alternative ways of quoting the same premium.

For instance, currency futures in Chicago are expressed in the reciprocal form, dollars per currency, and the futures option market adopts the same pricing convention. Thus the holder of one contract of a February 77 call has the right to buy 125 000 Swiss francs (the underlying value of one futures contract) at an exercise price of $0.77 per Swiss franc. However, in conventional European terms, this would be expressed as a call on Swiss francs struck at \$/sfr 1.2987 (1 divided by 0.77). If we assume the premium for this February 77 call is 2.33 (\$0.0233) per Swiss franc, then the premium amount per Swiss franc option contract would be:

$$\text{Sfr } 125\,000 \times \$/\text{sfr } 0.0233 = \$2912.50$$

Were this same trade to have been executed in the over-the-counter market, the premium would more likely have been expressed as a percentage of the strike price, in this case 3.026% ($2.33/77 \times 100 = 3.026$). The total premium amount (ignoring rounding) is the same as the above and is calculated by multiplying the underlying dollar amount by the percentage figure:

$$\text{Sfr } 125\,000 \times \$/\text{sfr } 0.77 = \$96\,250$$

$$\$96\,250 \times 0.3026 = \$2912.52$$

This would be the case if the option were purchased in either London or New York. But, if the option were purchased in Switzerland or Germany, also in the over-the-counter market, the premium would more likely be expressed in terms of Swiss francs per dollar rather than dollars per Swiss franc. This can be calculated by multiplying the percentage premium by the Swiss franc spot rate, say \$/sfr 1.2850:

$$0.03026 \times \text{sfr}/\$1.2850 = \text{sfr } 0.0389 \text{ per dollar}$$

This would normally be expressed as 3.89 centimes per dollar. The total premium, in Swiss francs, is therefore:

$$\$96\,250 \times \text{sfr}/\$0.0389 = \text{sfr } 3\,744.13$$

Components of the premium can be split into two parts, *intrinsic value* and *time value*.

Thus:

$$\text{an option premium} = \text{intrinsic value} + \text{time value.}$$

For example, if the forward outright rate of the dollar against Swiss francs is \$/sfr 1.6000, then for a dollar call (right to buy), Swiss franc put (right to sell) option, with a strike of 1.5700, the intrinsic value of the option would be 0.0300 dollars against Swiss francs. For a dollars put (right to sell), Swiss franc call (right to buy) option, with a strike of 1.5700, then the intrinsic value of the option is 0.0000 dollars against Swiss francs.

Intrinsic value is the advantage to the holder of the option of the strike rate over the forward outright rate.

Time value is a mathematical function of implied volatility, time to maturity, interest rate differentials, spot and the strike of an option.

Time value represents the additional value of an option due to the opportunity for the intrinsic value of the option to increase.

Also, intrinsic value for an American style option can be defined as the amount the option would be worth if it were exercised immediately. In other words, it is the difference between the strike price and the spot rate. For example, with spot sterling against the dollar at £/$ 1.8000, the $1.7500 call option has $0.05 intrinsic value. Another way of putting it is to say that the £/$ 1.7500 call is in-the-money by 5 cents. Any option trading less than intrinsic value presents a riskless profit for an arbitrageur.

Thus, intrinsic value is simply the amount the option would be worth on expiry, whereby a currency call option has value on expiry by the amount the spot rate is higher than the strike rate and whereby a currency put option has value in expiry by the amount that the spot rate is below the strike rate. Obviously, an option will not be worth any more than intrinsic value on expiry because there will be no inherent advantage in owning it. Only if there is some time remaining before expiry will the option have any value in addition to its intrinsic worth.

10.11 VOLATILITY

Volatility is a measure of the variability, but not the direction, of the price of the underlying – essentially the chances of an option being exercised.

Volatility is a statistical measure of the tendency of a market price or yield to vary over time. It is usually measured by the variance or annualised standard deviation of the price, rate, or return and is said to be high if the price, yield, or return typically changes dramatically in a short period of time. In valuing an option, volatility is one of the most important elements because it is usually the only valuation not known with certainty in advance. Thus, volatility is the degree of price movement in a currency. Volatility can be measured historically, but the aspect of volatility essential for option pricing is a forecast or expectation of spot volatility over the life of the option. This forecast is the primary focus of professional option dealers. All other inputs in option pricing models are either assets with tradable market prices (for example, spot or forward foreign exchange, interest rates), fixed constants (strike price) or simple deterministic variables, like time to expiration. Thus, the most variable parameter traded by option traders, as opposed to being hedged through existing markets, is this expected volatility, or the volatility "implied" by option prices.

Measures of volatility are thus:

- Historical or actual volatility is a measure of the actual variance of the assets value and is determined only for a specific time period. It is a source of information used to forecast volatility, that is, expected future volatility is often forecast from historical volatility;
- Implied volatility is derived from the price of the option in the market. Holding all other inputs in the pricing model constant, the implied volatility is the expected variance of the underlying as determined by the market through a given option value; and
- Forecast volatility is the variance of an asset's value that individual market participants expect to occur.

For the option buyer, volatility is opportunity value, that is, the chance that the option will be in-the-money at expiration and thus provide a profit. On the other hand, for the option seller, volatility is risk, that is, the chance that the option will be in-the-money at expiration and will thus lead to a loss.

10.12 BREAK-EVEN

The break-even point of an option position is used to quantify the profit/loss of an option buyer and the option seller. The calculation of the break-even rate is simple if the exchange rate and the option premium are expressed in similar terms.

For both the call option buyer and seller, the call break-even equals the strike plus premium, while for both the put option buyer and seller, the break-even is equal to the strike minus the premium.

11

The Currency Option Concept

	BUY the option **PAY PREMIUM**	**SELL** the option **RECEIVE PREMIUM**
Call option on the dollar and **Put** option on the yen:	**Obtain the RIGHT** to buy the dollars and to sell the yen **Risk** is to a positive move in volatility and a positive move in dollars	**Assume the OBLIGATION** to sell the dollars and to buy the yen **Risk** is to a negative move in volatility and a negative move in dollars
Put option on the dollar and **Call** option on the yen	**Obtain the RIGHT** to sell the dollars and to buy the yen **Risk** is to a positive move in volatility and a negative move in dollars	**Assume the OBLIGATION** to buy the dollars and to sell the yen **Risk** is to a negative move in volatility and a positive move in dollars
CONCEPTS	Protection till maturity is a **positive** factor. However, there is a cost now, which is a **negative** factor.	Reward now is a **positive** factor. However, there are risks till maturity, which is a **negative** factor.

12

The Currency Options Market

Foreign exchange options can be traded on formal exchanges or in the over-the-counter (OTC) market, i.e. between two parties. The exchanges, such as the Chicago Board Options Exchange, the London International Financial Futures Exchange or the Philadelphia Stock Exchange, provide standardised options or standardised contracts with fixed maturity dates, strike prices and contract sizes, although each exchange has its own contract specifications and trading rules. The OTC market differs from the listed market in a similar way to how the spot and forward foreign exchange market differs from currency futures markets. The OTC market offers a customised, or tailor-made product, where the underlying amount, expiry date, strike and even the option type (American or European) are a matter of negotiation. Thus, OTC option specifications are much more flexible to fit specific requirements. In the listed market, all such terms are standardised.

The OTC market is principally made up of banks and financial institutions, which make option prices to their clients, and to each other. The exchange traded market is a public market, where traders (who may be international banks) and private individuals own seats on the exchange, and meet together in a "room", "floor" or "pit" to trade currency options; whereby in the OTC market, trading is a private deal between two parties. Similarly, in the OTC market, settlement of option trades and the credit risk inherent in any deal is a matter between the financial institution and its counterparty. This is usually for the option premium, which is paid upfront by the buyer to the writer. The buyer, therefore, has a contingent claim on the writer until the option expires. In the listed market, all transactions are processed through a clearing house which acts as the counterparty to each deal, through a margining process (similar to that used in all futures markets) and the clearing house guarantees the performance of the contract.

12.1 EXCHANGE vs OVER-THE-COUNTER

Exchange traded options can be characterised by:

- Currencies are quoted mainly against dollars although recently some crosses have become available;
- Strike prices are at fixed intervals and quoted in dollars or cents per unit(s) of currency;
- Fixed contract sizes;
- Fixed expiry dates, generally at three-month intervals, e.g. delivery on the third Wednesday of March, June, September and December;
- Premium paid upfront and on the same day as the transaction;
- Options are usually American style.

Standard option

Put/Call:	Either
Underlying:	Bonds, interest rates, currencies, stocks, stock indices, commodities, etc.
Strike price:	Fixed
Expiry date:	Fixed
Payout:	At maturity of the option, it depends on the difference between the strike price and the market price

The main advantage of the listed market is the public auction system. The trader or hedger can be sure that the premium paid or received is publicly negotiated and displayed on market screen and published the following day in the financial press and is therefore "fair". By contrast, in the OTC option market, where the contract is between, say, the bank and its client, the buyer or writer has no way of telling whether the premium quoted is fair or otherwise. However, it has to be remembered that there are some occasions where the public auctions system is at a disadvantage to the OTC option market. For example, as liquidity is the greatest on the exchanges in the near-the-money strikes with medium maturities (two or three months), it may not be easy for a client holding an option position which has moved deep in- or far out-of-the-money to liquidate the position, particularly if the option had under a month to expire and the quantity is quite large. By contrast, the OTC option market maker will usually make a competitive price for the whole amount.

One other advantage of the traded option market is the clearinghouse system. In the OTC option market, where banks trade with each other and their clients according to their mutual assessment of credit risk, it is unfortunately very easy to "fill" a foreign exchange line. Once credit lines are "full up", not only is further option business between the two parties prohibited but also so may be other traditional forms of business, for example spot or forward foreign exchange. On the exchanges, however, the margining system allows market users the opportunity to buy or write options in substantial amounts without affecting credit lines. Thus, credit risk (the risk of the writer defaulting on the option) is therefore minimised and anonymity between counterparties can be preserved. It should be noted that currency options on the Chicago Mercantile Exchange (CME) are options on futures rather than options on the spot currency. Hence, if a call is exercised, the buyer receives a long futures position rather than a spot position and the opposite is the case for the buyer of a put. However, the margining process can be a disadvantage, in that the mark-to-market system ensures that losses are taken on a daily basis rather than on the expiration day of the option.

Over-the-counter options have the following characteristics:

- Strike rates, contract sizes and maturity are all subject to negotiation. An institution can structure its own option requirements, enabling it, for example, to make cross rate transactions;
- Maturities can be from several hours up to five years;
- The buyer has the direct credit risk on the writer;
- Only the counterparties directly involved know the price at which the option is dealt;
- The premium is normally paid with spot value from the transaction date with delivery of the underlying instrument also typically with spot value from expiry;
- Options can be either style but the majority are European style.

For example, Bank A buys from Bank B a 1.5700 European style sterling call/dollar put on 10 million pounds, with a maturity of six months. Bank A buys the option through the OTC market for a premium of $0.02 per £1 principal.

In this example:

Buyer:	Bank A
Writer (seller):	Bank B
Strike price:	1.5700
Principle amount:	£10 000 000
Expiry date:	6 months
Premium:	$200 000 (£10m × $0.02)

12.2 STANDARDISED OPTIONS

Currencies traded – the Philadelphia Stock Exchange (PHLX) lists six dollar-based standardised currency option contracts, which settle upon exercise in the actual physical currency, while the Chicago Mercantile Exchange (CME) lists 14 currency option contracts, which includes crosses, for example European euro against the Swiss franc.

Contract size – the amounts of currency controlled by the various currency options contracts are geared to the needs of the widest possible range of participants. For example, the sizes expressed in units of currency for each option on the PHLX are:

US dollar vs Australian dollar	50 000 Australian dollar (units)
US dollar vs British pound	31 250 British pound (units)
US dollar vs Canadian dollar	50 000 Canadian dollar (units)
US dollar vs European euro	62 500 European euro (units)
US dollar vs Japanese yen	6 250 000 Japanese yen (units)
US dollar vs Swiss franc	62 500 Swiss franc (units)

Exercise style – Both American and European style options are available for mid-month and month-end options. However, longer-term options are European style options only.

Expirations – the exchange offers a variety of expirations, including mid-month, month-end and some longer-term options. For example, currency options are available for trading with fixed quarterly months of March, June, September and December.

Exercise prices – prices are expressed in terms of American cents per unit of foreign currency. For example, a call option on euros with an exercise price of 95 would give the option buyer the right to buy euros at 95 cents per euro. On the exchange, exercise prices are set at certain intervals surrounding the current spot or market price for a particular currency. When significant price changes take place, additional options with new exercise prices are listed and commence trading. Also, strike price intervals vary for the different expiration time frames. They are narrower for the near-term and wider for the long-term options.

Premium quotation – premiums for dollar-based options are quoted in American cents per unit of the underlying currency (with the exception of Japanese yen which are quoted in hundredths of a cent). For example, a premium of 0.95 for a given European euro option is ($0.0095) per euro. Since each option is for 62 500 euros, the total option premium would be $593.75 (62 500 × $ 0.0097).

12.3 CUSTOMISED OPTIONS

Customised currency options can be traded on any combination of the currencies currently available for trading. Currently, the Australian dollar and the Mexican peso may be matched with the American dollar only, and must be denominated in American dollars.

Underlying currency – the underlying currency is that currency which is purchased (in the case of a call) or sold (in the case of a put) upon exercise of the contract.

Base currency – the base currency is that currency in which terms the underlying is being quoted, i.e. strike price.

Expiration/Last trading day – expirations can be established for any business day up to two years from the trade date. Customised option contracts expire at 10:00am Eastern Time on the expiration day in contrast with standardised options, which expire at 2:30pm Eastern Time on the expiration day. In addition, the exercise and assignment process for customised options is more akin to the OTC market in terms of expiration time frame. Unlike the process utilised for standardised options, exercise notices must be received by 10:00am Eastern Time and the writer is then notified of the number of contracts assigned.

Contract size – the underlying currency determines the contract size and is the same size as standardised contracts. In the case where the dollar is the underlying, the contract size is $50 000. Note that the Mexican peso is only available in the customised environment.

Underlying currency:

Australian dollar	50 000 Australian dollar (units)
British pound	31 250 British pound (units)
Canadian dollar	50 000 Canadian dollar (units)
European euro	62 500 European euro (units)
Japanese yen	6 250 000 Japanese yen (units)
Swiss franc	62 500 Swiss franc (units)
Mexican peso	250 000 Mexican peso (units)
American dollar	50 000 American dollars (units)

Exercise prices – exercise or strike prices may be expressed in increments out to four characters. For example, a $/£ option could have an exercise price of 1.5430.

Exercise style – European style only.

Minimum transaction size – since customised currency options were designed for the institutional market, there is a minimum opening transaction size, which equals or exceeds 50 contracts. For example, 55 contracts would be acceptable.

Contract terms – an option strike price may be expressed in either American terms or European terms (inverse terms). For example, an option in American terms would have exercise prices quoted in terms of dollars per unit of foreign currency. An option in European or inverse terms would have exercise prices quoted in terms of units of foreign currency per dollar.

Trading process – trading is conducted in an open outcry auction market, just as in standardised option contracts.

Premiums – premiums may be expressed either in terms of the base currency per unit of the underlying currency or in per cent of the underlying currency (based on contract size). For example, the premium for an option on the dollar versus the euro (dollar being the base currency and the euro being the underlying currency) could be expressed in American cents per euro or as a percentage of 62 500 euros.

Position limits – position limits are the maximum number of contracts in an underlying currency that can be controlled by a single entity or individual. Currently, position limits are set at 200 000 contracts on each side of the market (long calls and short puts or short calls and long puts) for each currency, except the Mexican peso, which is 100 000 contracts. For purposes of computing position limits, all options involving the dollar against another currency will be aggregated with each other for each currency (i.e. usd/eur and jpy/eur on the same side of the market will be aggregated – usd/eur long calls and short puts with jpy/eur short calls and long puts).

12.4 FEATURES OF THE LISTED MARKET

By choosing to trade on a regulated securities exchange, you can take advantage of an open and orderly secondary marketplace, where option positions can be adjusted or closed at any time while still enjoying the financial safeguards of the Options Clearing Corporation (OCC).

Open and orderly marketplace – prices in the crowd may be given by market makers (also referred to as registered options traders), specialists or floor brokers representing customer orders. A specialist, designated by the Exchange to represent a particular currency, is responsible for maintaining fair and orderly markets and disseminating the best-quoted prices for each series in standardised options. In addition, specialists are responsible for the proper execution of orders entrusted to them. Customised options do not have a specialist. Instead, market makers are assigned to particular currency pairs and are responsible for making two-sided markets. While standardised options are quoted continuously, customised options are only quoted upon request. Both standardised and customised options are marked-to-market daily.

Regulation – for instance with the PHLX, a self-regulatory organisation under the jurisdiction of the US Securities and Exchange Commission (SEC) sets and enforces rules to ensure the integrity of their markets. All currency options traded on the Philadelphia Stock Exchange are SEC regulated. The Exchange staff administers its own rules and regulations as well as the SEC rules. Various departments of the Exchange monitor and enforce regulations. The Market Surveillance Department oversees floor trading activity, conduct and trading practices to ensure compliance with Exchange and SEC regulations. The Examinations Department monitors the daily financial condition of floor brokers, market makers and specialists and serves as the Designated Examining Authority to audit selected member firms.

Liquidity – the combination of specialists, market makers and floor brokers guarantees that there is always a buyer or seller for all listed currency options. The centralised location of all interested parties provides depth, liquidity and competitive markets.

Position limits – the Exchange establishes position limits for each currency in order to prevent any one entity from gaining an undue amount of control over the underlying currency, which are approved by the US Securities and Exchange Commission.

Trading hours – for the PHLX, their currency options market is open for trading from 2:30am to 2:30pm Eastern Time, Monday through Friday (except for standardised Canadian dollar options, which trade from 7:00am to 2:30pm Eastern Time). This makes trading currency options possible during business hours in most key time zones. For the CME, there is open outcry trading from 7:20am to 2:00pm (central time) with Globex electronic markets being traded from 2:30pm to 7:05am, the following day. On Sundays, trading begins at 5:30pm.

Guarantee – the various regulatory and self-regulatory bodies that oversee options trading and the exchanges on which they are traded assure orderly markets. In addition, the fiduciary responsibility of a listed option is guaranteed by the Options Clearing Corporation (OCC), the only clearing-house worldwide to receive a "AAA" credit rating from the Standard and Poor's Corporation. OCC is the issuer, guarantor and clearer of all PHLX options. OCC is the intermediary between every buyer and seller, thereby serving as the counterparty to every trade and eliminating counterparty risk.

Margin – a significant contribution to the integrity of the listed option marketplace is the option writer's requirement to post margin – an amount of money or collateral deposited by a customer with his broker, by a broker with the clearing-house, or by a clearing member with the clearing-house, for the purpose of insuring the broker or clearing-house against potential loss on open option contracts. In a marketplace with margin requirements, option traders can avoid review of one another's credit every time they trade. It is the obligation of the customer to post or deposit margin due on currency options carried "short" (or written) in the customer's account on a marked-to-market basis with their respective broker. Brokerage firms guarantee the obligations of "shorts" or writers to the OCC, called "clearing members", that carry the accounts of writers or their brokers. Thus, there are customer obligations to the brokers and/or clearing members, and then clearing firm margin requirements to the OCC. Clearing firm margin or the amount that a clearing member is required to post at the OCC is different from customer margin.

Delivery and settlement – PHLX trades currency options that are physically settled – the exchange of one currency for another. Physically settled currency options are not automatically exercised at expiration, but rather the buyer must submit exercise instructions to their broker dealer. Subsequently, a writer or "short" will be assigned, which will result in the physical delivery of currency between the two clearing members.

Exercise/Assignment – on the CME, all in-the-money options are automatically exercised at expiration in the absence of contrary instructions. All American style CME foreign exchange options may be exercised until 7:00pm central time on any business day the option is traded. However, for Brazilian real options, this deadline is 7:00pm central time on the business day following termination of trading for expiring monthly options.

12.5 COMPARISONS

	Exchange	**Over-the-counter**
Contract specifications:	Standardised and customised	Customised
Regulation:	Securities and Exchange Commission (SEC)	Self-regulated
Type of market:	Open outcry, auction market	Dealer market
Counterparty to every transaction	Options Clearing Corporation (OCC)	Bank or broker
Transparency/Visible prices:	Yes	No
Orders anonymously represented in the market	Yes	No
required to mark positions daily	Yes	No

12.6 WHERE IS THE MARKET?

The OTC market is to be found in the major financial centres of the world, for example London, New York, Tokyo, Zurich, Paris and Frankfurt. In recent years substantial development has also taken place in Singapore, Hong Kong and Sydney. Although the exchange traded market is also to be found around the globe, the two principal centres of activity are Philadelphia ("Philly") and Chicago ("Merc").

"Philly" currency options are the most widely traded and most active of the markets on spot currencies. Both American and European style options are quoted. The Options Clearing Corporation, the largest clearing-house in America, clears the contracts. Options on currency futures are traded on the "Merc" (the Chicago Mercantile Exchange). Contracts are offered on all major currencies and the special feature of these options is not that they are American style, but that they can only be exercised into the underlying futures contract and not into the physical currency. Contracts are settled by the clearing-house of the IMM. There are other centres for currency option trading; however, liquidity is lower and daily volumes are much smaller.

12.7 CONCLUDING REMARKS

The easiest way to summarise is to mention the principal advantages and disadvantages of listed and over-the-counter options:

	Listed options	OTC options
Advantages	Public display Confidentiality Clearing-house (credit) Clearing-house margins allowed Individuals to write options	Flexibility Ease of access No margins Easy documentation Market hours Longer maturities Markets in most currencies
Disadvantages	Restricted number of currencies No maturities after one year Many exchanges Margins cumbersome Restricted hours Documentation	Lack of confidentiality No price display Greater credit risk

13
Option Pricing Theories

Historically, theorists have devoted a substantial amount of work developing a mathematical model for pricing options and, hence, a number of different models exist as a result. All make certain assumptions about market behaviour, which are not totally accurate, but which give the best solution to the price of an option. Professionals use these models to price their own options and to give theoretical fair value; however, actual market rates will always be the overriding determinant. In other words, an option is worth as much as someone is prepared to pay for it. Although the formula for pricing options is complex, they are all based on the same principles.

Historically, option pricing models have fallen into two categories:

- Ad hoc models, which generally rely only upon empirical observation or curve fitting and, therefore, need not reflect any of the price restrictions imposed by economic equilibrium; and
- Equilibrium models, which deduce option prices as the result of maximising behaviour on the part of market participants.

The acknowledged basis of modern option pricing formulae is the often-quoted "Black–Scholes" formula devised in the early 1970s to produce a "fair value" for options on equities. Of course, currency options differ because there is no dividend and both elements of the exchange carry interest rates that can be fixed until maturity. Therefore, various adaptations to the original Black–Scholes formula have been made for use in currency option pricing. The best known of these is the Garman–Kohlhagen adaptation, which adequately allows for the two interest rates and the fact that a currency can trade at a premium or at a discount forward depending on the interest rate differential.

American style options cause further problems in the pricing due to the probability of early exercise. In 1979, Cox, Ross and Rubinstein published a pricing model to take account of American style options. By using the same basics as Black–Scholes, they adopted what is now known as the "binomial" method for pricing such options. This same binomial model is now used alongside the Garman–Kohlhagen version to price currency options.

13.1 BASIC PROPERTIES

When looking at option prices, there are a few basic properties of options, which need to be considered:

- First, options cannot have a negative value to their holders. Since options are rights and these rights will only be exercised to benefit the holder, the option cannot be a liability to its holder.
- Second, options prices should not allow simple arbitrage, that is, it should not be possible to buy an American call or put and immediately exercise the option for a profit greater than the price paid for the option. This need not be true for European options, since the option

holder does not have the right to exercise until the maturity date.

- Third, American type options should be worth at least as much as European type options. Since American options have all the rights a European option has plus the right of early exercise, an American option will be as valuable as a European option if the right to early exercise is worthless and more valuable than a European option if the right of early exercise is valuable.

In addition to the currency price, the exercise price and the time to maturity, option values depend on the price volatility of the underlying currency, the risk-free rate of interest and any cash distributions made by the currency during the life of the option. For a call option, a higher current currency price should imply a greater value to the option holder. This is because a higher present currency price makes it more likely that on the expiration date, the market price of the currency will be above the exercise price. As this is precisely the condition under which the option will be exercised, the value of a call option increases as the present currency price increases. For put options, however, the effects of changes in the current asset price go in the opposite direction as it pays the holder of the put to exercise when the currency price is low, that is, the value of a put option decreases as the present currency price increases.

Thus, the effect of the exercise price, X, on the value of the call option is straightforward. Holding all other factors constant, a higher exercise price diminishes the profit from the exercise of the option. An increase in the exercise price would, therefore, lead to a decrease in the price of the call option. In the case of put options, a higher exercise price increases the profit from exercise of the option. Thus, put option prices increase with an increase in their exercise price.

The effect of an increase in time to maturity on the value of an option depends on the nature and type of option. There is an asymmetry nature to option contracts which causes the holder to benefit from increased uncertainty. The option holder stands to gain by a rise in uncertainty, and therefore the value of the call option increases as its time to maturity increases. Also, the present value of the exercise price decreases as the time to maturity increases. Therefore, the time left to maturity has a way of influencing option values. An American put option cannot logically decrease in value with an increased time to maturity but with a European put option, the net effect of these two influences is ambiguous, i.e. increased uncertainty increases value while the decreased present value of the exercise price decreases value.

An increase in the volatility of the currency price makes future currency prices more variable and increases the probability of large gains. Again, the asymmetry of the option contract allows the option holder to benefit from increased uncertainty since the option is effectively insured against downside risk.

13.2 THEORETICAL VALUATION

The price and subsequent value of an option are determined by a theoretical valuation based on several known and estimated factors. The time until maturity, the current foreign exchange spot and forward foreign exchange prices, the strike and the cost of funding the option premium are all readily available. Meanwhile, a market has developed which estimates the future volatility, or in other terms, the activity of the underlying cash product. The greater the anticipated movement, the greater the value of the option for a given fixed set of parameters. Options also increase in value the smaller the distance between the strike price and the forward foreign exchange rate, and the greater the time to maturity. For European and American options, most market participants accept the valuation put forward by Black and Scholes and, as such, option prices can be agreed once the factors are entered into the equation.

The theoretical model also calculates the risk associated with changes in any of the variables required for pricing the currency option. The *delta*, or hedge ratio of the option, is the degree to which the option value will change with a movement in the underlying currency. A dollar/Swiss franc option with a 20% delta would change in value by approximately 20 franc points for every 100 point spot move. While the delta is the first derivative of the price, *gamma* is the second one, or change in delta for every move in the spot foreign exchange rate. A 50-delta dollar call option with a 15% gamma would have a 65 delta if the dollar appreciated 1%.

It is this dynamic nature of the delta that allows an option to be a leveraged product with limited risk and unlimited profit potential. Profitable positions effectively grow in size while unprofitable trades are impacted less by adverse changes in the market.

The *vega* or volatility risk of an option is the extent to which the valuation will change with varying estimates of volatility. The *theta*, or time decay, is the decrease in value of the option as it approaches maturity, as an option is a constantly diminishing asset. Finally, every option has forward foreign exchange risk equivalent to the delta and an interest rate exposure based on changes in funding costs. The delta and interest rate risks can be hedged easily in the relevant markets. The dynamic nature of the other risks is the essence of the options market.

13.3 BLACK–SCHOLES MODEL

In 1973, Fischer Black and Myron Scholes published a paper describing an equilibrium model of stock option pricing that is based on arbitrage. This is made possible by their crucial insight that it is possible to replicate the payoff to options by following a prescribed investment strategy involving the underlying asset and lending/borrowing.

The mathematics employed in the Black–Scholes model is complex, but the principle is straightforward. The model states that the stock and the call option on the stock are two comparable investments. Therefore, it should be possible to create a riskless portfolio by buying the stock and hedging it by selling call options. The hedge is a dynamic one because the stock and the option will not necessarily move by the same amount, but by continuously adjusting the option hedge to compensate for movement in the underlying market and thus the overall position should be riskless. Therefore, the income received from investing in the call option premium will be offset exactly by the cost of replicating (hedging) the position. If the option premium is too high, the arbitrageur will make a riskless profit by writing call options and hedging the underlying stock. If too low, it should be possible to profit by buying the call option and selling sufficient stock.

Black and Scholes demonstrated that the option premium could be arrived at through an arbitrage process in a similar manner to that in which a currency forward rate can be derived through a formula linking the spot rate and the interest rate differential. Also, in the same way that a currency forward rate is not "what the market thinks the currency will be worth at a future date", but simply based on an arbitrage relationship, so the Black–Scholes model is not influenced by such factors as market sentiment, direction or apparent bias. In fact, an assumption of the model is that the market moves in a random fashion, in that, while prices will change, the chances of an up move against a down move are about even, and that future price movements cannot be predicted from the behaviour of the past.

The model:

$C = SN(d_1) - Ke^{(-rt)}N(d_2)$

C = theoretical call premium

S = current stock price

t = time until option expiration

K = option striking price

r = risk-free interest rate

N = cumulative standard normal distribution

e = exponential term (2.7183)

$$d_1 = \frac{\ln(S/K) + (r + s^2/2)t}{s\sqrt{t}}$$

$$d_2 = d_1 - s\sqrt{t}$$

s = standard deviation of stock returns

ln = natural logarithm

Plotted over a period of time, the distribution of prices takes on the characteristics of the "bell-shaped" curve. Such a distribution is a key assumption of the Black–Scholes model, yet with the foreign exchange markets in particular, it is a questionable one. Even with its economic liquidity and its global 24-hour structure, foreign exchange is by no means a perfect market. Frequently, there are times when prices do not behave in a normally distributed fashion. Such occurrences as wars, central bank intervention and unexpected political or economic news are all factors, which can and do disrupt the day-to-day business of the market.

Furthermore, in order to simplify the calculation process, Black and Scholes made other assumptions about market behaviour, which may vary from the real world. They assumed that volatility was known and constant, that interest rates were constant, that there were no transaction costs or taxation effects, that trading was continuous, that there were no dividends payable, and that options could only be exercised on the expiry date.

Interest rates will vary, of course, as will volatility and even the foreign exchange markets have a transaction cost in the bid/offer spread. Frequently, the market will become very thin or almost untradable during highly volatile periods. However, most of these assumptions can be relaxed without inordinately affecting the formulations of the pricing model and where the assumptions are more critical, other models have been developed.

13.4 EXAMPLES OF OTHER MODELS

As already has been mentioned, Black–Scholes is by no means the only model being used in the options market today. Theorists have devoted a substantial amount of time and effort developing mathematical models for pricing options and a number of different models exist as a result. All make certain assumptions about market behaviour, which are not totally accurate but which give the best solutions to the price of an option.

For example, in 1973, the *Merton* option pricing formula generalised the Black–Scholes formula, so it could price European options on stocks or stock indices paying a known dividend yield. The yield is expressed as an annual continuously compounded rate q. Values for a call price c or put price p are:

$$c = se^{-qt}\Phi(d_1) - xe^{-rt}\Phi(d_2)$$

$$p = xe^{-rt}\Phi(d_2) - se^{-qt}\Phi(-d_1)$$

where:

$$d_1 = \frac{\log(s/x) + (r - q + \sigma^2/2)t}{\sigma\sqrt{t}}$$

$$d_2 = d_1 - \sigma\sqrt{t}$$

Here, log denotes the natural logarithm, and:

- s = the price of the underlying stock;
- x = the strike price;
- r = the continuously compounded risk-free interest rate;
- q = the continuously compounded annual dividend yield;
- t = the time in years until the expiration of the option;
- σ = the implied volatility for the underlying stock;
- Φ = the standard normal cumulative distribution function.

Another example was in 1979, *Cox, Ross and Rubinstein* derived a pricing model, which could account for the early exercise provisions in American style options. Using the same parameters as in the Black–Scholes model, they adopted what is known as a "binomial" method to evaluate the premium. Making the assumption that the option market behaves efficiently and therefore the holder of a call or put option will exercise if the benefit of holding the option is outweighed by the cost of carrying the hedge, the binomial process involves taking a series of trial estimates over the life of the option, each estimate (or iteration) is a probability analysis of the likelihood of early exercise on any given day.

Also, in 1982, *Garman and Kohlhagen* extended the Black–Scholes model to cover the foreign exchange market, where they allowed for the fact that currency pricing involves two interest rates, not one, and that a currency can trade at a premium or discount forward depending on the interest rate differential. Like the Merton formula, the Garman and Kohlhagen formula applies only to European options. Values for a call price c or put price p are:

$$c = se^{-qt}\Phi(d_1) - xe^{-rt}\Phi(d_2)$$

$$p = xe^{-rt}\Phi(-d_2) - se^{-qt}\Phi(-d_1)$$

where:

$$d_1 = \frac{\log(s/x) + (r - q + \sigma^2/2)t}{\sigma\sqrt{t}}$$

$$d_2 = d_1 - \sigma\sqrt{t}$$

Here, log denotes the natural logarithm, and:

- s = the current exchange rate (units of domestic currency per unit of foreign currency);
- x = the strike exchange rate;
- r = the continuously compounded domestic risk-free interest rate;
- q = the continuously compounded foreign risk-free interest rate;
- t = the time in years until the expiration of the option;
- σ = the implied volatility for the underlying exchange rate;
- Φ = the standard normal cumulative distribution function.

13.5 PRICING WITHOUT A COMPUTER MODEL

Against all the above theories, there is a way to price an option without a computer model. This can be obtained by the following equation, which will give a good approximation for a European style option premium. The formula is:

$$\text{Price} = \text{BB} \times \text{forward outright rate}$$

This is where:

$$\text{AA} = \text{square root (days to expiry/365)} \times \text{volatility} \times 0.19947$$

and

$$\text{BB} = ((\text{AA} + 0.5) \times 2) - 1$$

This formula is where price is the premium for an at-the-money European option quoted in units per base currency.

13.6 EDUCATED GUESS

Another calculation relies heavily on probability theory. The principal concepts are expected value and the lognormal distribution. Since the future is unknown, an "educated guess" is about where the spot market might be in order to determine the value of that right today. Thus, rather than trying to predict the future spot rate, option pricing takes a systematic, mathematical approach to the educated guess.

In this case, expected value (EV) is the payoff of an event multiplied by the probability of it occurring. For example, the probability of rolling a six on one die is 1/6 or 16.67%. The EV of a game in which \$100 is paid for rolling a six and nothing for any other roll is:

$$(1/6 \times \$100) + (5/6 \times \$0) = \$16.67$$

where the expected value is the fair price for playing such a game.

An options premium can be thought of in the same way, although instead of six possible outcomes, there are hundreds. All the spot rates that might prevail are the options expirations. Each outcome will have a specific value. This will either be zero if the option is out-of-the-money or the difference between the closing spot and the strike price if the option is in-the-money. Each closing spot rate can also be thought of as having its own discrete probability. If, for each outcome, the value of that outcome is multiplied by its probability and then the results are added up, the sum would be the premium of the option. The expected value of an option (the probability – weighted sum of all its possible payoffs) is the fair price for buying the option.

13.7 THE PRICE OF AN OPTION

The price of an option is made up of two separate components:

$$\text{Option premium} = \text{intrinsic value} + \text{time value.}$$

Intrinsic value is the value of an option relative to the outright forward market price i.e. it represents the difference between the strike price of the option and the forward rate at which one could transact today. Intrinsic value can be zero but never negative.

There are six factors that contribute to this pricing of an option:

- Prevailing spot price;
- Interest rate differentials (forward rate);
- Strike price;
- Time to expiry;
- Volatility;
- Intrinsic value.

As described above, the best-known original closed-form solution to option pricing was developed by Fischer Black and Myron Scholes in 1973 (Black–Scholes model). Also, as was mentioned, in its simplest form, it offers a solution to pricing European style options on assets with interim cash payouts over the life of the option. The model calculates the theoretical, or fair, value for the option by constructing an instantaneously riskless hedge that is one whose performance is the mirror image of the option payout. The portfolio of option and hedge can then be assumed to earn the risk-free rate of return.

Central to the model is the assumption that markets' returns are normally distributed (i.e. have lognormal prices), that there are no transaction costs, that volatility and interest rates remain constant throughout the life of the option, and that the market follows a diffusion process. The model has the five major inputs:

- The risk-free interest rate;
- The options strike price;
- The price of the underlying;
- The option's maturity; and
- The volatility assumed.

Since the first four are usually determined, markets tend to trade the implied volatility of the option. For example, a six-month European style sterling put/dollar call with the spot rate at $/£ 1.7500 and forward points of 515, giving an outright forward of 1.6985 (1.7500–0.0515), will have an intrinsic value of 4.15 cents per pound.

While the Black and Scholes pricing formula looks formidable, it is important to understand that the formula is nothing more than the simple two-state option pricing model applied with an instantaneous trading interval.

If the strike price of the option is more favourable than the current forward price, the option is said to be in-the-money. If the strike price is equal to the forward rate, it is an at-the-money option and if the strike price is less favourable than the outright, the option is termed out-of-the-money.

For American style options, a similar definition applies except that the option's "moneyness" relative to the spot price also needs to be considered. Clearly, in the example above, an American style option would be in-the-money relative to the forward but not to the spot. Conversely, if the option had the same details except that it was a call on sterling, it would clearly be out-of-the-money under the European definition but as an American style option it would be in-the-money relative to the spot price. Naturally, the cost of the option would need to be considered in order to achieve a profitable early exercise of an American option and this leads to a phenomenon peculiar to American style options known as "optimal exercise". This is the point at which it becomes profitable to exercise an American style option early having taken account of the premium paid.

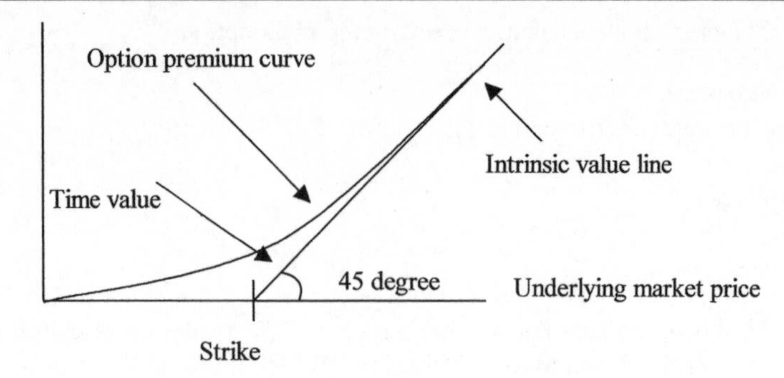

Figure 13.1

13.8 OPTION PREMIUM PROFILE

The graph shows in Figure 13.1 premium against spot at a given point in time. It can be seen that the time value call position is greatest when the option is at-the-money. This is because this represents the highest level of asymmetric risk, which is optimum risk reward profile.

The time value tends to zero as spot goes deep out-of-the-money and thus converges with the maximum loss expiry line and also as it goes deep in-the-money, converging with the unlimited profit expiry line. The change in the premium is not parallel to the change in the underlying value. The premium will change more rapidly when the option is near at-the-money and less rapidly when the option is in-the-money or out-of-the-money.

13.9 TIME VALUE AND INTRINSIC VALUE

Time value is a mathematical function of implied volatility, time to maturity, interest rate differentials, spot foreign exchange rate and the strike of an option.

The option premium can be split into two parts: intrinsic value and time value. The effect of an increase in time on an options premium is not linear. This is because the probability of a rise or fall in a currency's value does not increase on a straight-line basis. For example, all things being equal, the premium for an at-the-money three-month option is only worth about two-thirds more than for a one-month option (not three times its value). A one-year option is only worth about one-third more than a six-month option (instead of twice its value). As a consequence, the premium for at-the-money options declines at an accelerating rate towards expiry. Figure 13.2 demonstrates the time value premium delay.

Time value is affected by a number of factors:

- The time remaining to expiration;
- The volatility of the underlying spot market;
- The strike price of the option;
- The forward rate of the currency pair; and
- The current interest rates.

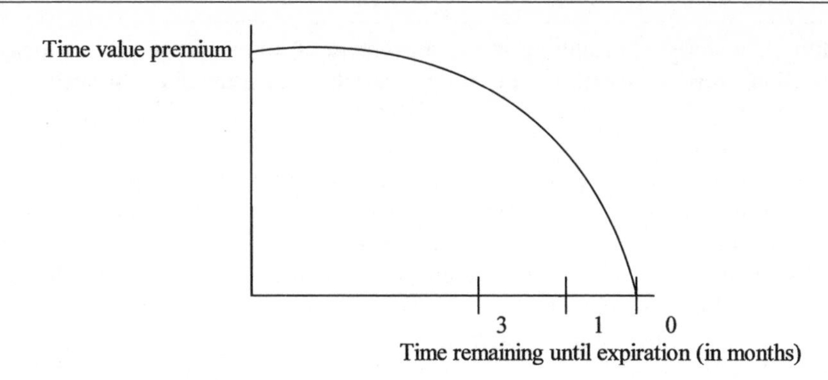

Figure 13.2

Intrinsic value is the advantage to the holder of the option of the strike rate over the forward foreign exchange outright rate.

An option is said to have intrinsic value where the strike price of the option is more favourable than the current market forward rate. As a general rule, the greater the intrinsic value of an option the higher its premium. Also, an option with some intrinsic value is described as being in-the-money, while an option with no intrinsic value is said to be out-of-the-money. However, where the strike price of the option is equal to the current forward rate the option is said to be at-the-money.

13.10 TIME TO EXPIRY

The time decay of an option is related to the time remaining in the option; in fact, it is proportional to the square root of the time remaining. The reason for this phenomenon is two-fold:

1. The longer the time to maturity, the greater is the chance that the exchange rate moves such that the option will be exercised. The rate at which the premium diminishes as the option approaches expiry is called the "time decay" and the rate of decay is exponential, i.e. the option loses time value more quickly approaching expiry than it does earlier in its life. At expiry, the option will have only intrinsic value and no time value.
2. The time value can be thought of as "risk premium" or the cost to the writer of hedging the uncertainty of exercise.

13.11 VOLATILITY

In essence, volatility is a measure of the variability (but not the direction) of the price of the underlying instrument, essentially the chances of an option being exercised. It is defined as the annualised standard deviation of the natural log of the ratio of two successive prices.

Volatility is a statistical function of the movement of an exchange rate. It measures the speed of movement within an exchange rate band, rather than the width of that band.

Historical volatility is a measure of the standard deviation of the underlying instrument over a past period and is calculated from actual price movements by looking at intraday price changes and comparing this with the average (the standard deviation). The calculation is not affected by the absolute exchange rates, merely the change in price involved. Thus, for example, the starting and finishing points for two separate calculations could be exactly the same but could give two very different levels of volatility depending on how the exchange rate traded in between. Thus, if the market has traded up and down erratically, the reading will be high. If instead it has gradually moved from one point to the other in even steps, then the reading will be lower.

Implied volatility is the volatility implied in the price of an option, i.e. the volatility that is used to calculate an option price. Implied volatilities rise and fall with market forces and tend to reflect the level of activity anticipated in the future, although supply and demand can at times be dominant factors. In the professional interbank market, two-way volatility prices are traded according to market perception and these volatilities are converted into premium using option models. Implied volatility is the only variable affecting the price of an option that cannot be directly observed in the markets, thus leading to the typical variations in price inherent in any marketplace.

Actual volatility is the actual volatility that occurs during the life of an option. It is the difference between the actual volatility experienced during delta hedging and the implied volatility used to price an option at the outset, which determines if a trader makes or loses money on that option.

In summary, implied volatility is a timely measure, in that it reflects the market's perceptions today. On the other hand, historical volatility is a retrospective measure of volatility. This implies that it reflects how volatile the variable has been in the recent past. But it has to be remembered that it is a highly objective measure. Implied volatilities can be biased, especially if they are based upon options that are traded in a market with very little liquidity. Also, historical volatility can be calculated for any variable for which historical data is tracked.

Volatility affects the time value or risk premium of an option, as an increase in volatility increases the time value and thus the price of the option. Likewise, a decrease in volatility lowers the price of the option. For example, consider the position of the writer of an option, whereby, say, a bank sells an option to a client, giving the client the right to purchase dollars and sell Swiss francs in three months' time. In order to correctly hedge the position, consider what will happen in three months' time. If the spot is above the strike price of the option, the client will exercise the option and the bank will be obliged to sell dollars and buy francs. However, if the spot is below the strike price, the client will allow the option to lapse. Hence the bank's initial hedge for the option will be to purchase a proportion of dollars in the spot market against this potential short dollar position. If the spot subsequently rises, the likelihood of the option being exercised will increase and so the initial hedge will be too small. Therefore, the bank will need to buy some more dollars, which it does at a rate worse than the original rate at which the option was priced, thereby losing money. Conversely, if the spot rate falls, this makes the option less likely to be exercised and the bank will then find itself holding too many dollars and will have to sell them out at a lower price than where they were purchased,

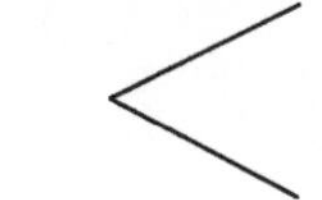

Figure 13.3

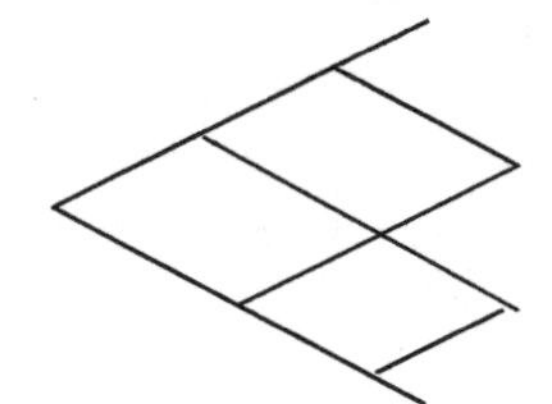

Figure 13.4

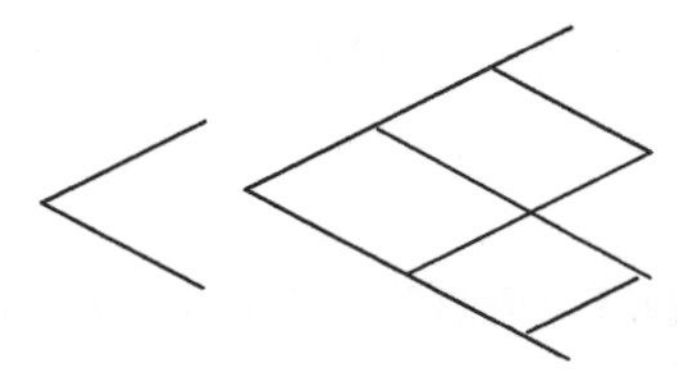

Figure 13.5

thus losing more money. These losses are called "hedging costs" and each time the spot market moves, the rehedging required will lose the bank money. In essence, the premium received by the writer is effectively the best estimate of these hedging costs over the life of the option.

It is clear to see that as volatility increases, market movement increases and so does the number of times the writer of the option must rehedge. Thus, the hedging costs of the option increases and as volatility rises, the price of the option will rise. Conversely, as volatility decreases, the number of times the writer of the option has to hedge also decreases and so lower hedging costs will be incurred.

It should be noted that longer-term options are more sensitive to volatility. For instance, say a volatility of 10% gives a certain range of outcomes over one time period. See Figure 13.3.

Given more time periods with the same volatility, the range of possible outcomes increases. See Figure 13.4.

An increase in volatility to 12% will have a larger impact on the range of outcomes in the second case due to the cumulative effect. See Figure 13.5.

The option pricing models make an incorrect assumption regarding the likelihood of exercise of low and high delta options. Pricing models currently in use assume a lognormal distribution of outcomes around the forward outright rate similar to the normal distribution shown in the graph (Figure 13.6). This is an approximation in all respects but it is particularly inaccurate for low and high delta options, where the outcomes are more likely to occur than the distribution would indicate. The volatility trader will, therefore, use a higher implied volatility, which gives a higher option price in order to give a closer estimate of their real value.

Another point to note is that sometimes a volatility quote is wider for low or high delta options. This is because as with gamma, volatility has more effect on 50 delta options than on lower or higher delta options. If the width of a volatility quote for an at-the-money option

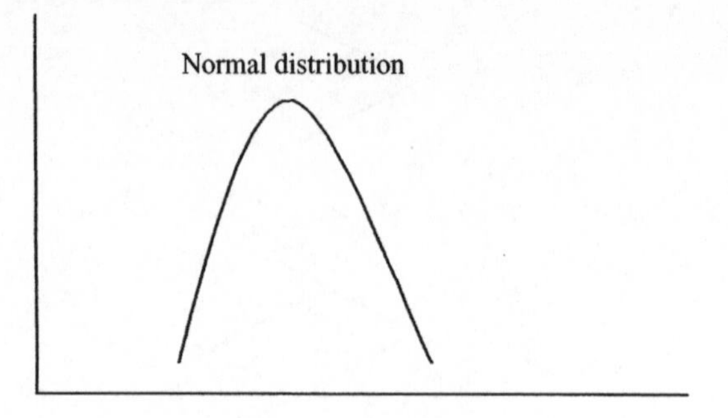

Figure 13.6

were maintained for, say, a 10-delta option, the option premium spread would be extremely narrow. For this reason, it is usual practice to widen these quotes to give a more usual price spread. As in all markets, however, it should be noted that supply and demand determine the prices quoted.

13.12 STRIKE PRICE AND FORWARD RATES

An option's time value is greatest when the strike price is at-the-money and the further in- or out-of-the-money the strike price is, the lower the time value is. This can be explained by again considering the hedging costs. If the option is originally at-the-money, it is said to have a 50 delta and therefore the initial hedge will be to buy or sell half the principal amount of the option. The delta of the option can be thought of as the probability of exercise, so a 50 delta gives a one in two chance of exercise. That is, maximum uncertainty. As the spot moves, the delta will change and require readjusting of the hedge in the spot market. The change in delta (or gamma) is greater for a 50-delta option than for an option with a much higher or lower delta, for example 80 or 20 delta. This is because the likelihood of exercise, and therefore the amount of hedge required, changes more rapidly. Thus, less readjustment is required for these high and low delta options, and consequently, fewer hedging costs are incurred for the low and high delta options. This leads to lower levels of risk premium or time value for in-the-money and out-of-the-money options.

13.13 INTEREST RATES

The currency interest rate is another factor that affects option premiums. As premium is usually paid upfront, it must be discounted to take account of the interest that would be earned by putting the premium on deposit. Thus the higher the domestic interest rate, the greater the discounting effect on the premium.

The effect of the interest rate differential on the option premium is not intuitively obvious, yet it is one of the most important components of the premium for a currency option. If the dollar interest rate rises in relation to the interest rate of the foreign currency, the premium of a currency call option will increase in value. This is because holding a foreign currency and buying a currency call option are alternative investments. On the one hand, the investor will sell (borrow) dollars and buy (invest in) a foreign currency in order to take advantage of a rise in that foreign currency. Alternatively, the trader could just simply buy a currency call option. If the dollar interest rate rises, the cost of borrowing dollars will increase, which will make the alternative of buying a currency call option more attractive. Consequently, the premium will rise.

This can equally be explained in terms of the forward value of a currency. If the dollar interest rate rises in relation to the foreign currency interest rates, and the spot rate remains the same (unchanged), covered interest rate arbitrage will ensure that the forward rate of the foreign currency will rise relative to the spot. Therefore, the call option on that currency will also rise in value. Of course, the dollar interest rate might remain the same but the interest rate of the foreign currency might fall. The effect on the interest rate differential and therefore on the value of the currency call option will remain the same, but the premium will rise.

The converse is true for currency put options, because an increase in the dollar interest rate in relation to the foreign currency interest rate will, given no change on the spot price, result in a rise in the forward value of the currency. Thus the holder of a put option on the currency will see the premium fall. Buying a currency put option is an alternative strategy to borrowing in that currency and investing in dollars. Hence, a rise in the dollar interest rate or a fall in the foreign currency interest rate makes the put option strategy less attractive and the put premium will fall.

The effect of interest rate differential changes on currency option premiums can be summarised as follows:

- Assuming the spot rate remains unchanged, a rise in dollar interest rates relative to the foreign currency interest rate, or a fall in the foreign currency interest rate relative to the dollar interest rate, will increase the premium for a currency call option and decrease the premium for a currency put option.
- Assuming the spot rate remains the same, a fall in the dollar interst rate relative to the foreign currency interest rate, or a rise in the foreign currency interest rate relative to the dollar interest rate, will decrease the premium for a currency call option and increase the premium for a currency put option.

13.14 AMERICAN vs EUROPEAN

For European options, intrinsic value is the value of an option relative to the outright forward market price, that is, it represents the difference between the strike price of the option and the forward rate at which one could transact today. Intrinsic value can be zero but is never negative. If the strike price of the option is more favourable than the current forward price, the option is in-the-money. If the strike price is equal to the forward rate, the option is at-the-money and if the strike price is less favourable than the outright forward, the option is out-of-the-money.

A similar definition applies for American style options, except that the options' "moneyness" relative to the spot price also needs to be considered. Naturally, the cost of the option needs to be considered in order to achieve a profitable early exercise and this leads to a phenomenon peculiar to American options known as "optimal exercise". This is the point at which it becomes profitable to exercise an American option early having taken account of the premium paid.

In fact, there are several occasions when it would be better to pay an extra premium and buy a more expensive American style option. For example:

1. When a trader is buying an option where the call currency has the higher interest rate and there is an expectation that the interest rate differential will widen significantly;

2. When a trader is buying an option where the interest rates are close to each other and there is an expectation that the call interest rate will move above the put interest rate; and
3. When a trader is buying an out-of-the-money option with interest rates as in both of the above and there is an expectation for it to move significantly into the money, then the American style option is more highly leveraged and will hence produce higher profits.

13.15 CONCLUDING REMARKS

The generally accepted pricing basis for options today is the Black–Scholes formula, which was devised in the early 1970s to provide a "fair value" for equity options. However, the foreign exchange markets needed something to take account of interest rates and the fact that there are no dividends due on currencies. Various adaptations of the Black–Scholes model emerged, of which the most popular one used today is the Garman–Kohlhagen model. This method makes allowances for the interest rates of the respective currencies and the fact that a currency can trade at a discount or premium forward relative to the other currency.

It has to be remembered that American style options differ due to the possibility of early exercise. The Cox, Ross and Rubenstein model is the generally accepted method for these, but they do not feature heavily in the over-the-counter market.

Overall, therefore, the industry norm is to use the Black–Scholes formula adapted by Garman–Kohlhagen for valuing over-the-counter European style currency options.

Thus, in summary, the factors, which are required to price an option, include:

1. Currency pair;
2. Call or put;
3. Strike rate;
4. Amount;
5. Style–European or American;
6. Expiration date and time (New York expiry or Tokyo expiry);
7. Prevailing spot rate;
8. Interest rates for both currencies;
9. Foreign exchange swap rate (calculated from the information in point 8); and
10. Volatility of the currency pair.

From the list, points 1 to 6 are chosen by the potential buyer/seller of the option. Points 7 to 9 are given by the market and lastly, point 10 is the only unknown factor. It represents the anticipated market volatility expected for the life of the option and is determined using the option pricing models discussed earlier.

14
The Greeks

The overview discussed in the next couple of chapters should help to clarify not only how the price of an option is influenced by changes in the underlying, the time to expiration and the implied volatility, but also how the market measures the impact of these variables on an option's price. Traders extensively use the "Greeks", a set of factor sensitivities, to quantify the exposure of portfolios that contain options. Each measures how the portfolio's market value should respond to a change in some variable.

The Greeks are a set of factor sensitivities used for measuring risk exposures related to options or other derivatives.

For speculative purposes, the value of an option needs to be known on a continual basis and, more importantly, the factors that change an option's value need to be understood. In analysing an option risk (or value), the market norm is to use letters of the Greek alphabet. Not surprisingly they are often referred to as the "Greeks" and they include delta, vega, theta, gamma and rho. (However, vega is not in the Greek alphabet, but is named after a star in the constellation Lyra). Sometimes, Vega has also been referred to as kappa. Also, four of the five are risk metrics. The exception here is Theta, because the passage of time is certain and thus entails no risk.

Therefore, these major "Greeks", which measure these risks and need to be taken into account before taking on any option position, are:

Vega/Kappa	Theta	Delta	Gamma	Rho
Measures the impact of a change in volatility	Measures the impact of a change in time remaining	Measures the impact of a change in the price of the underlying	Measures the rate of change in delta	Measures the sensitivity to an applicable interest rate

An option's price sensitivity to price changes in the underlying instrument is known as its delta.

14.1 DELTA

When an option trader sells or buys a currency option, they will use the foreign exchange market to hedge the exposure. The most common type of hedging is delta hedging.

Delta is the change in premium per change in the underlying. Technically, the underlying is the forward foreign exchange outright rate but as the option pricing model assumes constant interest rates, this is often calculated using the spot foreign exchange rate. For example, if an option has a delta of 25 and spot moved 100 basis points, then the option price gain/loss would be 25 basis points. For this reason, delta is sometimes thought of as representing the "spot sensitive" amount of the option.

Also, delta can be thought of as the estimated probability of exercise of the option. As the option pricing model assumes an outcome profile based around the forward foreign exchange outright rate, an at-the-money option has a delta of 50%. It falls for out-of-the-money options and increases for in-the-money options, but the change is non-linear, in that it changes much faster when the option is close-to-the-money.

Delta is the ratio a volatility trader would hedge against a particular option to cover the spot sensitivity.

Turning to calculus for the formal definition of delta, let 0 be the current time. Let $0p$ and $0s$ be current values for the portfolio and underlier. Delta is the first partial derivative of a portfolio's value with respect to the value of the underlier:

$$\text{delta} = \frac{\partial^0 p}{\partial^0 s}$$

This technical definition leads to an approximation for the behaviour of a portfolio.

$$\Delta^0 p \approx \text{delta}\ \Delta^0 s$$

Where $\Delta 0s$ is a small change in the underlier's current value, and $\Delta 0p$ is the corresponding change in the portfolio's current value. This is called the delta approximation.

An option is said to be delta-hedged if a position has been taken in the underlying in proportion to its delta. For example, if one is short a call option on an underlying with a face value of $1 000 000 and with a delta of 0.25, a long position of $250 000 in the underlying will leave one delta-neutral with no exposure to changes in the price of the underlying, but only if these are infinitesimally small.

As the underlying market moves throughout the life of the option, the delta will change, thus requiring the underlying hedge to be adjusted. Once the initial hedge has been transacted, calls and puts behave in precisely the same way, in terms of the hedging required.

For example, an at-the-money sterling call/dollar put option in £10 000 000, with a strike price of £/$ 1.7500, has an initial delta of 50. The option writer therefore buys £5 000 000 in the spot market to hedge the option position. If the spot rises to £/$ 1.7700, the delta will increase to, say, 60. Now, the writer needs to purchase an extra £1 000 000 to attain delta-neutrality. If the exchange rate then falls back again to the original rate, the option writer is overhedged and requires selling back £1 000 000 in order to remain delta-neutral. Clearly, as the option writer rehedges, losses will be incurred which will increase as volatility increases.

Another example could be where a trader sells a dollar call/Swiss franc put at $/sfr 1.5500 for six months in $10 000 000. The trader's risk is that in six months, the option is exercised and there will be a payout of dollars and a receipt of francs. The trader's hedge against this risk would therefore be to buy dollars and sell francs, thus hedging the delta amount because this represents the likelihood of exercise. If spot is $/sfr 1.5300 and the forward outright is $/sfr 1.5345, then the trader's hedging, ignoring time movement, would look like that shown in the following table, as the forward rate changes:

Forward $/sfr	Delta	Hedge	Total
1.5345	35	Buy $3.5 mill	+$3.5 mill
1.5500	50	Buy $1.5 mill	+$5.0 mill
1.5600	57	Buy $0.7 mill	+$5.7 mill
1.5200	30	Sell $2.7 mill	+$3.0 mill

Whether or not the trader looses money will depend on volatility. From the table above, it can be seen that hedging a short option position loses money, as the trader would be continually buying high and selling low. However, when the option was first sold, the trader received a premium for it – representing the estimated cost of hedging to the trader. If the volatility of the market is higher than the trader expected and then has to hedge more frequently, then the trader may lose more money hedging than originally gained on the premium. If, however, the market is less volatile than the assumption of the option price, the trader should lose less money hedging than received in premium and therefore make a profit overall.

If the trader had bought the option rather than sold it, the trader would then hope for increased volatility because the hedging exercise would be making money.

For example, the trader buys exactly the same options, a dollar call/Swiss franc put at $/sfr 1.5500 in $10 000 000. The trader's risk is now that there will be a long dollar position in six months, so the hedge will be to sell dollars and buy francs. As the forward outright rate moves, however, the delta of the option will move in exactly the same way as before. This follows as the option is the same and the delta does not depend upon who owns the option. In this case, therefore, the trader will be buying low and selling high and making money on the hedging. Just as before, this makes sense as the trader originally paid out a premium to buy the option, so the hedging is making back that premium. This time, the trader has bought volatility and hopes that volatility will in fact be higher than the rate at which the option was bought for. If it is, the trader will make more money hedging than was paid out in premium.

Hence, buying and selling volatility is like any other product in that there is a wish to buy at a low rate and sell at a higher rate to make a profit.

As another example, consider a short sterling call at £/$ 1.8100 position at 342 points. The loss profile corresponds to the loss profile on a short sterling cash position. Thus, a hedge on a short sterling call position would be to buy sterling cash. The value of the option will go up with sterling going up, but it is not a one-to-one relationship.

The delta ratio indicates the increase in value of the option for every increase in value of one point on the cash market. Thus the following rules on delta can be established. On a call option, delta will range from 0% when out-of-the-money to 50% at-the-money to 100% when deep in-the-money. Conversely, the delta of a put option goes from 0% when out-of-the-money to –50% at-the-money to –100% when deep in-the-money.

In the example above, the delta of the option is, say, 45%, which means that to hedge the position, an amount of sterling of 45% of the face value of the option will have to be bought. Therefore, if the option is for £1 000 000, a move up of 50 points on the rate will result in a loss of:

$$£1\,000\,000 \times 0.0050 \times 45\% = \$2250$$

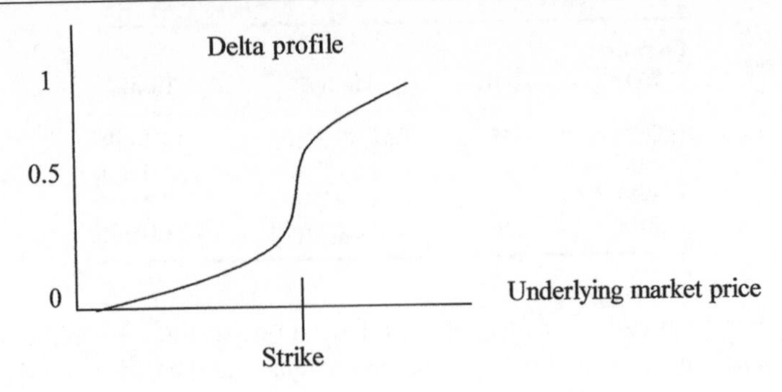

Figure 14.1

This will be offset by the long cash position of:

$$450\,000 \times 0.0050 = \$2250$$

The delta of an option does not remain constant and the new delta of this position is, say, 47%. In order to maintain a delta neutral position, the trader will have to buy another £20 000. Such a hedging strategy will enable the trader to keep the premium received initially when selling the option.

The graph in Figure 14.1 shows that delta is the gradient of the tangent of the curve of the premium in relation to the cash prices. This also reveals that delta will move more rapidly for an option with a short remaining life than for an option with a long remaining life.

In conclusion, basically, the delta of an option will change if any factor which influences the potential probability of exercise changes. These include spot foreign exchange price, volatility, time, and interest rates. Option traders use the delta as a guide to hedging. Taken simply, if a bank is short one option with a delta of 50%, the bank will hedge only half of the nominal amount of the option, as it only has a 50% chance of being exercised. This is known as "delta hedging". This is a simplistic example and in reality banks have large option books, which they hedge on a daily basis, but the principle applies no matter what the size of the portfolio.

Also, there are three points to keep in mind with delta:

1. Delta tends to increase as it gets closer to expiration for near or at-the-money options;
2. Delta is not a constant; and
3. Delta is subject to change given changes in implied volatility.

14.2 GAMMA

The rate of change of delta is called gamma and it will give a measure of the amount of change in the delta for a given change in the cash price. Therefore, it will provide an estimate of how much it will cost to delta hedge.

Gamma is the rate of change in an option's delta for a one-unit change in the underlying.

The cost of rebalancing the hedge is a consequence of the curvature of the premium curve against cash prices. The curvature is greatest at-the-money and reduces when in-the-money or out-of-the-money. This can be shown in the graph of Figure 14.2.

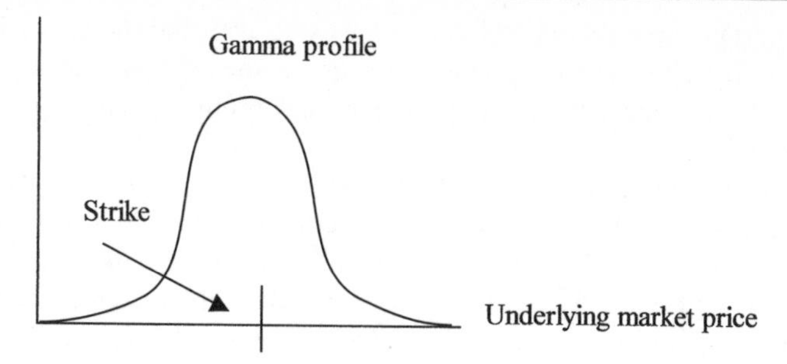

Figure 14.2

A short option position is called gamma negative. The higher the gamma, the less stable is the delta hedge. An initial conclusion is that it is more costly to hedge a short long dated option position than a short position of short dated options.

Thus, gamma is the change in delta per change in the underlying and is important because the option model assumes that delta hedging is performed on a continuous basis. In practice, however, this is not possible as the market gaps and the net amounts requiring further hedging would be too small to make it worthwhile. The gapping effect that has to be dealt with in hedging an option gives the risk proportional to the gamma of the option.

For a formal definition of gamma, again turn to calculus. Gamma is the second partial derivative of a portfolio's value $0p$ with respect of the value $0s$ of the underlier:

$$\text{gamma} = \frac{\partial^{2\,0}p}{\partial^{0}s^{2}}$$

By incorporating gamma, there can be an improvement to the approximation for how the portfolio's value should change in response to small changes in the underlier's value:

$$\Delta^{0}p \approx \frac{\text{gamma}}{2}\Delta^{0}s^{2} + \text{delta}\Delta^{0}s$$

This is called the delta–gamma approximation.

An option's gamma is at its greatest when an option is at-the-money and decreases as the price of the underlying moves further away from the strike price. Therefore, gamma is U-shaped and is also greater for short-term options than for long-term options.

By convention, gamma can be expressed in two ways:

1. A gamma of say 5.23 will mean that for 1% change in the underlying price the delta will change by 5.23 units, that is, from 50% to 55.23%; and
2. A gamma of 3% will mean that for a one-unit change in the underlying price, the delta will change by 3%, for example from 50% to 51.5%.

As an example of gamma hedging, from the previous section on delta hedging, as the forward outright rate moved from 1.5600 to 1.5200, the delta of the option moved from 57 to 30. The size of movement of the delta given this movement of the underlying is the gamma of the option by the definition "gamma is the change in delta per change in the underlying". The hedging the trader was required to do was to sell $1 700 000. In practice, the trader sold the full amount at a rate of $/sfr 1.5200. If the trader were able to hedge continuously as the model assumes, the trader would have sold the same amount, that is $1 700 000, but at an average rate of $/sfr 1.5450. This would obviously have been more profitable. From this example, it can be seen that the gapping effect works against the trader when there is a short options position (and therefore short gamma) and a repetition of the exercise would show that the gapping is in the trader's favour if there was a long options position being held (and gamma).

The value of gamma is, therefore, very important in determining sensitivity to spot movement and this gapping effect.

However, gamma is not the same for all options. Gamma is greater for short-term options than for long-term options. For example, assume a dollar call/Swiss franc put option with a strike of $/sfr 1.5500 and that there is one second to go to expiry. If the spot foreign exchange rate at the time is $/sfr 1.5501, the option is extremely likely to be exercised and the delta will be 100. If, in that second, the spot foreign exchange rate moved to $/sfr 1.5499, the option would not in fact be exercised and the delta would move to 0. Here, it can be seen that a 0.0002 move in the spot foreign exchange rate produced a change in delta from 100 to 0. If it was the same option but there was one year to maturity, a movement of 0.0002 in the spot foreign exchange rate would not significantly alter the likelihood that the option would be exercised, that is, the delta would not change noticeably.

Gamma is greater for at-the-money options that for options with deltas above or below 50. Assume an extreme example to see this effect. Using the same option of a dollar call/Swiss franc put, with a strike of $/sfr 1.5500 and there is a second to go before expiry. If the spot foreign exchange rate is at $/sfr 1.5500 and thus the option has a delta of 50, there would be the same situation as before when a 0.0001 movement in the spot foreign exchange rate created a movement of 50 in the delta. If, however, the spot were at $/sfr 1.5200, the delta of the option would be 0 and a movement even as large as 0.0200 would not increase that delta.

In conclusion, gamma is seen as a second-generation derivative, where the others considered are regarded as first generation derivatives in the pricing of an option, in that the others all consider the change that an external effect has on an option's value, such as a change in the spot foreign exchange rate. However, gamma measures the rate of change of the delta itself. Therefore it is literally the delta of the delta. Since the delta is the key pricing tool used by market participants in controlling the portfolio risk, to be able to work out the rate of change of this risk is very useful. Hence, gamma is a very important part of any option portfolio and is affected by three different factors: spot foreign exchange movement, time to maturity, and volatility.

Also, the three points to keep in mind with gamma are:

1. Gamma is smallest for deep out-of-the-money and deep in-the-money options;
2. Gamma is highest when the option gets near the money; and
3. Gamma is positive for long options and negative for short options.

14.3 THETA

Theta time decay is the effect of time passing on an option's value.

Theta is the depreciation of the time value element of the premium, that is, it measures the effect on an option's price of a one-day decrease in the time to expiration. The more the market and strike prices diverge, the less effect theta has on an option's price. Obviously, if you are the holder of an option, this effect will diminish the value of the option over time, but if you are the seller (the writer) of the option, the effect will be in your favour, as the option will cost less to purchase. Theta is non-linear, meaning that its value accelerates as the option approaches maturity. Positive gamma is generally associated with negative theta and vice versa.

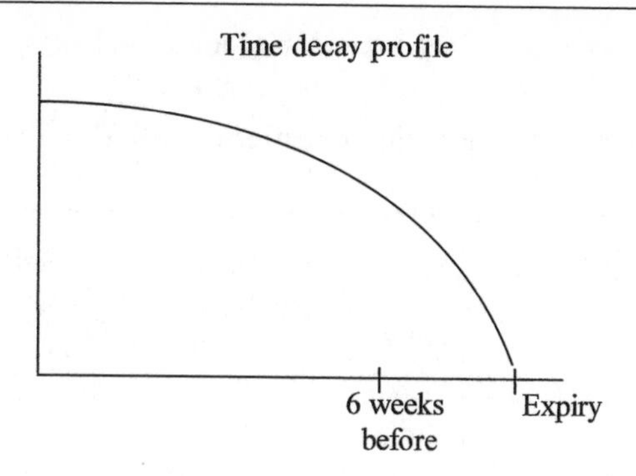

Figure 14.3

The rate at which the time value decays with respect to time is expressed as hundredths of a per cent per unit of time (day/week). Obviously, the theta factor plays in favour of a short option position. Shorter dated options have larger thetas as do those that are at-the-money. This effect will give rise to trading strategies referred to as a calendar spread.

To determine theta, assume t denotes time, and let tp denote the portfolio's value at time t. Formally, theta is the partial derivative of the portfolio's value with respect to time:

$$\text{theta} = \frac{\partial^t p}{\partial t}$$

where the derivative is evaluated at time $t = 0$. This technical definition leads to an approximation for the behaviour of a portfolio.

$$\Delta^t p \approx \text{theta}\Delta t$$

where Δt is a small interval of time, and Δtp is the change in the portfolio's value that will occur during that interval, assuming all other market variables remain the same.

The delta of an option does have an influence on the time decay of an option because the time value element of an option total value is maximum for at-the-money options. As the delta increases or decreases, the time value of the option decreases. Obviously, for options where there is very little time value, there will be very little time decay. If there is any doubt about which date to choose for an option maturity, as can be seen from Figure 14.3, there is little increase in time value for days at the far end of the option. To buy a slightly longer option therefore will not cost much more. However, if a trader waits until the option expires and then has to buy another option to cover the final period, the additional cost could be substantially more. For this reason, buying an option for the longest period needed is recommended.

In actual practice, traders do not use theta, but it is an important conceptual dimension. However, some additional points of note are:

1. Theta can be very high for out-of-the-money options if they contain a lot of implied volatility;
2. Theta is typically highest for at-the-money options; and
3. Theta will increase sharply in the last few weeks of trading and can severally undermine a long option holder's position, especially if implied volatility is on the decline at the same time.

14.4 VEGA

Vega is the rate of change of the option premium relative to a change in volatility of the option.

Vega, sometimes also called kappa, quantifies risk exposure to implied volatility changes. Vega tells us approximately how much an option price will increase or decrease given an increase or decrease in the level of implied volatility. Option sellers benefit from a fall in implied volatility, while option buyers benefit from an increase in implied volatility. Vega is greatest for at-the-money options and increase with the time to maturity. This is because the longer the time to maturity, the greater the possibility of exchange rate movements and therefore the greater the sensitivity of the option price to a change in volatility.

Vega is the first partial derivative of a portfolio's value $0p$ with respect to the value 0σ of implied volatility. This technical definition leads to an approximation for the behaviour of a portfolio.

$$\Delta^0 p \approx \text{vega}\Delta^0\sigma$$

Where here $\Delta 0\sigma$ is a small change in the implied volatility from its current value, and Δp is the corresponding change in the portfolio's value.

Thus, the more volatile the underlying price, the more expensive the option will become because of the uncertainty element. The ratio of how much the value of the premium changes for a 1% change in volatility is, thus, vega. Longer dated options have higher vegas and at-the-money options have higher vegas. It is expressed as a percentage change of dollars for a 1% change of volatility. For example, a vega of 1.0 means the option premium will appreciate by 1% in dollar or currency terms.

Some points to keep in mind with vega are:

1. Vega can increase or decrease even without price changes of the underlying because implied volatility is the level of expected volatility;
2. Vega can increase from quick moves of the underlying; and
3. Vega falls as the option gets closer to expiration.

14.5 RHO

The rho of an option measures the change in value given a change in interest rates.

It is generally considered to be the least important of the Greeks but nevertheless any option, be it a single position or a large portfolio, will be exposed to such a risk. This is because with OTC European style options, the price (in part) is derived from the forward foreign exchange rate. Therefore, if either of the two interest rates of the currency pair in the option should change, then the forward foreign exchange rate and hence the price will change. This can happen without a move in the spot foreign exchange price.

In formulating rho, let $0p$ and $0r$ be current values for the portfolio and underlier. Formally, rho is the partial derivative of the portfolio's value with respect to the risk-free rate:

$$\text{rho} = \frac{\partial^0 p}{\partial^0 r}$$

This technical definition leads to an approximation for the behaviour of a portfolio.

$$\Delta^0 p \approx \text{rho}\Delta^0 r$$

where $\Delta 0r$ is a small change in the risk-free rate, and $\Delta 0p$ is the corresponding change in the portfolio's value.

In summary, rho is the general term used for interest rate risk but it is broken down further. Rho usually refers to the base currency interest rate (usually dollars) and phi relates to the traded currency interest rates (for example, Swiss francs or Japanese yen).

14.6 BETA AND OMEGA

Some other Greek letters that are used do not actually measure an option's value but are more geared to looking at the use of options or risks associated with valuation methods. Briefly, they include beta and omega.

Beta represents the risk involved in hedging one currency pair against another, especially when sometimes currency pairs have a high correlation. For example, within the old European Monetary System (EMS) with the Deutschemark and the French franc. Some traders that had a dollar against the French franc position would have been happier hedging this exposure in the more liquid dollar against the Deutschemark market because it fairly closely correlated to the French franc. The risk here would have been if the Deutschemark against the French franc correlation had started to weaken.

Omega measures the translation profit/loss risk assumed by trading in currency pairs (which result in profits/losses in those two currencies) that are not the same as the reporting base currency for accounting purposes. An example would be an American bank that gets profits for its sterling against Swiss franc trades in either sterling or francs, yet has to convert these to dollars for the balance sheet.

15

Payoff and Profit/Loss Diagrams

The payoff and profit/loss diagrams are both useful aids in understanding options and are often used to show how options will perform at maturity. Once they have been mastered, they can provide a very useful method of determining net risk for a combination strategy at maturity. (Note: the "at maturity" is stressed as an option's total value and can fluctuate during its life, even if spot and the forward outright rate remain unchanged.)

A payoff diagram relates the payoff to an option position to the underlying currency price at expiration, which is how options will perform at maturity. Initially, the graph in Figure 15.1 represents a long position in the base currency of a currency pair.

The graph is drawn in this way to represent the fact that for the base currency, for example the dollar in $/sfr, if bought at $/sfr 1.6500, then a 0.0200 $/sfr profit will be realised at $/sfr 1.6700 and a 0.0200 $/sfr loss at $/sfr 1.6300. In the same way, a short position in the base currency can be represented in the graph shown in Figure 15.2.

The slope of the line is 45 degrees, to show that the relationship between spot and the profit and loss is 1–1. As all these graphs are being drawn at maturity, the two graphs (Figures 15.1 and 15.2) could represent a forward outright foreign exchange position or a spot foeign exchange position.

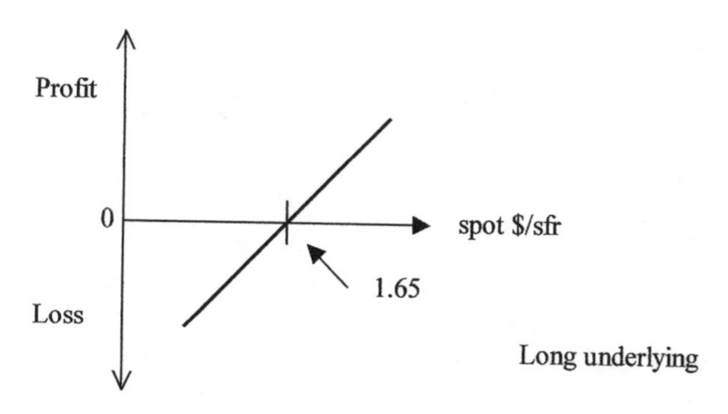

Figure 15.1

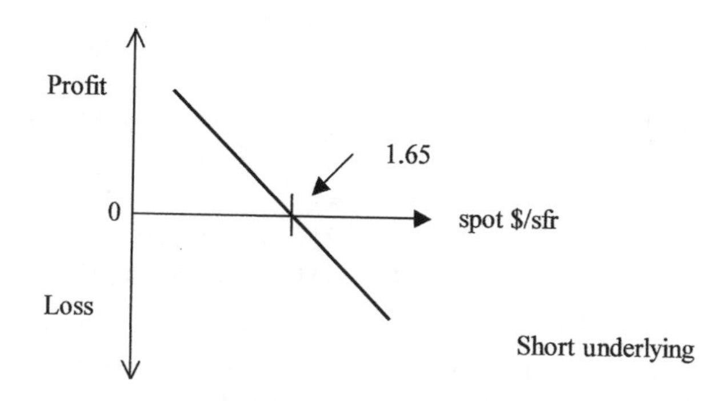

Figure 15.2

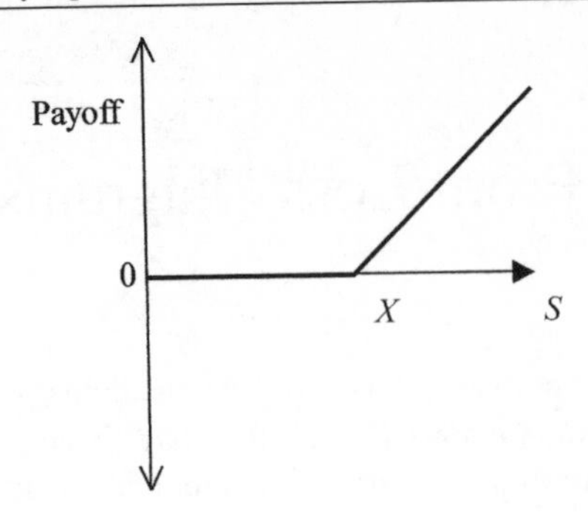

Figure 15.3

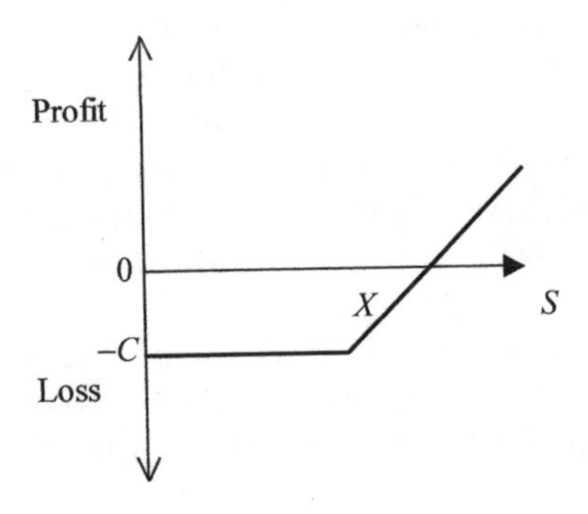

Figure 15.4

15.1 PAYOFF DIAGRAM

A payoff diagram relates the payoff to an option position to the underlying asset price at expiration. Figure 15.3 is the payoff diagram for the holder of a call option. Thus, if on the expiration date, the spot rate, *S*, of the currency pair is at or below the exercise price, *X*, the option is not exercised and the position has a zero payoff. If the currency price is above the exercise price, the option will be exercised and the position will realise a payoff of $S - X$. This is true for both American and European calls since at expiration they are equivalent contracts.

The payoff to the call option at expiration can also be represented as:

$$C = c = \text{Max}(0, S - X)$$

which says that the call option will be worth the maximum of zero and the difference between the then prevailing spot price, *S*, for the currency pair and the exercise price, *X*.

15.2 PROFIT DIAGRAM

Figure 15.4 is the profit diagram for the holder of a call option. This alternative convention of representing option positions, again at expiration, takes account of the price, *C*, paid for the option and thus indicates the net profit or loss to the position.

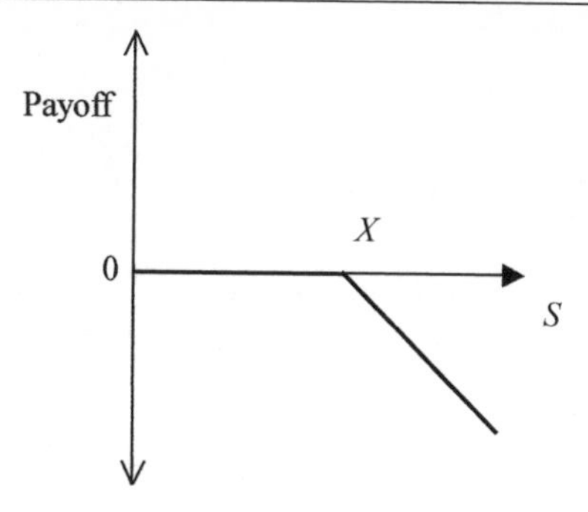

Figure 15.5

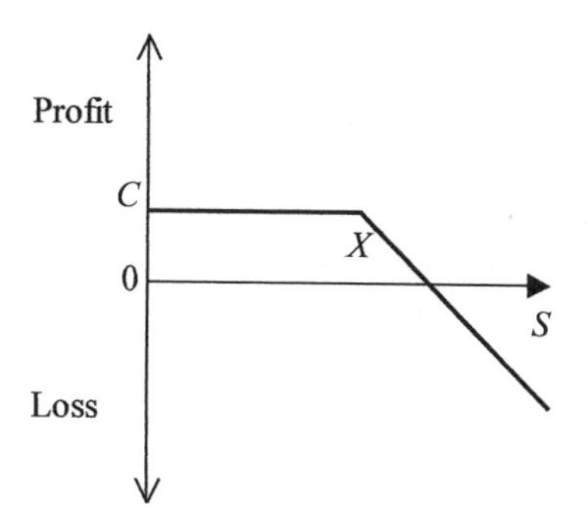

Figure 15.6

15.3 THE OPTION WRITER

For every holder, or buyer, of an option there must be an option writer or seller. Figures 15.5 and 15.6 are the payoff and profit diagrams, respectively, for the option writer. If the spot price, S, of the currency pair is above the exercise price, X, the option will be exercised and the writer is obligated to deliver the currency pair to the holder of the option in exchange for the exercise price. Thus, the writer incurs a loss of $S - X$ on the transaction.

If the currency pair price is below the exercise price, the option is not exercised and the writer does not incur a loss. Note, that while the payoff diagram shows only the payoff at expiration to the writer's position, the profit diagram takes into account the call price, or premium C, initially received by the writer of the call option.

If the payoff, or profit, diagrams of the option holder and writer are "added", they, not surprisingly, cancel each other out. The option market is a zero-sum game, when the option holder profits, the option writer loses and vice versa.

15.4 PUT OPTION

The same analysis can be applied to put options. In this case, if the spot price, S, is above the exercise price, X, on the expiration date, then the holder of the put option will not exercise since this would result in an immediate loss. If the currency pair is less than the exercise price, then the holder of the put will exercise and realise a payoff of $X - S$. This is true for both American and European puts, since at expiration they are equivalent contracts. Hence, the payoff of a put

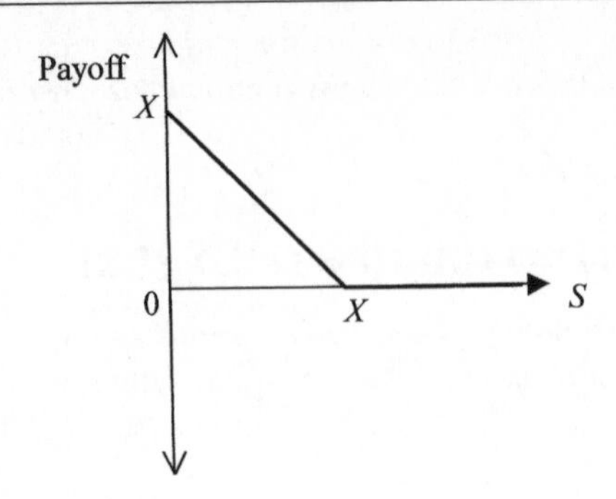

Figure 15.7

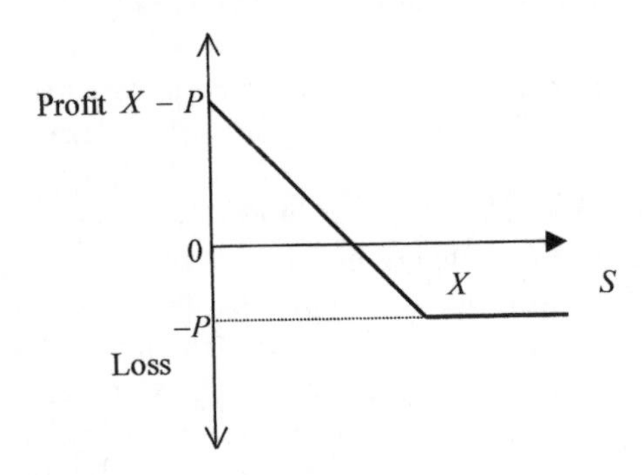

Figure 15.8

option at expiration can also be represented as:

$$P = p = \text{Max}(0, X - S)$$

where the value of an American put option will be represented as "P" and the value of a European put option is represented as "p", which says that the put option will be worth the maximum of zero and the difference between the exercise price, X, and the then prevailing spot price, S. In the case of put options, the option is termed out-of-the-money when the currency pair price is greater than the exercise price X (just the opposite to the case for call options). When the currency pair price is less than the exercise price X, the option is termed in-the-money.

Figure 15.8 is the profit diagram for the holder of the put option. Again, this representation of the option position at expiration takes account of the price P, paid for the option.

15.5 PUT OPTION WRITER

The payoff and profit diagrams for the put option writer are depicted in Figures 15.9 and 15.10. Again, the payoff or profit diagrams for the put option holder and writer sum to zero.

15.6 BASIC OPTION POSITIONS

Thus, in simplistic terms, the graph for purchasing a base currency will look like Figure 15.11.

If the spot at maturity is at or below the strike, the option will be worthless but the option buyer would have paid the premium. If, however, the spot at maturity is above the strike, there will be a profit as for a spot foreign exchange position but less the premium paid.

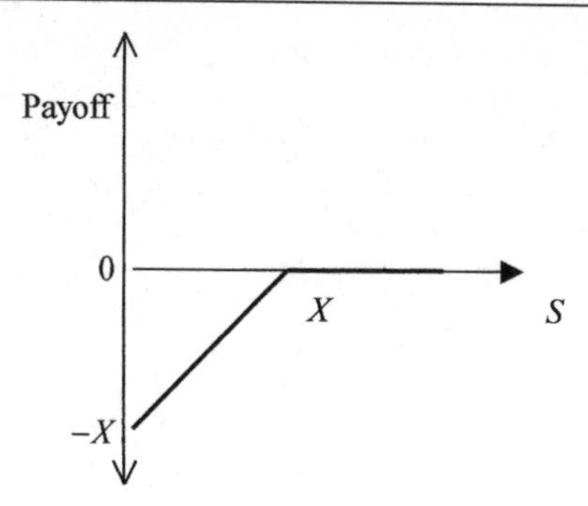

Figure 15.9

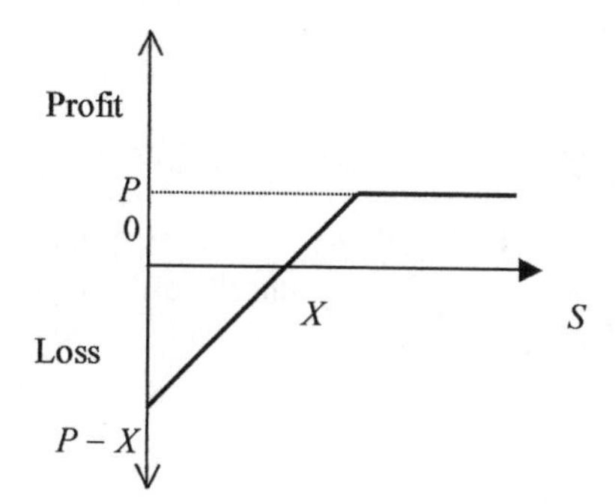

Figure 15.10

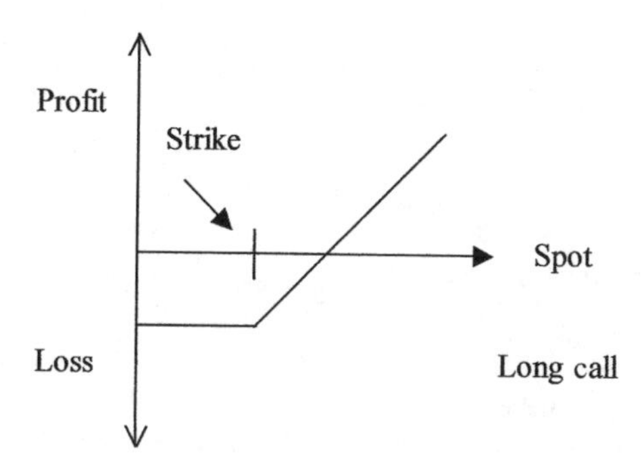

Figure 15.11

If the buyer buys a currency pair put, the graph will be similar but with profit occurring as the base currency falls as shown in Figure 15.12.

If a currency pair call is sold, the graph will be as shown in Figure 15.13.

In this case, the premium represents a profit as it is being paid to the writer. If the spot foreign exchange rate at maturity is at or below the strike, the holder of the option will not exercise and the premium will be kept. If, however, the spot foreign exchange rate at maturity is above the strike, the holder will exercise and the writer will realise a loss as for a spot foreign exchange position less the premium received.

Following on, if a currency pair put is sold, the graph will be as shown in Figure 15.14.

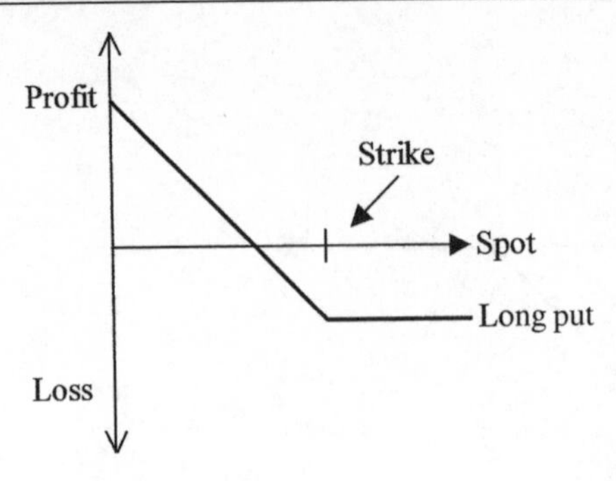

Figure 15.12

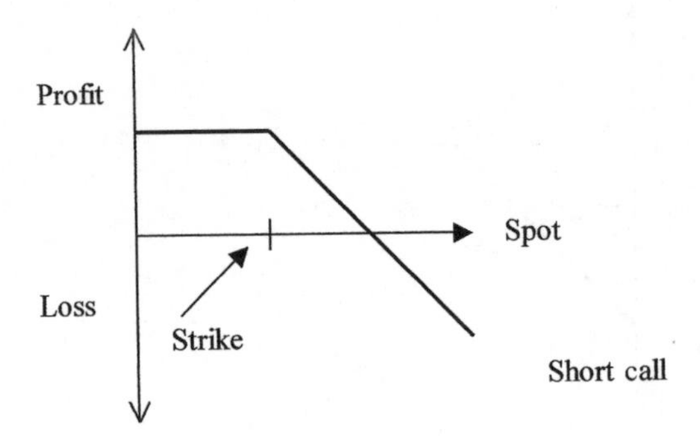

Figure 15.13

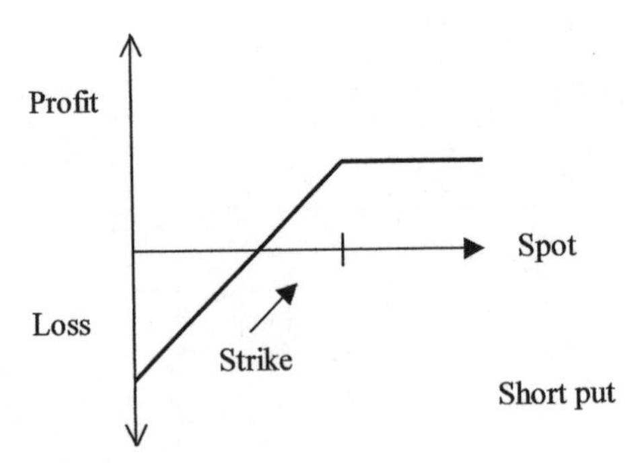

Figure 15.14

15.7 GRAPH ADDITION

If graphs are added together, it is possible to see the resulting exposure of the combined position. To do this, the profit and loss of each position has to be calculated at a particular spot exchange rate at maturity and then plot the sum.

For example, if a trader is long the base currency, say dollar in $/sfr at say $/sfr 1.5500, a trader could buy a dollar put/Swiss franc call at $/sfr 1.5500 to the same maturity date to hedge the position. From this, the two graphs would look like Figure 15.15.

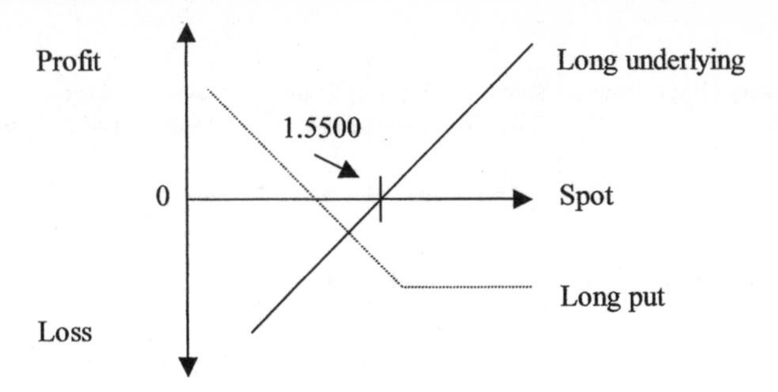

Figure 15.15

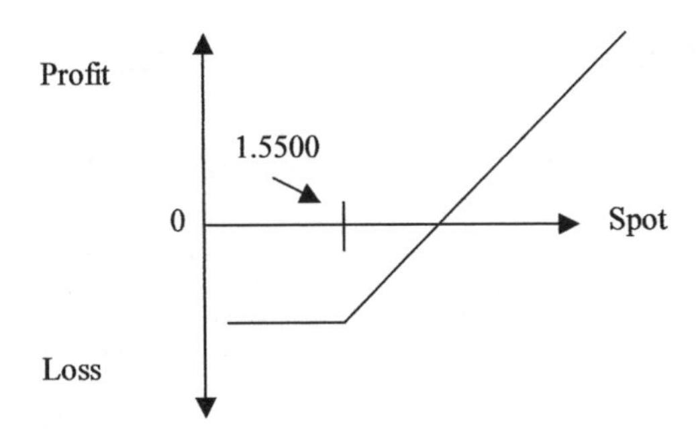

Figure 15.16

The resulting graph would then be as shown in the Figure 15.16.
If the profit and loss is calculated, then it is easy to see why:

Spot at maturity $/sfr	P/L on long $ position	P/L on long $ put	Resulting p/l
1.5100	−0.0400 $/sfr	+0.0400 $/sfr – premium	Premium
1.5300	−0.0200 $/sfr	+0.0200 $/sfr – premium	Premium
1.5500	0	Premium	Premium
1.5700	+0.0200 $/sfr	Premium	0.0200 – premium
1.5900	+0.0400 $/sfr	Premium	0.0400 – premium

When the difference between the strike and the spot is equal to the premium that is the breakeven point.

15.8 PROFIT/LOSS PROFILES FOR TEN POPULAR OPTION STRATEGIES

Figure 15.17 shows the profit/loss profiles for ten popular option strategies. All the profiles represent the option value at expiration of the option. (It should be noted that for the profit/loss column, there is an increase in spot prices from left to right and −ve denotes negative and +ve denotes positive.)

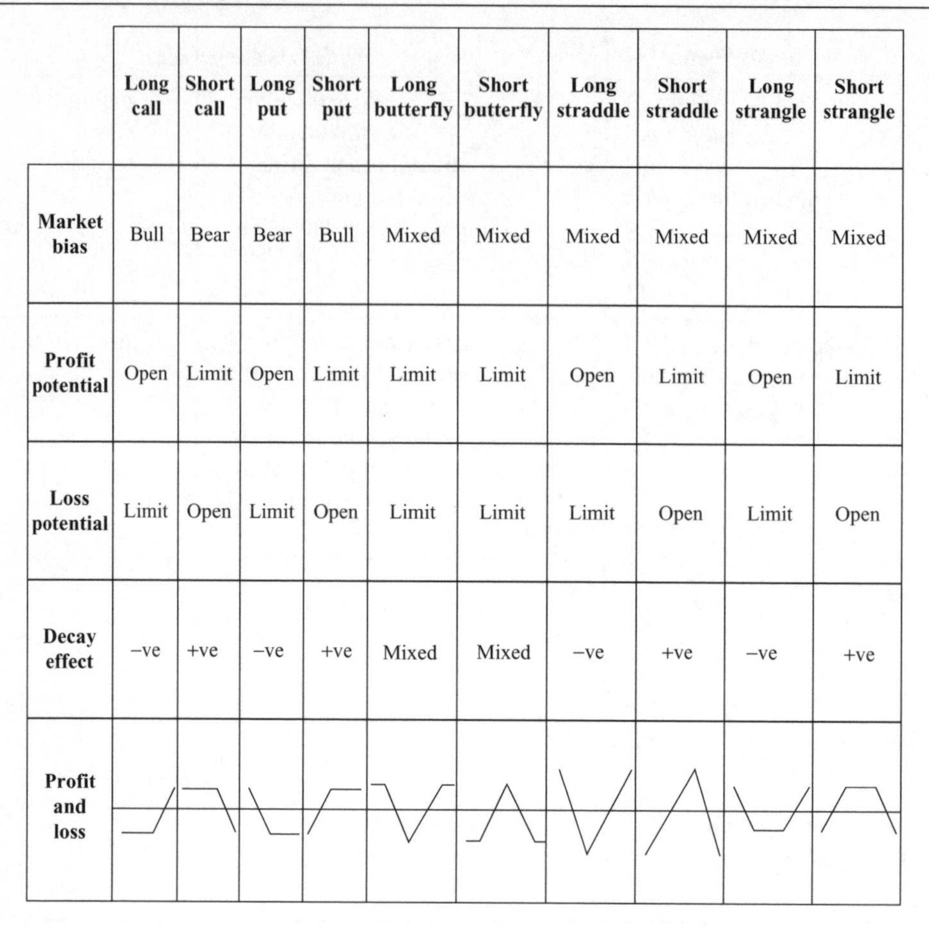

	Long call	Short call	Long put	Short put	Long butterfly	Short butterfly	Long straddle	Short straddle	Long strangle	Short strangle
Market bias	Bull	Bear	Bear	Bull	Mixed	Mixed	Mixed	Mixed	Mixed	Mixed
Profit potential	Open	Limit	Open	Limit	Limit	Limit	Open	Limit	Open	Limit
Loss potential	Limit	Open	Limit	Open	Limit	Limit	Limit	Open	Limit	Open
Decay effect	−ve	+ve	−ve	+ve	Mixed	Mixed	−ve	+ve	−ve	+ve
Profit and loss										

Figure 15.17

15.9 CONCLUDING REMARKS

Once payoff profiles have been mastered, they can provide a very useful method of determining net risk for a combination strategy at maturity. The "at maturity" is stressed as an option's total value and can fluctuate during the options life, even if the spot foreign exchange rate and the forward outright foreign exchange rate remain unchanged.

To summarise, if, for example, in simple terms, a trader feels sterling will move higher, the trader can:

1. Buy sterling spot of forward – buying sterling cash will give unlimited profit potential as well as unlimited loss potential;
2. Buy a sterling call – a buy call position would provide unlimited profit potential if it rises over and above a rate to cover the cost of the premium. Downside loss is limited to the premium should sterling fall; or
3. Sell a sterling put – if the view were that sterling would remain relatively stable, the sales of a put would be a good strategy, since the trader would receive a premium upfront. The loss potential remains, however, unlimited should sterling move down.

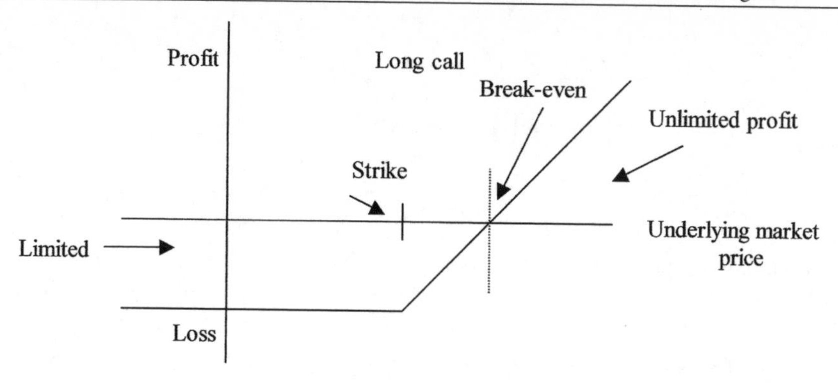

Figure 15.18

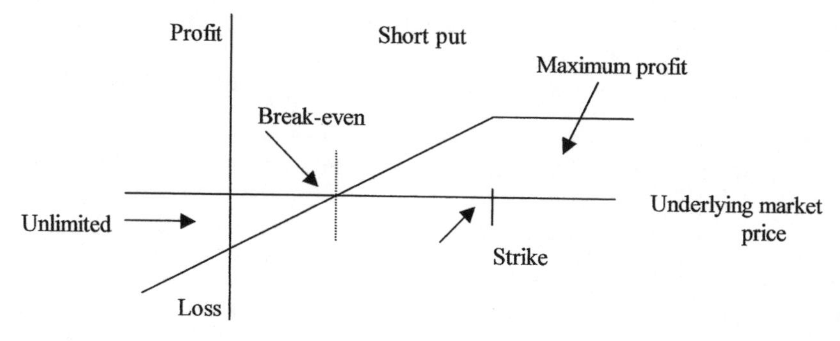

Figure 15.19

The payoff diagram in Figure 15.18 is a long sterling call option and the payoff diagram in Figure 15.19 is for a short sterling put option.

16

Basic Properties of Options

There are some basic simple properties that options exhibit. First, options cannot have negative value to their holders. Since options are rights and these rights will only be exercised to benefit the holder, the option cannot be a liability to its holders.

Second, option prices should not allow simple arbitrage, that is, it should not be possible to buy an American call or put option and immediately exercise it for a profit greater than the price paid for the option. In other words, the value of American calls and puts cannot be less than their in-the-money value. This need not be true for European call and put options, since the option holder does not have the right to exercise until the maturity date.

A third property that option prices must exhibit is that American style options must be worth at least as much as European style options. Since American options have all the rights European options have plus the right of early exercise, an American option will be as valuable as a European option if the right to early exercise is worthless and more valuable than a European option if the right of early exercise is valuable.

16.1 OPTION VALUES

In addition to the currency price, the exercise price and the time to maturity, option values depend on the price volatility of the underlying currency, the risk-free rate of interest. The question then is how will option values respond to changes in these determinants of option value?

For a call option, a higher current currency pair price should imply a greater value to the option holder. This is because a higher present currency pair price makes it more likely that on the expiration date, the market price of the currency pair will be above the exercise price. As this is precisely the condition under which the option will be exercised, the value of a call option increases as the present currency pair price increases. However, for put options, the effects of changes in the current currency pair price go in the opposite direction as it pays the holder of the put to exercise when the currency pair price is low. That is, the value of a put option decreases as the present currency pair price increases.

The effect of the exercise price, X, on the value of the call option is straightforward. Holding all other factors constant, a higher exercise price diminishes the profit from the exercise of the option. An increase in the exercise price would, therefore, lead to a decrease in the price of the call option. In the case of a put option, a higher exercise price increases the profit from exercise of the option. Thus, put option prices increase with an increase in their exercise prices.

The effect of an increase in time to maturity on the value of an option depends on the type of option. The call option holder will get the full benefit from favourable outcomes and simply not exercise if the outcome is unfavourable. This asymmetry in the nature of the option contract causes the holder to benefit from increased uncertainty. However, the present value of the exercise price also decreases as the time to maturity increases. Therefore, the time left to maturity has a second way of influencing option values. For the call option, this decrease in present value augments the time effect, that is, increased uncertainty, and the call option value unambiguously increases. An American put option cannot logically decrease in value with an increased time to maturity but with a European put option, the net effect of these influences is ambiguous. That is, increased uncertainty increases value while the decreased present value of the exercise price decreases value.

16.2 PUT/CALL PARITY CONCEPT

The payoff diagrams introduced in the preceding chapter can be used to demonstrate another useful property of options. In essence, there is a special relationship between puts and calls, which allows an option user to create synthetic positions. Thus, using a combination of a call option and a put option at the same strike gives a long position in the underlying, as seen from the diagram in Figure 16.1 of a long call option and a short put option.

There exists an arbitrage relationship between the exercise price, the foreign exchange rate and the call and put option premium. This link is known as put/call parity.

As shown, the two options produce a cash position, because at any point, one of the options will be exercised and the base currency will be received. Buying a put and selling a call will achieve a short cash position.

The relationships, which can be achieved using this put call parity, can be stated as:

Long put + Long cash = Long call
Long call + Short cash = Long put
Short put + Short cash = Short call
Short call + Long cash = Short put

What is significant about the above is that the two combinations/portfolios have identical expiration values. Irrespective of the value of the underlying at expiration, each portfolio will have the same value as the other.

If the two portfolios are going to have the same value at expiration, then they must have the same value today. Otherwise, an investor could make an arbitrage profit by purchasing the less expensive portfolio, selling the more expensive one and holding the long short position to

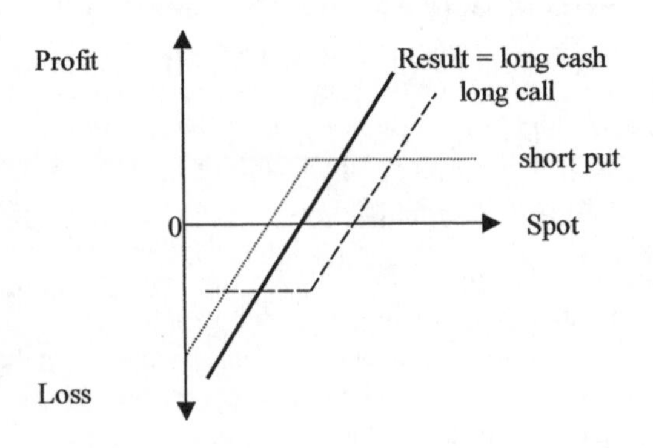

Figure 16.1

expiration. Accordingly, we have the price equality:

$$c + PV(x) = p + s$$

where:

- c = the current market value of the call;
- $PV(x)$ = the present value of the strike price x, discounted from the expiration date at a suitable risk-free rate;
- p = the current market value of the put;
- s = the current market value of the underlying.

This is the put call parity. Note that it is not based on any option pricing model. It was derived purely using arbitrage arguments. It applies only to European options, since a possibility of early exercise could cause a divergence in the present values of the two portfolios.

As an example, consider the following options:

First, a sterling put/dollar call option at £/$ 1.8100, where the spot rate is at £/$ 1.8000 and the forward sterling rate is £/$ 1.7940, with a price of 462/500 (points). Second, a sterling call/dollar put option at £/$ 1.8100, where the spot rate is £/$ 1.8000 and the forward rate is £/$ 1.7940, but for a price of 300/337. Both options are assumed to be European style.

If a trader buys the call at 337 and sells the put at 462, there is a credit of 125 points (462 –337). This is the same as being long the forward at 1.8100 – 0.0125 = 1.7975. This is about the same price as where the trader could have bought the forward if it were not for the bid/offer spread. If the trader bought the put at 500 and sold the call at 300, there would have a 200 point debit and this would have resulted in a short position in the forward at 1.8100 – 0.0200 = 1.7900. Thus the difference between this and the forward is again the fact that the trader is paying the spread of 40 points.

Another example, consider a six-month European style option whereby the six-month forward sterling foreign exchange rate in each case is £/$ 1.7500.

1. If the $1.75 call premium is 5 cents, then the same strike, same style $1.75 put option premium must also be 5 cents.
2. If the $1.70 call premium is 7.5 cents, then the same strike, same style $1.70 put premium must be 2.5 cents.
3. If the $1.73 put option premium is 4 cents, then the same strike, same style $1.73 call premium must be 6 cents.

Thus, according to the put/call parity, the put premium can be derived given the strike price, the call premium and the forward foreign exchange rate. Alternatively, the call option premium can be derived given the strike price, the put premium and the forward foreign exchange rate. The formula is expressed as:

$$\text{Call premium} - \text{put premium} = \text{forward} - \text{strike}$$

This may also be expressed as:

$$\text{Put premium} = \text{call premium} - (\text{forward} - \text{strike})$$

or:

$$\text{Call premium} = \text{put premium} + (\text{forward} - \text{strike})$$

If the $1.70 call premium is 7.5 cents, then the $1.70 put option premium is:

$$7.5 \text{ cents} - (1.75 - 1.70) = 2.5 \text{ cents}$$

If the $1.73 put option premium is 4 cents, then the $1.73 call premium is:

$$4 \text{ cents} + (1.75 - 1.73) = 6 \text{ cents}$$

Arbitrage possibilities can arise if forward foreign exchange rates, put options and call options fall out of line. This is quite possible in the over-the-counter market but much less likely on the exchanges where the locals are actively arbitraging. When the arbitrage is done to create a synthetic long against a natural short, this is referred to as a "reversal", while the opposite is called a "conversion".

(Note: usually, various combinations of synthetic longs and shorts relate to European style options since there is an added disadvantage to American style options, in that as they can be exercised early, they may create an unfavourable cash flow situation which could affect any arbitrage possibilities.)

Thus, for the same strike, same amount, and same date:

BUY CALL & SELL PUT = LONG Forward foreign exchange position
BUY PUT & SELL CALL = SHORT forward foreign exchange position

It is important to remember that no matter where the spot is at expiry, either the put or the call will be exercised. Thus, as an example, the purchase of a dollar put and the sale of a dollar call will equal the outright forward sale of dollars. Also, it does not really matter that much whether calls or puts are traded, but it is important to remember "base interest rate" risk due to the timing difference between upfront premium and forward foreign exchange profit.

16.3 SYNTHETIC POSITIONS

If a trader takes the payoff diagrams at expiry representing risk reward, and combines them, the trader may produce synthetic positions, as already mentioned in the preceding chapter. For example, a long underlying and a long call option are equivalent to a long put option, so if on the one hand a put option is trading at a given level and on the other hand the spot plus long call option gives a level cheaper than that of the put, it is possible to buy the synthetic and sell the natural to create the arbitrage or just to provide a cheaper put option for a portfolio.

Figures 16.2 and 16.3 illustrate various combinations. Both relate to European style options since there is an added disadvantage to American style options in that if they are exercised early, they may create an unfavourable cash flow situation, which could affect any arbitrage opportunities.

As in the example above with put/call parity, if the $1.7000 call option were bought for 7.5 cents and sterling sold forward at a rate of $1.7500, the resulting transaction is exactly the equivalent of buying a $1.7000 put for 2.5 cents. Thus:

1. Buy $1.70 call for 7.5 cents and sell sterling at $1.75.
2. Buy $1.70 put for 2.5 cents.

If, at expiry, spot sterling is trading at £/$ 1.50:

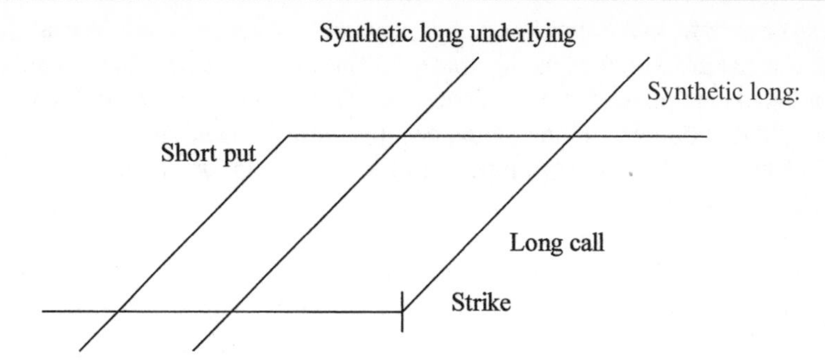

Figure 16.2

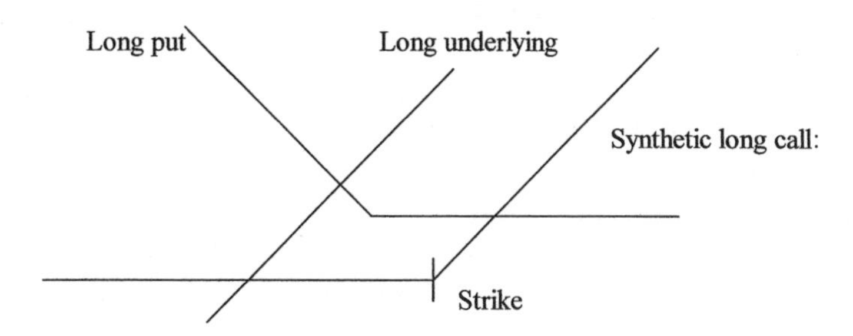

Figure 16.3

1. Foreign exchange profit = 25.0 cents (\$1.75 − \$1.50)
   Less call option premium = 7.5 cents (call abandoned)
   Net profit = 17.5 cents
2. Long \$1.70 put gross profit = 20 cents (\$1.70 − \$1.50)
   Less put option premium = 2.5 cents
   Net profit = 17.5 cents

Because the combination of a long call option and a short foreign exchange position gives the identical exposure to a long put option with the same strike, such a trade is usually known as a synthetic long put. As mentioned before, various other types of synthetic positions can be created:

$$\text{Synthetic short put} = \text{long forward} + \text{short call}$$

For example, buy sterling forward at a rate of \$1.7500 and sell a \$1.7500 call for 5 cents is equal to a synthetic short \$1.75 put for 5 cents.

$$\text{Synthetic long call} = \text{long forward} + \text{long put}$$

For example, buy sterling forward at a rate of \$1.75 and buy \$1.73 put for 4 cents is equal to a synthetic long \$1.73 call for 6 cents.

$$\text{Synthetic short call} = \text{short forward} + \text{short put}$$

For example, sell sterling forward at a rate of \$1.75 and short \$1.73 put for 4 cents is equal to a synthetic short \$1.73 call for 6 cents.

As can be seen from the above, it is always possible to convert calls into puts and vice versa, through a forward foreign exchange trade. For instance, it is possible to convert a long call position into a long put position or a short put into a short call option. But, it is not possible to convert a short option into a long option position, or a short call into long calls or puts. Nor is it possible to convert a long option position into a short option, a long put into a short put or short call, for example.

17 Risk Reversals

The risk reversal quoted in the options market represents the preference for puts or calls prevailing at that time. It indicates the relative value of similar delta puts and calls, for example 0.25 delta dollar puts against 0.25 delta dollar calls. This preference is expressed as a volatility percentage, for example 0.2/0.5% for dollar puts Swiss franc calls, indicating that the trader will wish to earn a spread of 0.5% to sell the dollar puts and buy the dollar calls. It also means that the trader will pay away a spread of 0.2% to do the opposite. The risk reversal arises for a number of reasons, but the primary reason is one of supply and demand.

The risk reversal can therefore be an indicator of directional sentiment, thus if dollar puts are favoured, it is likely that the market is one that is bearish on the dollar.

Options thus favoured on the risk reversal will command a higher volatility price, thereby increasing the premium of the option. For example, dollar puts might be more "expensive" than dollar calls. It is important to remember that puts and calls with deltas much less than 0.50 will have a large implied volatility differential.

17.1 UNDERSTANDING RISK REVERSALS

Understanding risk reversals in currency options trading is an invaluable tool for both traders and hedgers. At this stage, it is important to review how options are priced in the over-the-counter market. Market makers in options make prices and trade off implied volatility. As an example, a sample of at-the-money forward volatilities might be:

Dollar/Swiss franc	
1 month	14.3/14.8
3 month	14.2/14.6
6 month	13.6/14.0
12 month	13.0/13.5

When options are at-the-money forward, volatility traders are willing to buy one-month franc calls or franc puts based on a volatility of 14.3% and are willing to sell one-month franc calls or franc puts at 14.8%.

Since the likelihood that spot will be higher or lower than the forward price is 50–50, option traders are indifferent as to whether they buy puts or calls on their volatility bid or sell puts or calls on their volatility offer. However, when option strike prices are not the same as the forward foreign exchange outright, the likelihood of exercise is no longer 50–50 and option traders are no longer willing to quote the same volatility prices for both puts and calls. Indeed, the Black–Scholes pricing model that is used to price currency options makes several assumptions about market behaviour.

These assumptions are that the markets trade according to mathematical models, which clearly is not the case. This leads to an undervaluing of options that are far out-of-the-money (and also deeply in-the-money options) as too low a probability of exercise is assigned to these options. In order to compensate for this, it is necessary to raise the volatility bid for an out-of-the-money option (and also for deeply in-the-money options) and to widen the volatility spread.

Theoretically, out-of-the-money puts and calls with the same probability of exercise (delta) would trade at the same volatility price. However, directional spot foreign exchnage and volatility views held by the options market frequently distort the market. As a result, out-of-the-money calls may trade at a higher volatility price than out-of-the-money puts or vice versa. In other words, the options market is taking a view on the direction of the dollar. Risk reversals for out-of-the-money options might be quoted as:

Dollar/Swiss franc (R/R)	
1 month	0.5%/1.0%
2 month	0.3%/0.9%
8 month	0.2%/0.8%
12 month	0.1%/0.4%

The top lines are interpreted as dollar/franc risk reversal with dollar calls over dollar puts. This means that option traders are demanding a higher volatility price to sell out-of-the-money dollar calls than they would sell out-of-the-money dollar puts. In the one-month time period, a trader would sell a dollar call at a spread of 1.0% over where they would buy the out-of-the-money dollar put.

For example, consider the following:

One-month forward outright	$/sfr 1.6000
OTM dollar call strike	1.6300
OTM dollar put strike	1.5700

If the trader is selling the out-of-the-money dollar call, the trader will want to earn 1.0% volatility more than the out-of-the-money dollar put being bought. In other words, volatility prices may be:

Sell OTM dollar call strike	1.6300	15.0%
Buy OTM dollar put strike	1.5700	14.0%
Spread		1.0%

If the trader is going to buy the out-of-the-money dollar call, the trader is willing to pay more for it in volatility than what might be paid on the out-of-the-money dollar put. For example:

Buy OTM dollar call strike	1.6300	14.5%
Sell OTM dollar put strike	1.5700	14.0%
Spread		0.5%

Please note that the level of volatility set for each option is not as important as the spread between the buy and the sell.

17.2 IMPLICATIONS FOR TRADERS

As mentioned already, out-of-the-money puts and calls with the same mathematical probability of exercise will not always trade at the same volatility price because option traders have taken a view on the direction of the dollar. From the previous example, market demand for out-of-the-money dollar calls has exceeded market demand for out-of-the-money dollar puts causing out-of-the-money dollar calls to trade at a higher price than the out-of-the-money dollar puts. Option traders, therefore, believe that the dollar could trade higher in the near term. The stronger the conviction of a higher dollar, the higher the risk reversal. If the market has no strong view, the level of the risk reversal tends towards zero. This implies that out-of-the-money puts and calls would trade at similar volatilities. When the options market starts to believe in a lower dollar, out-of-the-money puts will start to trade over out-of-the-money dollar calls.

17.3 IMPLICATIONS FOR HEDGERS

For people who are looking to hedge their underlying foreign currency positions using options, risk reversals are most often used to price option structures, such as range forwards (also called cylinders, zero-cost options and collars). If a hedger has a foreign currency receivable and therefore needs to buy dollars at some future date, there might be an interest in protecting this exposure within a certain range without paying a premium. To create a range forward, a hedger would buy an out-of-the-money dollar call and sell an out-of-the money dollar put with the premium that would be paid on the call being offset by the premium that would be received on the put. In many cases, the hedger might determine the strike for the option that needs to be bought and would ask the trader to calculate at what strike the option would have to be sold, so that the net premium would be zero. From the above example, the hedger would have to pay a spread of 1.0% volatility more for the option needed to be bought than would be received for the option that needed to be sold. The greater the spread that the hedger must pay on the risk reversal, the less attractive the range.

For example:

Exposure:	Swiss franc receivable (long francs and short dollars)
Hedge:	range forward (zero premium)
Assumptions:	one-month forward outright 1.000

	Strike	Volatility
Buy one-month dollar call:	1.6300	15.0%
Sell one-month dollar put:	???	14.0%

Where ??? = 1.5762

This example shows that the hedger will be able to buy dollars at a price no worse than 1.6300, but no better than 1.5762.

If there is now the assumption that there is no spread, that is, a risk reversal of 0.0%:

	Strike	Volatility
Buy one-month dollar call:	1.6300	14.5%
Sell one-month dollar put:	???	14.5%

Where ??? = 1.5714

In this scenario, since the risk reversal is 0.0%, the hedger is able to buy dollars at 1.5714 (a more favourable rate than 1.5762).

Finally, if the risk reversal flips, so that dollar puts trade over dollar calls, the result might be:

	Strike	Volatility
Buy one-month dollar call:	1.6300	14.0%
Sell one-month dollar put:	???	15.0%

Where ??? = 1.5663

In this case, the hedger is actually earning the spread on the risk reversal which allows the dollars to be bought as low as 1.5663.

As can be seen from the above example, the purchaser of the strategy is not always "paying away" the spread on the risk reversal. If the dollar puts start to trade over the dollar calls, a hedger with foreign currency receivables will actually be able to buy out-of-the-money dollar calls at a cheaper volatility price than selling the out-of-the-money dollar puts.

Thus, in summary, for hedgers to hedge a foreign currency payable, the hedger would buy a dollar put and pay for the protection by selling a dollar call for the same premium. The hedger would obviously prefer the most favourable range in which to benefit from a rising dollar (the widest range with the highest possible dollar call strike price, when the dollar calls are richer than dollar puts). The hedger would therefore benefit from a greater risk reversal spread of dollar calls over puts. As illustrated above, this opportunity may arise when the market is expecting a greater risk of a rising dollar.

Conversely, to hedge a foreign currency receivable, the hedger would buy a dollar call and pay for protection by selling a dollar put for the same premium. The hedger would prefer the most favourable range in which to benefit from a falling dollar (again the widest range, but with the lowest possible dollar put strike price, when dollar puts are richer than dollar calls). The hedger would therefore benefit from a greater risk reversal spread of dollar puts over calls. As illustrated above, this opportunity may arise when the market is expecting a greater risk of a weaker dollar.

17.4 CONCLUDING REMARKS

The volatility market reflects the perceived risk to option market makers that the option will be exercised. Thus, if the risk of exercise is greater, volatilities are priced higher. Conversely, if the risk of exercise decreases, volatilities are priced lower. Thus, risk reversals are traded as a volatility spread between call and put volatility and are quoted as either dollar puts over dollar calls or dollar calls over dollar puts. Alternatively, franc calls over franc puts or franc puts over franc calls.

Obviously, like all markets, market conditions and expectations affect the pricing of risk reversals. If the market anticipates a greater risk of a higher dollar, there will be a demand for dollar calls over the demand for dollar puts and thus, the dollar call price increases. Hence, the option market maker will price risk reversal volatility higher for dollar calls over dollar puts. This means that risk reversal spread will be greater than zero.

If the market anticipates a greater risk of a weaker dollar, there will be a demand for dollar puts over the demand for dollar calls and thus the dollar put price increases. Therefore, the option market maker will price risk reversal volatility higher for dollar puts over dollar calls.

If the market has no strong view, the level of risk reversal tends towards zero, which implies that calls and puts would trade at similar volatilities.

Market Conventions

18.1 OPTION PRICE

How should one ask for an option price? The required pieces of information, in the preferred order, are as follows:

- The two currencies involved and which is the put and which is the call, e.g. dollar put, Swiss franc call;
- The period, e.g. two months or the expiry or delivery date, e.g. expiry 12 December, for delivery 14 December;
- The strike, e.g. 1.5010;
- The style, e.g. European or American style;
- The amount, e.g. 10 million dollars.

There are many ways of stating the period, but usually, if one date is stated, it is assumed to be the expiry date but it is much safer always to specify. In the same way, if a 10-day option is requested, it is assumed that the required option has an expiry date 10 days from the current date. If, however, an option is requested with a period in terms of months or years, e.g. three months, the dates of the option are worked out as follows:

- Calculate the spot foreign exchange date for that currency pair, using the same conventions as the spot foreign exchange market.
- Take the period, e.g. three months from that date, using the forward market conventions.

This gives the delivery date. The expiry date will then usually be two working days before that. The exceptions occur in any currency pair where spot is not two working days, for example the Canadian dollar, where the expiry date would be one working date before the delivery date.

Please note that with cross currencies and dates involving American holidays or in any cases where there may be confusion, it is always best to quote both the expiry and delivery dates required.

In asking for an option price, always state which currency is the call and which is the put. For example, does dollar/Swiss franc ($/sfr) put mean a dollar put or a Swiss franc put? On the option exchanges and in the OTC interbank market, this would usually refer to a Swiss franc put/dollar call. However, most corporations would probably mean a dollar put. For this reason, always state the case in full, e.g. dollar/call Swiss franc put or vice versa.

18.2 WHAT RATE TO USE?

As for a person who is pricing up the requested option, the following should be used:

	Option bought		Option sold	
	Call	Put	Call	Put
Intrinsic value:				
Strike	As specified in the contract			
Forward rate	Bid	Offer	Offer	Bid
Spot rate	Bid	Offer	Offer	Bid
Swap rate	Bid	Offer	Offer	Bid
Swap days	Spot date → Settlement date			
Local interest rate	Offer	Bid	Bid	Offer
Foreign interest rate	Bid	Offer	Offer	Bid
Time value:				
Option days	Deal date → Expiry date			
Local interest rate	Offer		Bid	
Volatility	Bid		Offer	
Option price:	Bid		Offer	

18.3 LIVE PRICE

In dealing with options, there are two main means for counterparties to enter into a transaction: live pricing or volatile pricing/quotation.

What does a 'live price' mean? The price of an option is obviously dependent on the spot foreign exchange price in the market. As an option trader needs to delta hedge the option straight away, the spot at which the trader can hedge is the rate the trader uses to price the option. If a price is being quoted live it means that the person asking for the price will be quoted a premium price for the option and the option trader will take the risk if spot foreign exchange moves during the transaction.

With live pricing, the price is usually quoted as a percentage of the principal of the option. When multiplied by the face amount, the actual premium can be determined. An example is the purchase of a dollar Japanese yen option for 1.25% on \$300 000, or 375 000 yen. If paid in yen, the same option could be quoted as 170 yen points. The price terms quoted for the option depends on the currency in which the premium will be paid and on which currency the face amount is quoted. Live pricing is most typically used by those hedging a pre-existing exposure or taking a directional view on the market. As no delta hedge is exchanged, the trade is subject to even small variations in the cash price. The alternative to dealing live is to deal 'with delta'. This means that the person asking the price will deal the delta hedge with the option trader as well as the option.

In the case of a volatility quote, the dynamic element of the cash market is frozen as soon as the counterparties agree on a volatility at which contracts will be exchanged. Spot and forward foreign exchange rates, interest rates, strike and volatility are agreed and a premium is calculated through the valuation model. A delta hedge is exchanged along with the option contract. Most market makers quote in volatility terms when dealing with each other and other market professionals, as it eliminates the need to deal in the cash market.

18.4 PRICING TERMS

Normally, the premium is quoted as a percentage of the base currency amount of the option. However, in the interbank market, it is normally quoted as pips per currency amount of the option. For example, if the option is a dollar/Swiss franc option, the premium can be quoted in the following ways:

- Per cent of the first currency amount of the option;
- Per cent of the second currency amount of the option;
- Second currency in terms of the first currency; and
- First currency in terms of the second currency.

For example, assume a dollar/Swiss franc option with a strike of 1.5800 in an amount of \$10 000 000 (spot \$/sfr 1.6200). Then, the pricing in terms of (1)–(4) above could be:

1. 1.16% of Swiss franc;
2. 1.13% of dollars;
3. 0.0072 dollars per Swiss franc; and
4. 0.0183 Swiss francs per dollar.

In other words, \$113 000 or sfr183 000.

18.5 PREMIUM CONVERSIONS

How can one form of premium be quoted to another? The following formula can be used:

BC = base currency (commodity currency)
NBC = non-base currency (terms currency)

(a) % BC = % NBC × strike/spot
(b) % NBC = % BC × spot/strike
(c) NBC/BC = % NBC × strike
(d) BC/NBC = % BC/strike

For example, if a Swiss franc/dollar option costs 2.05% dollar amount, spot is 1.5500 and the strike of the option is 1.5200, then:

$$\text{Swissfranc/dollar} = 0.0205 \times 1.5500 = 0.031775$$

or

318 Swiss franc pips per dollar

18.6 SETTLEMENT

Normally, settlement takes place in full, e.g. if a dollar put (right to sell)/Swiss franc call (right to buy) option is exercised, the full amount of the dollars will be paid to the option writer and the exerciser will receive the full amount of Swiss francs from the option writer. As mentioned before, settlement takes place on the delivery date unless the option is American and has been exercised early, in which case settlement takes place spot from the date the option is exercised.

Is it necessary to settle both amounts in full? No – it is possible to "net settle" the option. This means that only the profit on the option is paid from the writer to the holder of the option. If this is decided at the time of exercise, the writer will normally quote the holder a spot foreign exchange rate and if this rate is acceptable, the option profit will be determined accordingly. If net settlement is agreed at the time of the original deal, it may be necessary to have a more formal arrangement for determining the profit on the option at the time of exercise.

18.7 HOW IS AN OPTION EXERCISED?

It is sufficient that the option writer/seller receives notice (for example, by telephone, Internet, fax, Reuters Dealing) of exercise before the exercise time on the expiry date. This time is 3:00pm London time, 3:00pm Tokyo or 10:00am New York time. If, for some unknown reason the option holder misses the exercise time, if an option is very in-the-money, a few minutes leeway is usually accepted by the option writer.

18.8 RISKS

It is important to note that there is a significant difference between the expectations and the risks assumed by the three main different players in the currency options market. The first group, investors, typically look to use options in order to improve the risk/rewards ratio compared with entering a spot foreign exchange transaction. As such, the investor is concerned with the total cost of the option, from which it can easily be determined by how far the market must move in order to profit. Therefore, the primary interest is usually on the delta, or magnitude of the position, and how moves in the market will impact their daily profits and losses. The volatility level is of lesser concern.

The second group, hedgers, are primarily concerned with protecting an existing exposure from adverse movements in the currency market. Often, these corporate treasuries are hedging profits from overseas offices or costs from international purchases. Performance is compared with benchmark foreign exchange rates or cost effective levels. In the past, such risks were generally hedged in the forward foreign exchange market, locking in acceptable rates without any potential for profits. Options now provide the protection required while offering opportunities to profit from beneficial movements in the foreign exchange rate.

Third, volatility traders, for example banks and other professional players, have sufficient capital to perform the important task of establishing competitive and liquid markets in currency options for the users mentioned above. As such, the options trader may hold hundreds of open options positions. The primary risk being managed is of movements in the price of volatility, and the relationship between the time decay and the gamma positions.

As the market for currency options has expanded, the number of speculators in the volatility market has also increased. Before computer systems were widely available to manage the complex and dynamic risks of an option portfolio, profits in the market were primarily transaction oriented, with most of the risk eventually falling into the hands of a small number of institutions. However, there are now many market participants who are willing to assume risk positions and there is a broad spectrum of players ranging from a pure market maker with little risk to a pure position taker making use if the available liquidity.

Also, the following risks should be taken note of:

- Credit risk – in selling an option to a client, there is no real credit risk if the option expires worthless, i.e. it is not exercised. There is a transaction related risk if it is exercised, which is similar to risk on a spot settlement thus requiring a credit line to be in place in advance of the transaction. The client pays an upfront premium.
- Market price risk – because an option buyer enjoys the dual benefits of insurance and upside potential, the option writer is subject to a greater amount of market/price risk when it sells options than when it sells forward foreign exchange contracts. To compensate for this risk, the option writer charges the upfront premium.
- Country risk – similar to that for foreign exchange forwards and swaps, in that given the time span involved, there could be an unexpected event in a foreign country, which could affect the liquidity of that currency.

18.9 CONCLUDING REMARKS

In summary, options are not merely insurance contracts against exchange risk but they are above all financial assets that can be bought and sold just like tradable securities. Options may be combined so that their asymmetric payouts tailor a defined risk profile. Some combinations are primarily trading strategies, but option combinations can also be a useful tool. For example, for investors to construct a strategy allowing them to take advantage of a particular view that they have about a market direction. Other strategies allow purchasers to give up some of the benefits they may have received in market movements in return for a reduced premium payment. It must be remembered that by buying a call and simultaneously selling a put with the same maturity date and the same strike is equivalent to entering into a forward contract. But above all, remember the following risk profile of options:

Long option : unlimited profit potential – limited risk
Short option : unlimited risk – limited profit potential

Basic Option Glossary

Actual volatility The actual volatility that occurs during the life of an option

American option An option a purchaser may exercise for early value at any time over the life of the option up to and including its expiration date

Assignment Notification to the option writer requiring him to fulfil his contractual obligations to buy or sell the currency

At-the-money forward An option with an exercise price equal to the currency forward rate

At-the-money spot An option with an exercise price equal to the currency spot rate

Black-Scholes model The original closed-form solution to option pricing developed by Fischer Black and Myron Scholes in 1973. In its simplest form, it offers a solution to pricing European style options on assets with interim cash payouts over the life of the option. The model calculates the theoretical, or fair, value for the option by constructing an instantaneously riskless hedge, that is, one whose performance is the mirror image of the option payout. The portfolio of option and hedge can then be assumed to earn the risk-free rate of return. The model has five major inputs: the risk-free interest rate, the option's strike price, the price of the underlying, the option's maturity, and the volatility assumed. Since the first four are usually determined, markets tend to trade the implied volatility of the option

Break-even point The foreign exchange rate or currency futures price at which a strategy neither makes nor loses money

Buyer One who buys an option

Call option An option which gives the holder the right to buy, and the writer the obligation to sell, a predetermined amount of a currency to a predetermined date at a predetermined exchange rate

Clearing-house An organisation which matches and guarantees option trades on an exchange

Conversion arbitrage A riskless strategy involving the buying of a currency and the simultaneous buying of a put and writing of a call option, both normally European style and of the same strikes and expiration

Covered write A strategy involving the buying of a currency and the writing of a call option, or the selling of a currency and the writing of a put option

Credit premium The premium received when an option is written

Debit premium The premium paid when an option is purchased

Delta Measures the impact of a change in the price of the underlying

Delta hedging An option is said to be delta hedged if a position has been taken in the underlying in proportion to its delta. The delta of an option is altered by changes in the price of the underlying and by its volatility, time to expiry, and interest rates. Therefore, delta hedge must be rebalanced frequently. This is known as *delta-neutral hedging*

Discount A term used to describe an option, which is trading for less than its intrinsic value

Downside protection For covered calls the "cushion" against loss provided by the option premium received

Early exercise The exercise of an option before its expiration date

European option An option where the purchaser has the right to exercise only at expiration

Exchange-traded market The organised marketplace for option trading purposes

Exercise The process by which the holder of an option elects to take delivery of (call) or to deliver (put) a currency according to the contract terms

Exercise price, exercise rate The price at which the option holder has the right to buy or sell the underlying currency or currency futures contract

Expiration cycle In the exchange traded options market, the time frame in which listed options run

Expiration date The last day on which a holder of an option can exercise

Expiration time In the over-the-counter market the latest time an option may be exercised. This is usually 3pm London time or 10am New York time , or 3pm Tokyo time, on that particular day

Fair value Usually refers to the value of an option premium according to a mathematical model

Gamma Measures the rate of change in delta

Garman–Kohlhagen model A model developed to price European style options on spot foreign exchange rates. The model is similar to the Black–Scholes model except for the addition of an extra interest rate factor for the foreign country

Hedge ratio The ratio of options to buy or sell against a spot position in order to create a riskless hedge

Historical volatility A measure of the standard deviation of the underlying instrument over a past period and is calculated from actual price movements by looking at intraday price changes and comparing this with the average (the standard deviation)

Holder One who has bought an option

Implied volatility The volatility implied in the price of an option, i.e. the volatility that is used to calculate an option price

In-the-money Describes an option whose strike price is more advantageous than the current market price of the underlying

Intrinsic value The value of an option relative to the outright forward market price, i.e. it represents the difference between the strike price of the option and the forward rate at which one could transact today

Margin, initial margin The amount required to be put up as collateral by the option writer to the clearing-house. It is equivalent to a performance bond. Should the option position move against the writer, then variation or maintenance margin would be required

Mark-to-market The daily adjustment of an account to reflect accrued profits and losses

Option A contract between the buyer (or holder) of the option and the seller (or writer) of the option. This contract describes the rights of the option holder and the obligations of the option writer

Out-of-the-money Describes an option whose underlying is above the strike price in the case of a call, or below it in the case of a put

Over-the-counter market The customised option market usually traded directly between banks and their customers or with other banks

Payoff diagram Relates the payoff to an option position to the underlying currency price at expiration, which is how options will perform at maturity

Premium The amount of money paid by a buyer and received by a seller for an option

Put option An option giving the holder the right to sell and the writer the obligation to buy, a predetermined amount of currency to a predetermined date at a predetermined exchange rate

Put/call parity The link where there exists an arbitrage relationship between the exercise price, the foreign exchange rate and the call and put option premium

Riskless trade Involves the selling of a currency and the simultaneous buying of a currency call and writing of a currency put option, both normally European style and of the same strikes and expiration

Rho Measures an option's sensitivity to a change in interest rates. This will have an impact on both the future price of the option and the time value of the premium. Its impact increases with the maturity of the option

Seller One who sells/writes an option

Settlement date Two business days following exercise. It is the day on which the currencies involved in the option transaction are exchanged

Spread The strategy involving the simultaneous buying and selling of options on the same currency

Strike, strike rate/price The price at which the option holder has the right to buy or sell the underlying currency or currency futures contract

Stochastic volatility Refers to models in which volatility is permitted to change randomly. Models that incorporate stochastic volatility tend to reduce the value of at-the-money options and increase the value of out-of-the-money options because large movements are more probable than with the Black–Scholes model

Synthetic position When a trader takes the payoff diagrams at expiry representing risk reward, and combines them

Theta Measures the impact of a change in the time remaining

Time decay See Theta

Time value The amount by which an option premium exceeds its intrinsic or in-the-money value

Underlying The variable on which an option contract is based

Vega Measures the impact of a change in volatility

Volatility A statistical function of the movement of an exchange rate. It measures the speed of movement within an exchange rate band, rather than the width of that band

Writer One who sells an option

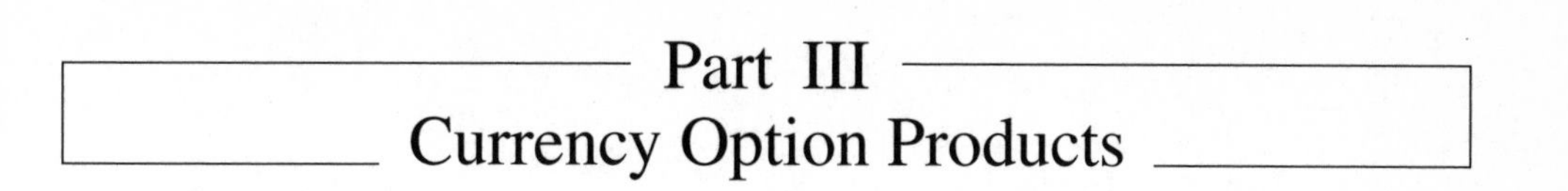

Part III
Currency Option Products

Vanilla Options

The following are examples of the first generation of currency options and are today classed as "vanilla" options, or standard options.

19.1 LONG OPTIONS

Call option – for example, buy a dollar call/Swiss franc put option with a strike of 1.5500 for expiry in three months' time. Assume the premium to be 0.0353 \$/sfr pips. If, at maturity, the spot foreign exchange rate is below \$/sfr 1.5500, say at \$/sfr 1.5375, then the option will be allowed to expire and the dollars will be bought in the market at the prevailing spot foreign exchange rate. The cost, of course, will be the premium paid of 0.0353 \$/sfr pips. However, if at maturity the spot foreign exchange rate is above \$/sfr 1.5500, say at \$/sfr 1.5848, then the option will be exercised and the position will then be long dollars at \$/sfr 1.5500, for a cost of 0.0353 \$/sfr pips. See Figure 19.1.

Put option – for example, buy a dollar put/Swiss franc call option with a strike of 1.5500 for expiry in three months' time. Again, assume the premium to be 0.0353 \$/sfr pips. If, at maturity, the spot foreign exchange rate is below \$/sfr 1.5500, the option will be exercised and the position will then be short dollars at \$/sfr 1.5500, for a cost of 0.0353 \$/sfr pips. However, if the spot foreign exchange rate is greater than \$/sfr 1.5500 at maturity, the option will be allowed to expire and the dollars will be sold in the market at the prevailing spot foreign exchange rate. The cost, again, will be the premium paid of 0.0353 \$/sfr pips.

The above two options are suitable for taking part in any favourable movement of the spot foreign exchange rate, while hedging 100% of the risk. Also, they are only of use if there is no resentment to paying the premium. It should be noted that the amount of the premium could be altered by the strike rate chosen. Hence, the total risk is limited to the premium paid.

19.2 SHORT OPTIONS

Put option – for example, sell a dollar put/Swiss franc call option with a strike of 1.5500 for expiry in three months' time. Assume the premium to be 0.0353 \$/sfr pips. If at maturity, the spot foreign exchange rate is below \$/sfr 1.5500, say at \$/sfr 1.5375, then the option will be exercised by the holder (buyer) against the writer (seller) and the writer will be long dollars at \$/sfr 1.5500, but for receipt of the premium of 0.0353 \$/sfr pips. However, if at maturity the spot foreign exchange rate is above \$/sfr 1.5500, say at \$/sfr 1.5848, then the option will be allowed to expire and the writer keeps the premium of 0.0353 \$/sfr pips. See Figure 19.2.

Call option – for example, sell a dollar call/Swiss franc put option with a strike of 1.5500 for expiry in three months' time. Again, assume the premium to be 0.0353 \$/sfr pips. If at maturity, the spot foreign exchange rate is below \$/sfr 1.5500, the option expires and the writer (seller) keeps the premium of 0.0353 \$/sfr pips. However, if the spot foreign exchange rate is greater than \$/sfr 1.5500 at maturity, the option will be exercised by the purchaser against the

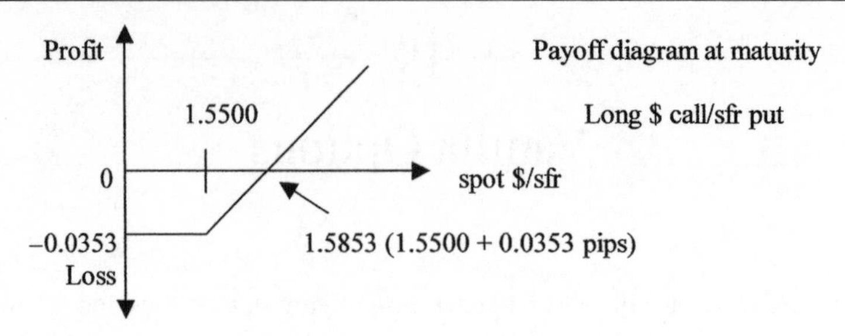

Figure 19.1

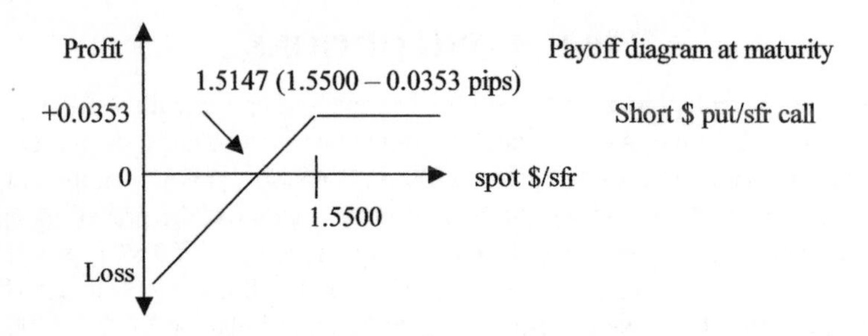

Figure 19.2

writer. Here, there will be an opportunity loss but the writer has the premium hopefully to use to offset against this possible loss.

These short options are suitable if:

- A trader wishes to receive a premium; and
- If there is a strong view on the future direction of the spot foreign exchange rate.

It should be noted that if there is no delta hedge and the position is held to maturity, then a short option position is no more risky than a forward outright position.

19.3 STRADDLE

In this strategy, the definition of a straddle is to buy a put and a call option with the same strike for the same period or sell a put and a call option with the same details. For example:

- Buy a dollar call/Swiss franc put, with a strike of 1.5500, for expiry three months for a premium of 0.0535 $/sfr pips; and
- Buy a dollar put/Swiss franc call, with a strike of 1.5500, for expiry three months for a premium of 0.0535 $/sfr pips.

If, at maturity, the spot foreign exchange rate is less than $/sfr 1.5500, the dollar put is exercised and the dollar call expires. The dollars are sold at $/sfr 1.5500 and they can then be bought back at the prevailing spot foreign exchange rate in the market. However, it must be remembered that two premiums have been paid, totalling 0.0706 $/sfr pips (0.0353 × 2). If the spot foreign exchange rate is above $/sfr 1.5500 at maturity, the dollar call is exercised and the dollar put is allowed to expire. The dollars would have been bought at $/sfr 1.5500 and then sold into the spot foreign exchange market at the prevailing rate. Again, remember that two premiums have been paid, totalling 0.0706 $/sfr pips.

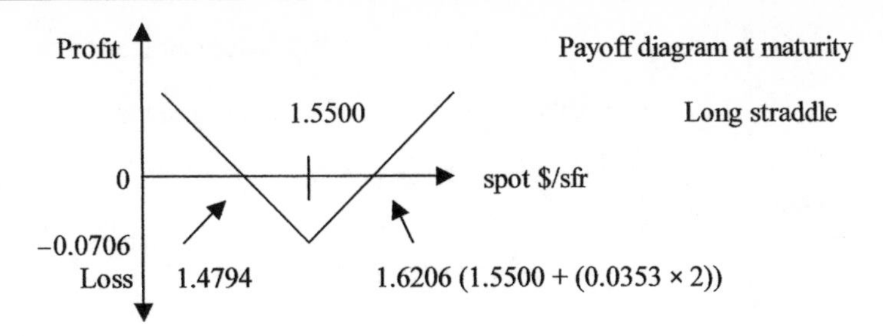

Figure 19.3

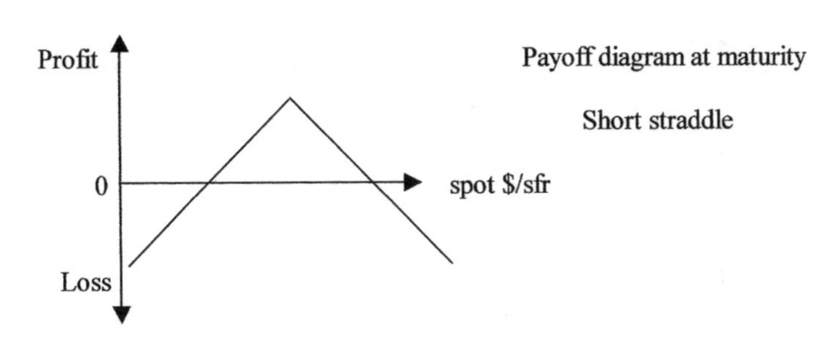

Figure 19.4

Straddles are bought when there is an expectation of a large move in the spot rate but there is uncertainty as to the direction of this move. Also, there has to be no aversion to paying the premium. On the other hand, straddles are sold when there is an expectation that there will be little movement in the spot foreign exchange market and there is a desire to receive the premiums. More risk is involved in selling straddles, as the maximum loss is unlimited in either direction.

The following should be noted:

- Long straddle = maximum loss at strike; while
- Short straddle = maximum profit at strike.

19.4 STRANGLE

The definition for a strangle is to buy a put and a call option but with different strikes for the same period or to sell a put and a call with different strikes but for the same period. The strikes are assumed to be out-of-the-money unless otherwise stated.

For example:

- Buy a dollar call/Swiss franc put with a strike of 1.5600 for expiry in three months' time for a premium cost of 0.0370 $/sfr pips; and
- Buy a dollar put/Swiss franc call with a strike of 1.5400 for expiry in three months' time for a premium cost of 0.0307 $/sfr pips.

If, at maturity, the spot foreign exchange rate is below $/sfr 1.5400, the dollar put is exercised and the dollars would have been sold at $/sfr 1.5400. The dollars can then be bought back in the prevailing spot foreign exchange market. However, two premiums of 0.0614 $/sfr pips would have been paid. If the spot foreign exchange rate at maturity is above $/sfr 1.5600, the dollar call is exercised and the dollars would have been bought at $/sfr 1.5600, which can then

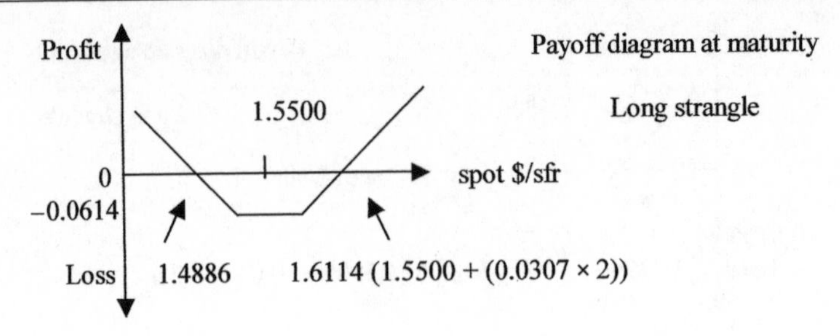

Figure 19.5

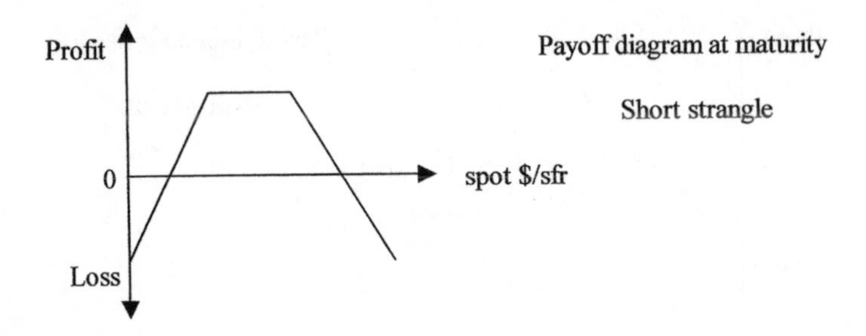

Figure 19.6

be sold back in the market at the prevailing spot foreign exchange rate. Again, the premium of 0.0614 $/sfr pips would have been paid. If, at maturity, the spot foreign exchange rate is between $/sfr 1.5400 and $/sfr 1.5600, neither option will be exercised and just the premium would have been paid.

Traders would buy strangles if there is an expectation for the spot foreign exchange rate to break out of its trading range but there is a certain amount of uncertainty as to the direction, plus there is no aversion to paying two premiums. Strangles are sold when there is an expectation for a trading range and there is a desire to receive two premiums. Obviously, there is more risk involved in selling strangles, as the maximum loss is unlimited.

The following should be noted:

- Long strangle = maximum loss between strikes; and
- Short strangle = maximum profit between strikes.

19.5 CYLINDER

The definition for this strategy is to buy a put option and sell a call option, or vice versa, with different strikes but for the same period. The strikes are assumed to be out-of-the-money unless otherwise specified.

For example:

- Buy a dollar call/Swiss franc put option, with a strike of 1.5600, expiry in three months' time; and
- Sell a dollar put option/Swiss franc call option with a strike of 1.5400, again with expiry in three months' time.

Assume both premiums are 0.0307 $/sfr.

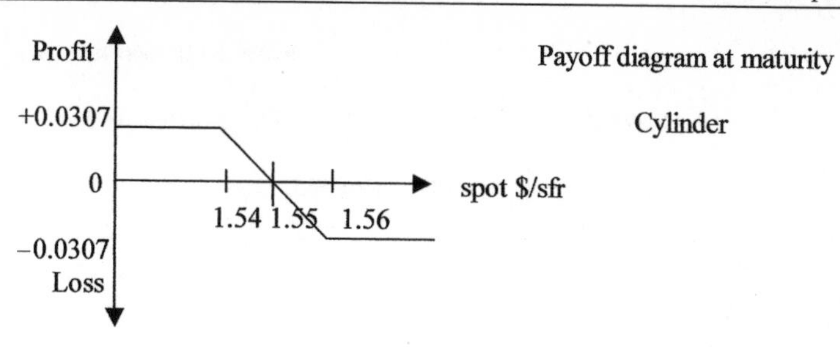

Figure 19.7

At maturity, if the spot foreign exchange rate is less than $/sfr 1.5400, the dollar put is exercised and the dollars would have been bought at $/sfr 1.5400. No premium was paid or received. If the market, at maturity, is between $/sfr 1.5400 and $/sfr 1.5600, neither option is exercised and no premium has been paid or received. If at maturity the spot foreign exchange rate is higher than $/sfr 1.5600, the dollar call option is exercised and the dollars would have been bought at $/sfr 1.5600. Once again, no premium has been paid or received.

This strategy tends to be used when there is a wish to minimise the premium paid plus a need to hedge an existing position. Also, there has to be a willingness to cap the maximum profit for the benefit of being hedged, where there is a belief that there won't be much profit above the level at which the upside has been capped.

It should be noted that a cylinder is often constructed so that there is no net premium to pay. This is called a zero-cost cylinder. Thanks to put/call parity, the effect of a cash position and the cylinder is the same as buying and selling a put or buying and selling a call, which is termed a put or call spread.

19.6 COLLAR

A collar is the opposite to a cylinder and is the simultaneous purchase of an out-of-the-money call and sale of an out-of-the-money put (or cap and floor in the case of interest rate options). The premium from selling the put reduces the cost of purchasing the call. The amount saved will depend on the strike rate of the two options. Of course, if the premium raised by the sale of the put exactly matches the cost of the call, the strategy will be zero cost. When combined with an outright forward foreign exchange position, this will lock the hedger into a range of values.

19.7 PARTICIPATING FORWARD

With this strategy, buy a put option and sell a call option, or vice versa, with the same strike for the same period but in different amounts. The strike of the option bought must be out-of-the-money for zero cost.

For example:

- Buy a dollar call/Swiss franc put option with a strike of 1.5700 for three months' time in an amount of 10 million dollars. Assume the premium is 1.70% of the dollar amount; and
- Sell a dollar put option/Swiss franc call option with a strike of 1.5700, again for three months' time but in an amount of 5.75 million dollars. Here, assume the premium is 2.96% of the dollar amount.

This represents a participation of 42.6%.

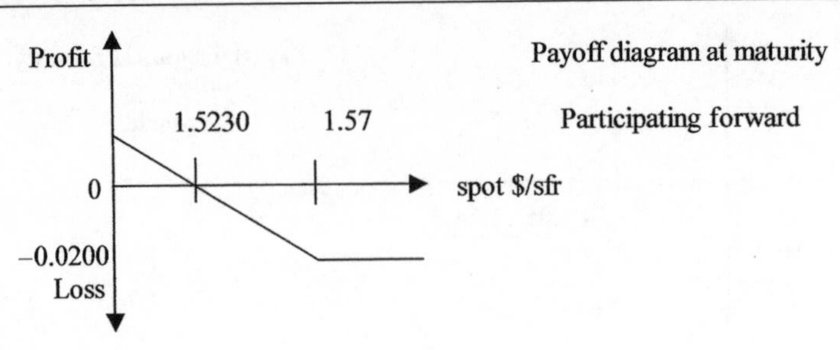

Figure 19.8

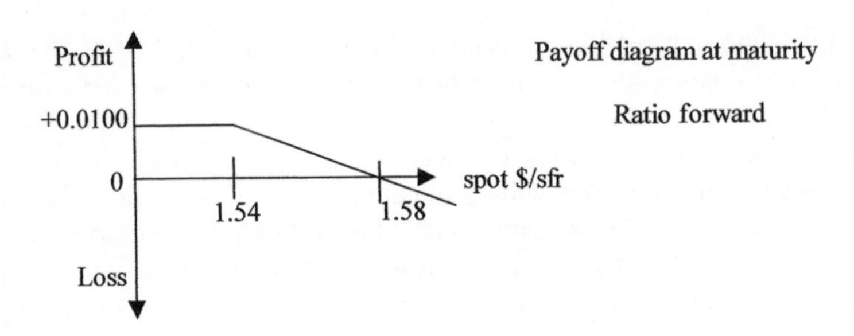

Figure 19.9

If, at maturity, the spot foreign exchange rate is less than $/sfr 1.5700, the dollar put is exercised and 5.75 million dollars would have been bought at $/sfr 1.5700. Any remaining dollars needed can then be bought at the prevailing foreign exchange market rate. If, at maturity, spot is higher than $/sfr 1.5700, the dollar call will be exercised and 10 million dollars would have been bought at $/sfr 1.5700. See Figure 19.8.

This strategy is used when there is a desire to minimise the premium paid and the position needs to be hedged and there is a willingness to give up some participation in the profit for the benefit of being fully hedged. Also, there has to be a belief that there will not be a significant profit potential in the underlying position.

Usually, a participating forward is constructed in such a way that there is no net premium to pay. In addition, either the strike or the required participation in the profit can be mentioned at the initial price request and the writer can calculate the rest.

19.8 RATIO FORWARD

For this option strategy, buy a put option and sell a call option or vice versa with the same strike for the same period but in different amounts. The strike of the option bought must be in-the-money for zero cost.

For example, assume the position is short dollars and long Swiss francs:

- Buy a dollar call/Swiss franc put with a strike of 1.5400, for three months' time, in an amount of 7.5 million dollars. Assume the premium is 2.58% of the dollar amount.
- Sell a dollar put/Swiss franc call with a strike of 1.5400, for three months' time in an amount of 10 million dollars for a premium of 1.935% of the dollar amount.

This represents a ratio of 1.33.

If, at maturity, the spot foreign exchange rate is less than \$/sfr 1.5400, the dollar put is exercised and the 10 million dollars would have been bought at \$/sfr 1.5400 against the existing short position. However, if the spot foreign exchange rate at maturity is greater than \$/sfr 1.5400, the dollar call is exercised and 7.5 million dollars would have been bought at \$/sfr 1.5400 to be used against the existing short dollar position. The remaining 2.5 million dollars will then be bought at the prevailing spot foreign exchange rate. See Figure 19.9.

This strategy is used when there is a desire to minimise the premium paid and there is a wish to achieve a better rate than the forward foreign exchange outright rate but there is a willingness to be hedged on only part of the amount. Also, there is a belief that there will not be much movement against the existing underlying position.

It should be noted that usually, a ratio forward is constructed such that there is no net premium to pay. Also, the ratio forward gives a partial hedge at levels that are at a rate better than the forward foreign exchange outright rate.

19.9 ADDED EXTRAS TO VANILLA OPTIONS

Rebate options enable part or all of the upfront cost of a vanilla option to be recovered if the underlying exposure moves in the hedger's favour and the option cover is thus no longer required. They offer the same initial level of protection as an equivalent vanilla option but will usually cost more than the corresponding vanilla option, depending on the amount and rebate level required. This increased cost needs to be weighed against the additional benefits offered by the rebate option if spot moves strongly in the purchaser's favour.

For example, take the case of a British manufacturer who is due to pay a Swiss supplier 3 million francs in two months' time. Assuming a spot gbp/sfr rate of 2.20 and a two-month outright forward foreign exchange rate at 2.1955, then a vanilla currency option of a sterling put/franc call, with a strike of 2.1955, could cost 61 gbp pips or £18 300 (3 000 000 × 0.0061).

Assume also that this British manufacturer is not highly averse to paying an option premium to cover its foreign exchange exposures, but in this case they are concerned that sterling may rebound strongly against the Swiss franc over the coming weeks, thus "wasting" the option premium. The exposure could be left unhedged with the manufacturer being able to take advantage of any sterling strengthening but left exposed in the case of any continued sterling depreciation.

Alternatively, the manufacturer could purchase a rebate option, paying, for example, £23 500 upfront for the option cover, but receiving a rebate of £100 000 if 2.2550 is reached. With a reduced rebate of £5 000, the rebate option could cost £20 900.

Thus, if sterling does strengthen against the Swiss franc, trading at gbp/sfr 2.2550 over the life of the option, the manufacturer will receive the rebate amount. With the spot foreign exchange rate at this higher level, the underlying option is likely to be relatively uncostly to replace. On the other hand, if gbp/sfr 2.2550 is not reached during the life of the option, the manufacturer has obtained the same benefit as under a vanilla option, although at a higher cost, which the British company has been happy to accept in return for the rebate should gbp/sfr 2.2550 trade.

Obviously, the increased cost needs to be weighed against the additional benefits offered by the rebate option if the spot foreign exchange rate moves strongly in the hedger's favour.

Mini premium options enable the upfront cost of a vanilla currency option to be potentially reduced or eliminated completely, without giving up any of the protection afforded by the option. Instead of giving up some of the cover afforded by the option, as is the case with knock-out option strategies, the hedger receives a reduced cost by agreeing to pay a larger premium than that payable for the vanilla option in the event of a trigger(s) level being reached. If the entire trigger levels trade, during the life of the option, the total cost (upfront premium plus premium paid at the trigger levels) will always be more than that of purchasing a vanilla option at the outset.

Enhanced collars enable hedgers to protect an underlying foreign exchange exposure at known "best" and "worst case" rates, while retaining full flexibility between these two extremes. This is achieved by buying and selling options with strikes either side of the forward foreign exchange rate, commonly at zero total cost. In effect, enabling the hedger to benefit from favourable foreign exchange movements beyond the cap/floor level of a vanilla collar option, so long as a specified limit rate is not reached at any point during the life of the option. This structure is achieved by the hedger buying a vanilla option struck at the "worst case" rate (cap/floor) and selling a knock-in option struck at the "best case" rate (cap/floor), with the knock-in at the limit rate.

If the limit rate is not reached during the life of the option, the hedger is simply long the vanilla option. The exposure is still protected at the worst case rate and the hedger may be able to deal at a better rate than the original best case rate, depending on the level of the underlying spot rate in the market at expiry. If the limit rate is reached (hit) during the life of the option, then the short option position knocks in and the hedger will be left with a vanilla collar with fixed cap and floor levels.

For example, assume a British company is due to pay an American supplier 2 million dollars in three months' time. The budget rate for the British company is gbp/$1.6000 and the sterling dollar spot foreign exchange rate is gbp/$ 1.6500 and an outright forward foreign exchange rate of 1.6475.

The British company could consider hedging its exposure to the dollar via a "forward extra" option. This would protect the exposure at a "worst case" rate of gbp/$ 1.6200, while allowing the company to benefit from any sterling appreciation, so long as gbp/$ 1.7580 does not trade, in which case the exposure will be locked-in at gbp/$ 1.6200.

Alternatively, an enhanced collar could be entered into at zero cost. With the worst case (floor) rate at gbp/$ 1.6200 and a best case (cap) rate at gbp/$ 1.6600, a limit rate of gbp/$ 1.7275 is obtained. The exposure is protected at gbp/$ 1.6200 and the company is able to benefit from any appreciation of sterling above the cap rate, so long as gbp/$ 1.7275 does not trade. If gbp/$ 1.7275 is reached during the life of the option, at any time, the cap at gbp/$ 1.6600 knocks in and the company will be left with a gbp/$ 1.6200–gbp/$ 1.6600 vanilla collar option.

In comparison, a zero-cost vanilla collar with a floor at gbp/$ 1.6200 could give a cap level at gbp/$ 1.6725.

Since enhanced collar options offer the same downside protection but greater upside potential than a vanilla collar option, with the same cap and floor levels, the option will in all cases cost more in terms of upfront premium. The further away the limit rate chosen is, the greater will be the difference between the two prices.

Therefore, in order to achieve a zero-cost structure, the cap and floor levels will be slightly worse than those on a zero-cost vanilla collar option. This is achieved by moving in the best case rate, the worst case rate, or both.

20

Common Option Strategies

In the previous chapter, the different types of vanilla options were briefly explained. In order to take the discussion one stage further and to look at options in more depth, the three tables below and the following comments summarise the profit and loss potential along with the effect time decay has on a position. It should be noted that terms such as "strangle" and "condor" are in fact generic terms that the professionals in the market use.

Directional options:

	Market bias	Profit potential	Loss potential	Decay effect
Long call	Bull	Open	Limited	Hurts
Short call	Bear	Limited	Open	Helps
Long put	Bear	Open	Limited	Hurts
Short put	Bull	Limited	Open	Helps
Bull spread	Bull	Limited	Limited	Mixed
Bear spread	Bear	Limited	Limited	Mixed

Precision options:

	Market bias	Profit potential	Loss potential	Decay effect
Long straddle	Mixed	Open	Limited	Hurts
Short straddle	Mixed	Limited	Open	Helps
Long strangle	Mixed	Open	Limited	Hurts
Short strangle	Mixed	Limited	Open	Helps
Long butterfly	Mixed	Limited	Limited	Mixed
Short butterfly	Mixed	Limited	Limited	Mixed
Long condor	Mixed	Limited	Limited	Mixed
Short condor	Mixed	Limited	Limited	Mixed

Call ratio spread	Mixed	Limited	Mixed	Mixed
Put ratio spread	Mixed	Limited	Mixed	Mixed
Call ratio backspread	Mixed	Mixed	Limited	Mixed
Put ratio backspread	Mixed	Mixed	Limited	Mixed

Locked trade option:

	Market bias	Profit potential	Loss potential	Decay effect
Box or conversion	Neutral	Absolute	Absolute	Neutral

Figure 20.1 provides a quick fix on what happens in an options position. For example, if a trader expects prices to go up, the trader can buy a call option and have limited risk or sell a put option and have unlimited risk.

Figure 20.2 is used with each strategy, which of course shows the profit/loss scale on the left vertical axis. The horizontal zero line in the middle is the break-even point. Therefore,

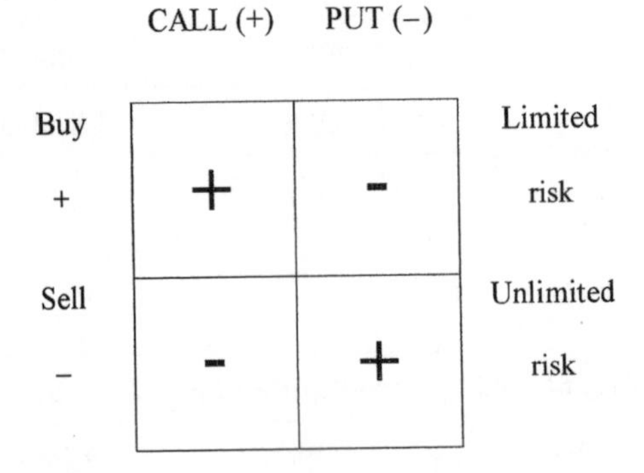

Figure 20.1

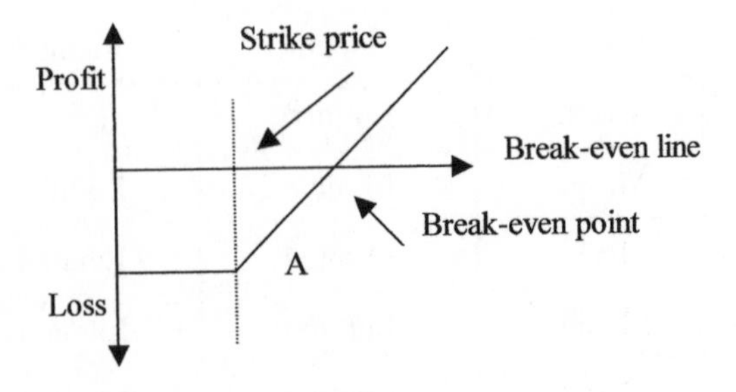

Figure 20.2

anything above that line indicates a profit, anything below it, losses. The scale along the bottom would represent the price of the underlying instrument, with lower prices to the left and higher prices to the right. "A", "B", "C" etc. in the diagrams indicates the strike price(s) involved.

20.1 DIRECTIONAL OPTIONS

Long call options are used when a trader is very bullish (positive) on the markets. The more bullish the trader is, the more out-of-the-money (higher) should be the option bought. No other position gives the trader as much leveraged advantage in a rising market (with limited downside risk). As the market rises, the potential profit increases and the loss is limited to the amount paid for the option, i.e. to the amount of the premium paid. The position is a wasting asset, in that as time passes, the value of the position erodes towards the expiration value. If volatility increases, erosion slows and as volatility decreases, erosion speeds up.

Short call options are used when a trader firmly believes the market is not going up. The trader should sell out-of-the-money (higher strike) options if they are only somewhat convinced, sell at-the-money options if the feeling is one of confidence that the market will stagnate or fall. If in doubt about the market stagnating, then a trader will sell in-the-money options for maximum profit. Profit is limited to the premium received, while the losses increase as the market rises. Because the risk is open-ended, the position must be watched closely. The position is a growing asset. As time passes, the value of the position increases as the option loses its time value. The maximum rate of increasing profits occurs if the option is at-the-money.

Long put options are used when a trader is very bearish (negative) on the market. The more bearish the trader is, the more out-of-the-money (lower) should be the option bought. No other position gives the trader as much leveraged advantage in a falling market (with limited upside risk). As the market falls, so profit increases. The loss is limited to the amount paid (premium)

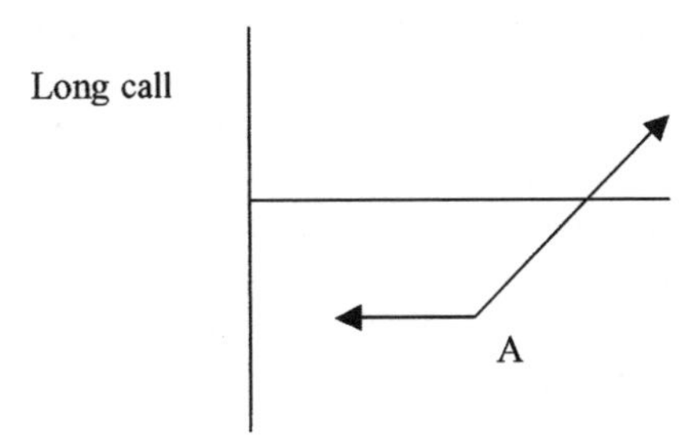

Figure 20.3

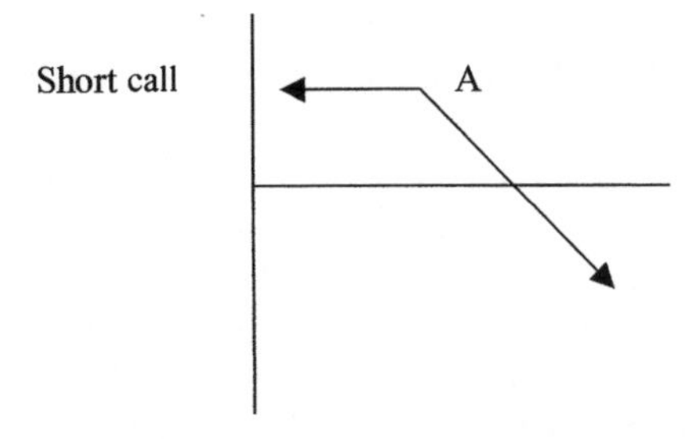

Figure 20.4

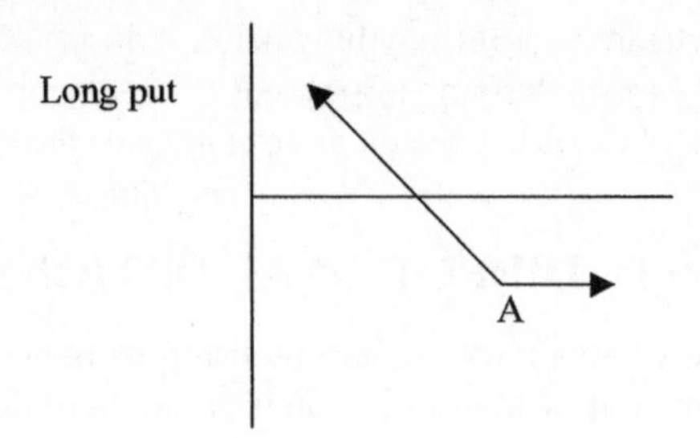

Figure 20.5

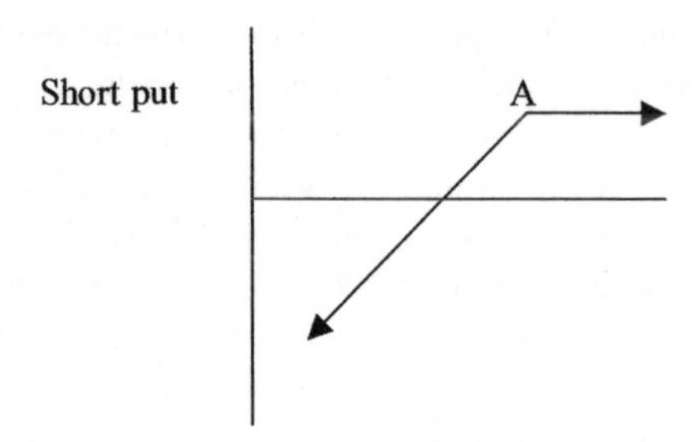

Figure 20.6

for the option. The position is a wasting asset. As time passes, the value of the position erodes towards expiration value. If volatility increases, erosion slows and as volatility decreases so erosion speeds up.

Short put options are used when a trader firmly believes the market is not going down. If the trader is only somewhat convinced, the trader will sell out-of-the-money (lower strike) options. However, the trader will sell at-the-money options if the opinion is one of confidence that the market will stagnate or rise. If there is any doubt about the market stagnating, then sell in-the-money options for maximum profit. Profit is limited to the premium received from the sale and any loss will increase as the market falls. Because risk is open-ended, the position must be watched closely. Also, the position is a growing asset. As time passes, the value of the position increases as the option loses its time value. Maximum rate of increasing profits occurs if the option is at-the-money.

Bull spread options are used when a trader thinks the market will go up somewhat or at least is a bit more likely to rise than fall. This is a good position to have if a trader wants to be in the market but is unsure of the bullish expectations. Profit potential is limited but in return there is limited loss. If the market is midway between A and B, then there is no time effect. At B, profits increase at a faster rate with time. At A, losses increase at maximum rate with time.

Bear spread options are used when a trader thinks the market will fall somewhat or at least is a bit more likely to fall than rise. This is a good position to have if a trader wants to be in the market but is unsure of the bearish expectations. Profit potential is limited, reaching maximum at expiration if the market is at or below A. By accepting limited profits, the trader can gain a limit to the risk as well. Losses, at expiration, increase as the market rises to B, where they stabilise. If the market is midway between A and B, then there is no time effect. At A, profits increase at a faster rate with time. At B, losses increase at maximum rate with time.

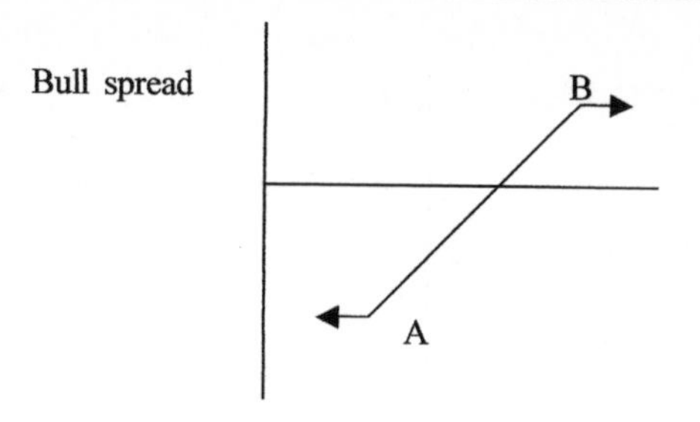

Figure 20.7

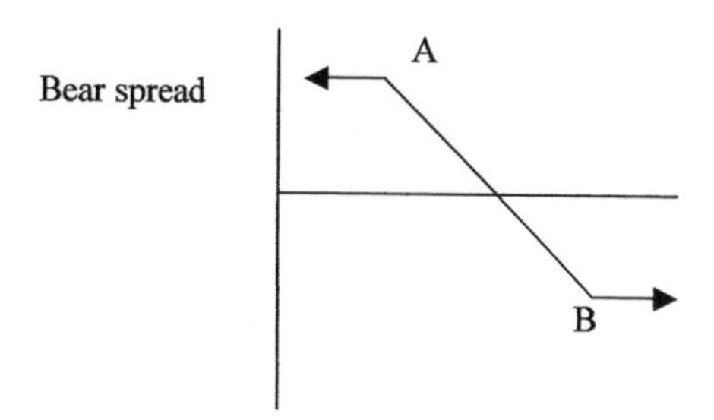

Figure 20.8

20.2 PRECISION OPTIONS

Long straddle options are used when the market is near A and there is an expectation that the markets will start to move but there is uncertainty as to the direction. This is an especially good position to have if the market is quiet and then starts to zigzag sharply, signalling a potential eruption. Profit is open-ended in either direction. At expiration, break-even is at A, plus or minus the cost of the spread. However, the position is seldom held to expiration because of increasing decay levels with time. Loss is limited to the cost of the spread with maximum loss being incurred if the market is at A at expiration. Decay accelerates as the options approach expiration. For this reason, the position is adjusted to neutrality by frequent profit taking. It is normally taken off well before expiration.

Short straddle options are used if the market is near A and there is an expectation that the market is stagnating. Because the trader will be short options, the trader will reap profits as they decay, as long as the market remains near A. Profit is maximised if at expiration the market is at A and the loss potential is open-ended in either direction. The position must therefore be closely monitored and readjusted to neutrality if the market begins to drift away from A. Because they are only short options, the trader will pick up time value decay at an increasing rate as expiration nears, maximised if the market is near A.

Long strangle options are used when the market is stagnant and the market is within or near A–B range. If the market explodes either way, the position will make money, but if the market continues to stagnate, then the position will lose less than with a long straddle. Profit is open-ended in either direction and break-evens are at A minus the cost of the spread and B plus the cost of the spread. However, the spread is not usually held to expiration. Loss is limited and in its most common version, loss is equal to net cost of the position. Maximum loss is incurred if, at expiration, the market is between A and B. Decay accelerates as the option

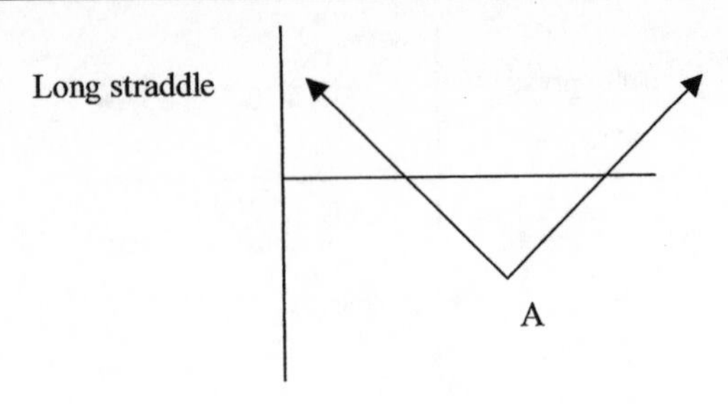

Figure 20.9

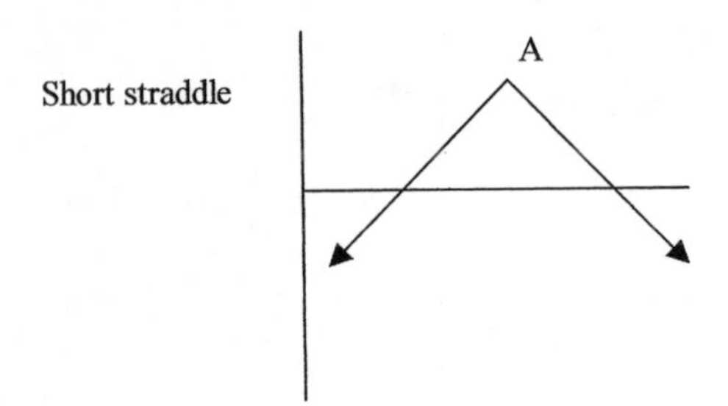

Figure 20.10

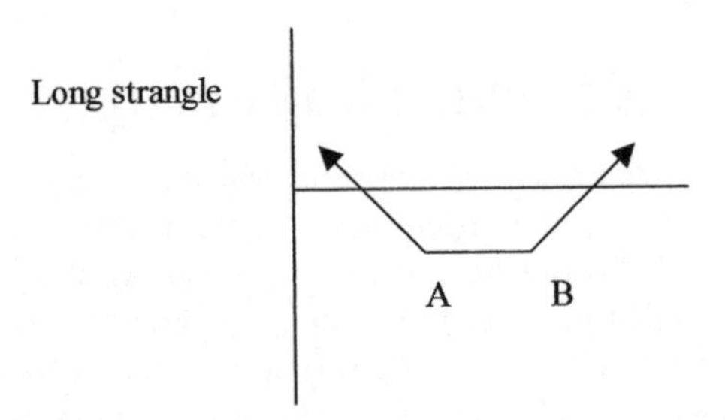

Figure 20.11

approaches expiration but not as rapidly as with long straddles. To avoid the largest part of decay, the position is normally taken off prior to expiration.

Short strangle options are used when the market is within or near A–B range and, though active, is quieting down. If the market goes into stagnation, the position makes money. If it continues to be active, there is a slightly less risk than with a short straddle. Maximum profit is realised if the market, at expiration, is between A and B.

Potential loss is open-ended. Although less risky than a short straddle, the position is not riskless. It got its name during the April 1978 IBM price swings, when a number of good traders holding this position were wiped out. Because the position is one of only short options, the trader will pick up time value decay at an increasing rate as expiration nears and is maximised if the market is within A–B range.

Long butterfly options are one of the few positions that may be entered into advantageously in a long-term options series. The rule of thumb is that a trader will enter into this option type when, with one month or more to go, cost of the spread is 10% or less of B–A (20% if a strike exists between A and B). Maximum profit occurs if the market is at B at expiration. That profit

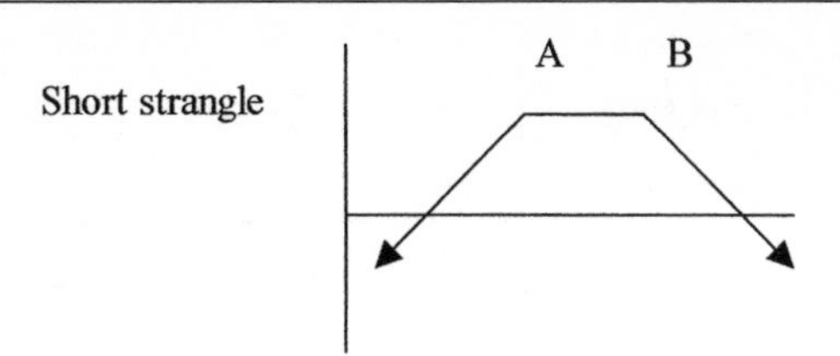

Figure 20.12

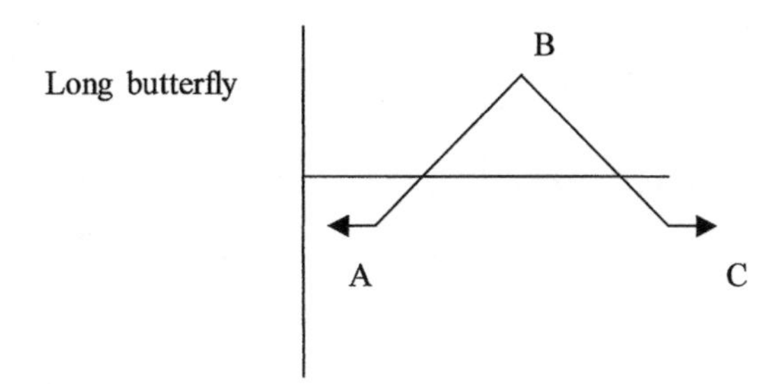

Figure 20.13

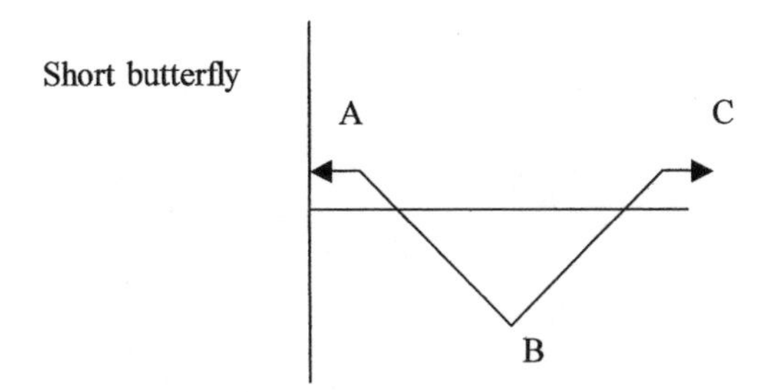

Figure 20.14

would be B–A-cost of doing the spread. This profit develops, almost totally, in the last month. Maximum loss, in either direction, is the cost of the spread. This is a very conservative trade and break-evens are at A plus the cost of the spread and at C minus the cost of the spread. Decay is negligible until the final month, during which time the distinctive pattern of the butterfly forms. Maximum profit growth is at B. If the trader is away from the A–C range entering into the last month, the trader may want to liquidate the position.

Short butterfly options are used when the market is either below A or above C and the position is overpriced with one month or so left. Also, this option strategy can be used when there is only a few weeks left and the market is near B and there is an expectation of a move in either direction. Maximum profit is credit for which the option spread is put on. This occurs when the market, at expiration, is below A or above C, thus making all options in-the-money or all options out-of-the-money. Maximum loss occurs if the market is at B at expiration. The amount of the loss is B–A-credit received when setting up the position. Break-evens are at A plus initial credit and at C minus initial credit. Decay is negligible until the final month, during which time the distinctive pattern of the butterfly forms. Maximum loss is at B.

Long condor options are entered into in far-out months. It is worth twice the average of A–B–C and B–C–D butterflies because it has twice the profit area. Maximum profit is realised

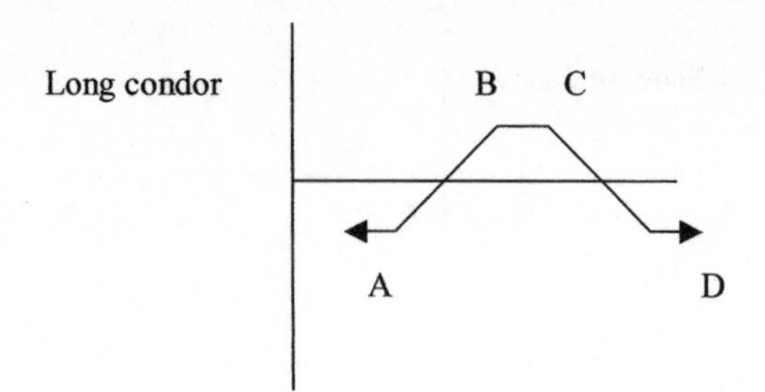

Figure 20.15

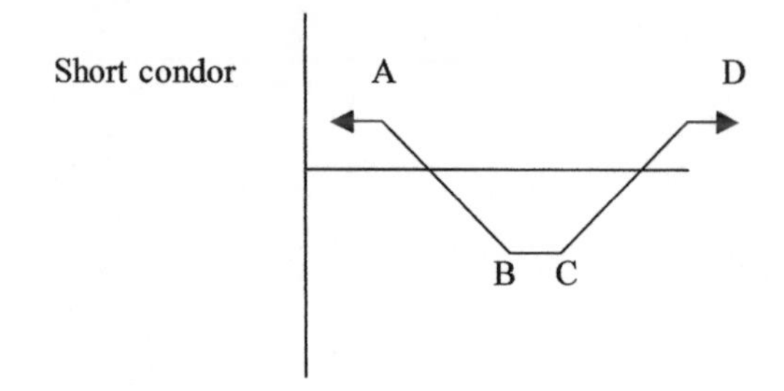

Figure 20.16

if the market is between B and C at expiration. Break-evens are at A plus the cost of the condor and D minus the cost of the condor. Maximum loss occurs if the market is below A or above D at expiration. Decay is negligible until the final month, during which time the "super butterfly" condor develops its characteristic shape. Maximum profits occur in B–C range.

Short condor options are normally entered into when the market, with less than one month to go, is between B and C but the trader thinks there is a good potential for a strong move outside of that range. Maximum profit will occur if the market is below A or above D at expiration. Maximum loss will occur if the position is held to expiration and, at that time, the market is between B and C. Decay is negligible until the last month, during which time the distinctive condor pattern emerges. The loss accelerates via decay with the market between B and C.

Call ratio spread options are usually entered into when the market is near A and the user expects a slight rise in the market but also sees a potential for a sell-off. Maximum profit is realised if the market is at B at expiration. Loss is limited on the downside but is open-ended if the market rises. The rate of loss, if the market rises beyond B, is proportional to the number of excess shorts in the position. If the market is at B, profits from option decay accelerate the most rapidly with passage of time. At A, there is the greatest rate of loss accrual by decay of long positions.

Put ratio spread options are usually entered into when the market is near B and there is an expectation that the market will fall slightly but also there is a potential for a sharp rise. Maximum profits are realised if the market is at A at expiration. Loss is limited on the upside but is open-ended if the market falls. The rate of loss, if the market falls below A, is proportional to the number of excess shorts in the position. If the market is at A, profits from option decay accelerates the most rapidly with passage of time. At B, there is the greatest rate of loss accrual by decay of long positions.

Call ratio backspread options are normally entered into when the market is near B and shows signs of increasing activity, with greater probability to the upside. For example, if the last major

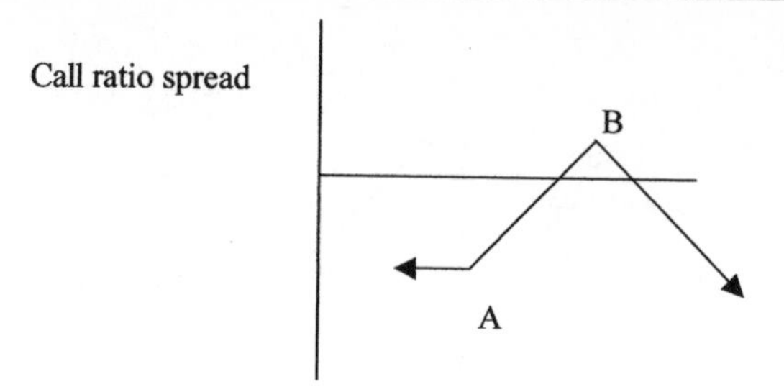

Figure 20.17

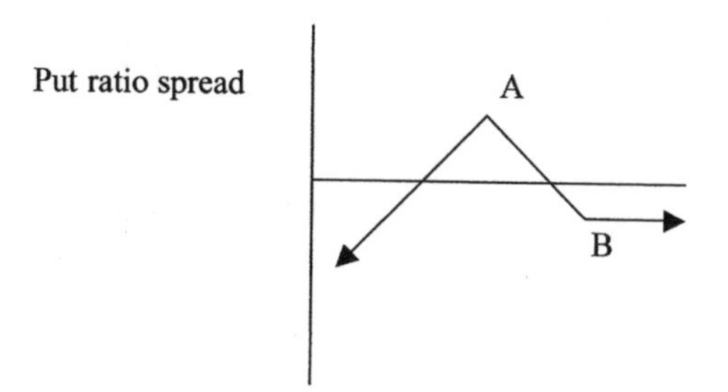

Figure 20.18

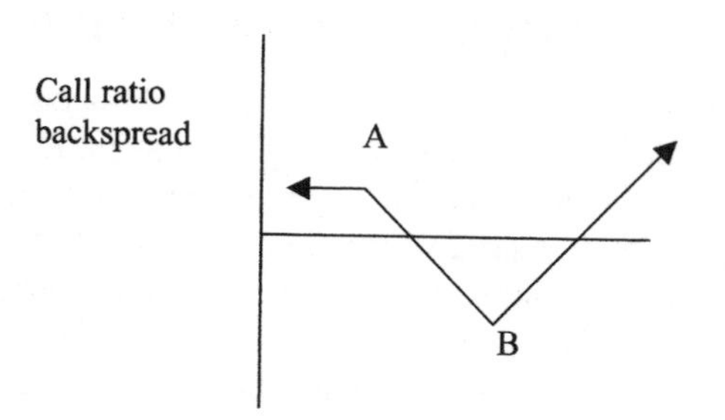

Figure 20.19

move was down, followed by stagnation. Profit is limited on the downside but open-ended in a rallying market. Maximum loss is realised if the market is at B at expiration. However, this loss is less than for the equivalent long straddle, the trade-off for sacrificing profit potential on the downside. If the market is at B, loss from decay will accelerate the most rapidly. Therefore, it is wise to exit early as the market is near B as you enter the last month. At A, there is the greatest rate of profit accrual by decay of short options.

Put ratio backspread options are normally entered into when the market is near A and shows signs of increasing activity, with greater probability to the downside. For example, if the last major move was up, followed by stagnation. Profit is limited on the upside but open-ended in a collapsing market. Maximum loss is realised if the market is at A at expiration. This loss is less than for the equivalent long straddle, the trade-off for sacrificing profit potential on the upside. If the market is at A, loss from decay will accelerate the most rapidly. Therefore, the trader will want to exit early if the market is near A as the position enters the last month. At B, there is the greatest rate of profit accrual by decay of short options.

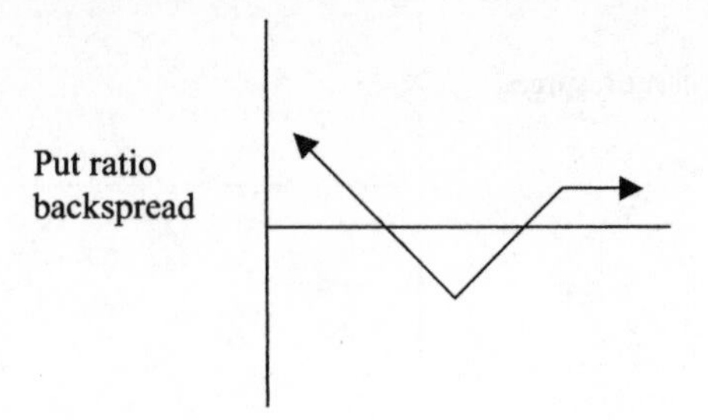

Figure 20.20

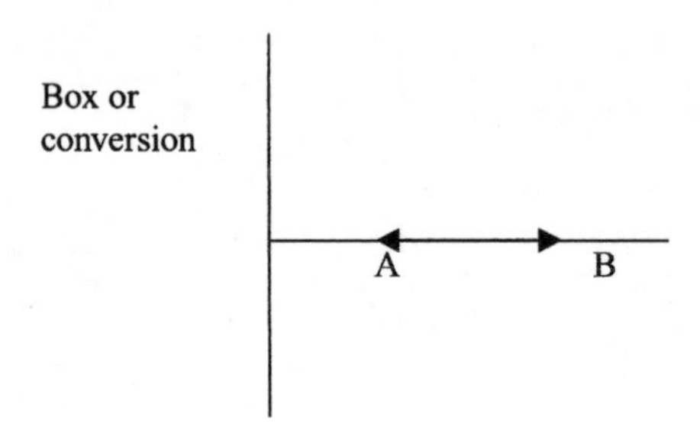

Figure 20.21

20.3 LOCKED TRADE OPTIONS

Box or conversion options are referred to as "locked trades" because their value at expiration is totally independent of the price of the underlying instrument. If a trader can buy them for less than that value or sell them for more, the trader will make a profit (ignoring any potential costs). This type of option will be used when a market gets out of line enough to justify an initial entry into one of these positions. This does occasionally happen. However, this option strategy is most commonly used to "lock" all or part of a portfolio by buying or selling to create the missing "legs" of the position. These are alternatives to closing out positions at possibly unfavourable prices.

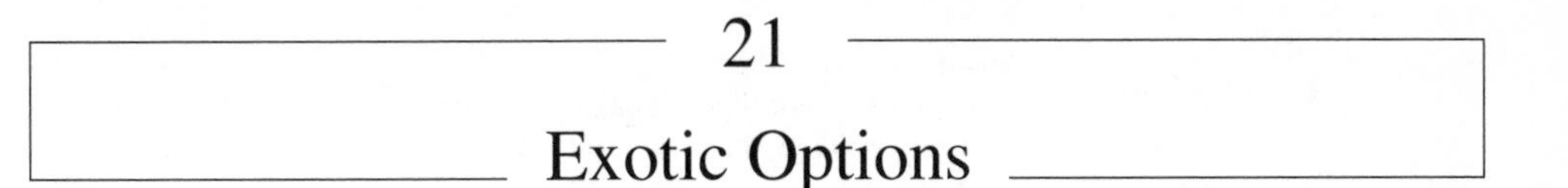

21 Exotic Options

Over the last few years, options have become an important tool for investors and hedgers in the foreign exchange market. With the growing sophistication of market participants, new ways of expressing views on the market or reducing hedging costs have evolved in the form of exotic options. Today, it is possible to do virtually any sort of option imaginable, the only limit seems to be price, as some of the more involved strategies become so expensive that it is not worth doing them. However, overall the growth of the exotic options market over the past few years has shown first how the technical side of the market has progressed and second how client sophistication has also developed.

Almost every day the main players of the markets are developing new exotic options, with exotic sounding labels; however, the better-known classed exotics are mentioned below.

21.1 BARRIERS

Barrier options are one of the groups of options that are known as "path dependent" options. They are essentially a European style option with fixed maturity, fixed call and put currencies and fixed strike price but with an additional "trigger" level. There are a number of different types of barrier options but their common feature is that they are either activated or terminated if a predetermined spot foreign exchange rate, or trigger level, is traded at any time before the expiry date. Barriers can be split into two general groups:

- Standard knock-ins and knock-outs; and
- In-the-money knock-ins and knock-outs.

With *standard barrier* options, there is a reduction in the premium associated with this additional trigger level feature (relative to the equivalent European style option). This trigger level must be placed out-of-the-money relative to the option. This means below the spot foreign exchange price for a call on the base currency and above the spot foreign exchange price for a put on the base currency. The closer the trigger level is to the spot foreign exchange price, the greater the reduction in premium of the knock-out and vice versa for the knock-in. Hence, the more likely the option is to be knocked out, the cheaper the option will be. Conversely, for a knock-in option, the less likely the option will be activated, the cheaper the cost will be.

For *in-the-money knock-ins and knock-outs*, the pricing is quite different. This group of options are terminated or activated, as the option is moving further into the money leading to unusual pricing and payoff profiles. In-the-money knock-out options can look very inexpensive but this is due to the fact that the purchase of one of these types of options assumes a very directionally specific view. Likewise, the price of an in-the-money knock-in can be very similar to that of the European style option, although it should not be any more expensive.

Examples of the payoff profiles of knock-ins and knock-outs are shown in graphs of Figure 21.1.

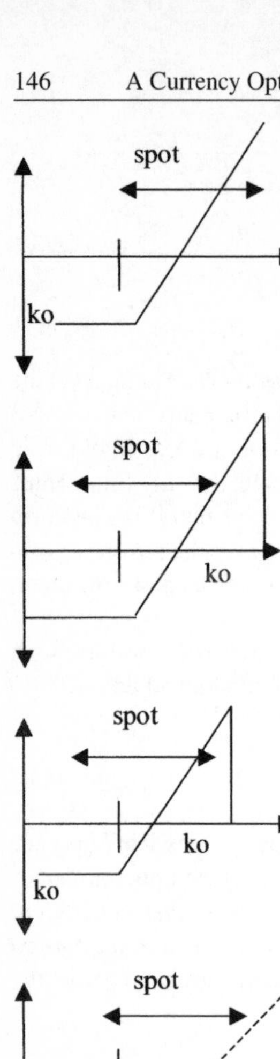

Out-of-the-money knock-out:
A standard option that automatically cancels out if spot trades through a predetermined knock-out level. This level is set below the initial spot for a call option, and above spot for a put.

In-the-money knock-out:
A standard option that automatically cancels out if spot trades through a predetermined knock-out level. This level is set above the initial spot for a call option, and below spot for a put.

Double knock-out:
A standard option that automatically cancels out if spot trades through either one of two predetermined knock-out levels. One of the knock-out levels is set above the initial spot and the other one below spot – hence there is both an out-of-the-money and an in-the-money knock-out with these options.

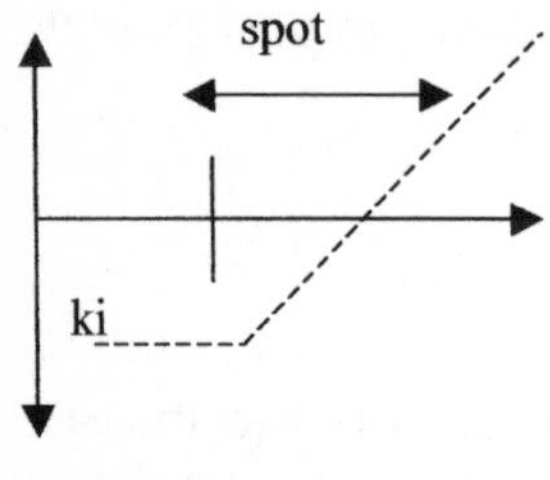

Out-of-the-money knock-in:
A standard option that can only be exercised upon expiry providing that spot has previously traded through a predetermined knock-in level. This level is set below the initial spot for a call option and above spot for a put.

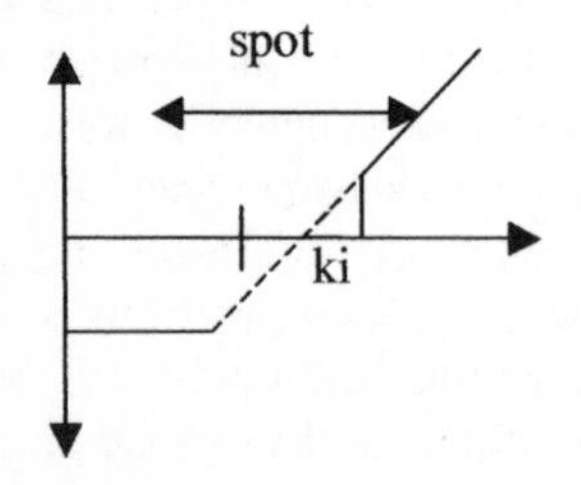

In-the-money knock-in:
A standard option that can only be exercised upon expiry providing that spot has previously traded through a predetermined knock-in level. This level is set above the initial spot for a call option and below spot for a put.

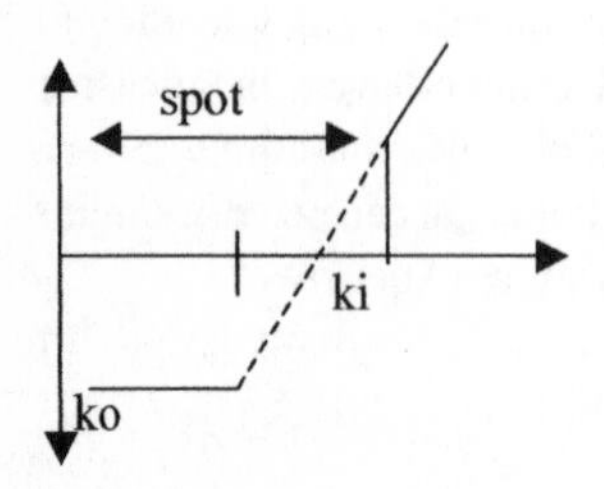

Knock-in/Knock-out:
A standard option that automatically cancels out if spot trades through a predetermined knock-out level and in addition can only be exercised upon expiry providing that spot has previously traded through a predetermined knock-in level. The knock-out level is set below the initial spot for a call option and above spot for a put. Similarly the knock-in level is set above spot for a call and below spot for a put.

Figure 21.1

Barrier options are mainly used as a means of adding an extra dimension of flexibility and can provide enormous opportunities for profit due to the large gearing available in addition to the ability to limit losses, if the option is purchased. For position takers, as knock-out options can be tailored to have lower premiums compared to the equivalent vanilla option, the gearing can be increased and therefore the potential for profit. In addition, the knock-out level can also be used as a stop loss since if a particular level is reached, for example a chart point, a trader may decide to close out an existing position. By providing a contrasting risk profile, knock-in options complement the opportunities provided by knock-out options. In addition, for risk managers, the strike level of a knock-in or knock-out option will set the level of protection.

As an example, for a knock-out option, consider a Swiss company who purchases raw materials from an American company. The raw materials will cost 1 million dollars and will be paid for in three months' time. Obviously, the Swiss company is exposed to the risk that over the three months, the dollar will strengthen and consequently cost more in Swiss francs. The company wants to protect itself against a rise above $/sfr 1.4700 compared to the current spot foreign exchange level of $/sfr 1.3500.

The Swiss company could purchase a European option, dollar call/franc put for three months with a strike rate of 1.4700, in the notional amount of 1 million dollars with an assumed premium cost of 1.97% of the dollar amount. The beauty of this course of action is that it is simple and the Swiss company will benefit fully from a fall in the dollar.

Alternatively, the Swiss company could purchase a knock-out option with exactly the same details as the European option above, but with a knock-out rate of 1.3250. Assuming a premium cost for this option of 0.98% of the dollar amount, this option will now provide a protection level of $/sfr 1.4700 as before, but at half the cost of the standard currency option. If the option is knocked out at $/sfr 1.3250, the hedge would cease. However, $/sfr 1.3250 is a more favourable rate than the original spot rate of $/sfr 1.3500. The Swiss company can then choose to rehedge using another knock-out with more favourable rates. If the option does not knock out and is exercised at $/sfr 1.4700, then the Swiss company would be better off compared to the standard option, since the premium was half as much.

As an example of a knock-in option, assume following a period of sharp declines in the dollar against the yen, the exchange rate has reached $/jpy 120.00. Also, assume a trader believes that there is scope for a further decline to $/jpy 115.00. Additionally, the trader also believes that this would be followed by large-scale intervention by the Japanese authorities, which would rapidly move the exchange rate sharply higher.

The trader could wait until $/jpy 115.00 is reached before purchasing a standard vanilla option, for a dollar call/yen put. However, if the trader is confident that $/jpy 115.00 will be reached, then a dollar call/yen put with a knock-in rate of $/jpy 115.00 could be purchased. As there is no actual guarantee that this rate will be achieved, the knock-in option is considerably cheaper to purchase. Thus, the trader has been able to tailor a specific view on the market into an efficient and cost effective option strategy.

Window options are an add-on to the barrier options. Essentially any barrier option can have a "window" applied to it, which will make it slightly more expensive, but this extra cost can be justified by allowing the purchaser a more suitable trade. In fact, the window refers to the period during the option's life for which the barrier is valid.

An example could be a euro call/dollar put option, with a strike of 1.1300, with a reverse knock-out at a rate of eur/$ 1.1900 with an expiry of three months with the knock-out active for the first month only. The purchaser of this option would believe that the euro would strengthen versus the dollar, but slowly at first or not at all for the first month. Then after that, there will be a greater move upwards, possibly breaking eur/$ 1.1900. By having the window during the first month for the knock-out, the premium is reduced and thereafter the option becomes a normal euro call/dollar put as the knock-out disappears. In fact, the window can be placed anywhere during the option's life span.

21.2 AVERAGE RATES

Average rate options were actually the first "exotic" option to be developed in the foreign exchange markets. There are two distinct types:

- Average price; and
- Average strike.

The two have both differing characteristics and quite different applications.

Unlike a European style currency option, the *average price* option is a cash-settled instrument and is exercised against the average of a series of exchange rate fixings rather than the spot foreign exchange rate on the expiry date. The frequency of the fixings is agreed in advance and can be daily, weekly, two-weekly, monthly or quarterly, or in fact any regularly spaced interval. The strike price of the option is set in a similar manner to that of a European style option. There is a premium saving on the average price option compared to the European style option, which arises from the nature of the pricing and is largely due to the inherently lower volatility of an average compared to the volatility of the underlying.

The *average strike* option differs from the average price option in that the strike price is not set until the expiry date of the option. At maturity, the strike price is set to be the average of a series of exchange rate fixings taken over the lifetime of the option. Again, this can be any regularly spaced interval. The option is then exercised against the spot foreign exchange rate at expiry and can be either cash settled or physically settled.

The average price option is used extensively as a corporate hedging tool, allowing a series of cash flows to be hedged using a single option and at a lower overall cost than a string of European style options. For instance, allowing a company to set its budget rate for its foreign exchange at the start of a financial year for an entire series of payments. The average rate for all these payments is then guaranteed, while there still remains the possibility of achieving a significantly better rate. Thus, an average rate option has a number of advantages over a series of currency options:

- Simplicity – a single average rate option will cover any number of specified payments;
- Flexibility – an average rate option can fix for any regularly spaced interval;
- Cost effective – the cost of an average rate option is typically less than the cost of transacting a series of currency options to cover each individual payment date; and
- Choice – the purchaser can select any date for the fixings to take place, for example the tenth of each month.

On the other hand, the average strike option can be used to hedge specific currency exposures linked to commercial contracts or as a speculative tool. However, the applications are not as broad as that of the average price option.

As an example, consider a British company who has a transaction exposure and who has an agreement with one of its subsidiaries in Switzerland to provide parts at a fixed Swiss franc price. Payments are made by the subsidiary on the tenth of every month and will be for 1 million francs. The payments will continue for 12 months. The company is concerned that sterling will appreciate against the franc from the current level of gbp/sfr 2.2300 to more than gbp/sfr 2.3000. Above this level, it will not be profitable for the company to supply the parts. The company decides to purchase the following average rate option:

Notional amount:	sfr 1 million
Strike rate:	gbp/sfr 2.3000
Option period:	12 months
Call:	sterling
Put:	Swiss francs
Fixings:	monthly
Premium:	1.43% of sfr amount
Fixing reference:	Reuters at 11am

On the tenth of each month, the company receives 1 million francs, which it then sells at the prevailing spot foreign exchange rate at 11am. Since the fixing reference is also at 11am on the same day, the company will have a match between the spot foreign exchange rate for the transaction and the fixing rate. At the end of the 12-month period, the average rate is calculated from the 12 individual fixings. If the average rate is below the strike rate of gbp/sfr 2.3000, then the company will have had the benefit of transacting at an average rate of below the strike rate over the period. If, on the other hand, the average rate is above the strike rate, the company will be compensated for the difference between the average rate and the strike rate.

For instance, if the average rate of the 12 fixings is gbp/sfr 2.3700, then the option writer/seller will make a payment to the purchaser of:

sfr 12 000 000 divided by 2.30 minus sfr 12 000 000 divided by 2.37 = £154 100.16

Average rate options can also be used for hedging translation exposure. For example, consider a multinational Japanese company who has a number of subsidiaries, including one in America. The company is concerned about the affects of a depreciation in the dollar affecting the strength of its balance sheet. The exchange rate used for the balance sheet valuation at year-end is the average rate over the year calculated on a monthly basis.

A conventional hedge would be to use foreign exchange forwards. However, this course of action would be deemed inappropriate since there would be a physical exchange of dollars for yen, whereas the effects of the exchange rate only affect the value on the balance sheet and do not apply to a physical transaction and would thus have an impact on the company's cash flow. Also, a series of currency options would also be considered not to be suitable, since the foreign exchange rate to be protected is the average foreign exchange rate and not an exchange rate on a particular date.

In this case, an appropriate solution would be for the Japanese company to purchase an average rate option with monthly fixings. If at the end of the financial year the average rate is worse than the rate set for protection, then the company will be compensated with a cash payment. Thus, the average rate option avoids having any physical exchanges of cash, which would be the case if the forward foreign exchange route were taken.

21.3 LOOKBACK AND LADDERS

The lookback option allows the holder, at expiry, to "look back" over the lifetime of the option and to select the most favourable exchange rate. There are two different types:

- Optimal rate lookback; and
- Optimal strike lookback.

With the *optimal rate lookback*, the strike price of the option is fixed on the initial deal date and at expiry will pay out against the high (low) of the spot rate during the option's lifetime, regardless of the spot rate on the expiry date. The high (low) is typically determined using a fixing rate and an appropriate reference source. Also, the option would usually be cash settled. Clearly, this option has greater potential for a larger positive payout than a European style option of the same strike and so the premium cost will be greater than that of the European.

In essence, this option structure offers the option buyer the "benefit of hindsight" and produces a payout equivalent to the highest intrinsic value achieved over the life of the option. In addition, an optimal rate call option gives the option buyer a payout equal to the difference between the option strike and the highest spot rate over the option's lifetime. Similarly, an optimal rate put option gives the option buyer a payout equal to the difference between the option strike and the lowest spot rate over the option's lifetime.

For example, with a dollar against the euro spot foreign exchange reference rate of eur/$ 1.1525 and an expiry date of three months, with the strike set at-the-money spot, the premium costs could be:

	European vanilla option	Lookback option
Dollar call/euro put	2.17% of dollar amount	4.04% of dollar amount
Dollar put/euro call	1.51% of dollar amount	3.28% of dollar amount

In fact, hedgers would use an optimal rate option to ensure that they obtain the best possible intrinsic value at expiry in return for a quantifiable upfront cost, while an investor would use this option type to take positions on actual market volatility. If volatility increases over the option period, the payout on the option should more than offset the premium paid, although the upfront cost can be relatively high.

As an example, an investor has a view that the dollar is about to weaken against the Swiss franc and that $/sfr 1.3500 will not trade over the coming three months (assume a spot reference of $/sfr 1.3300). Thus, the investor decides to sell an optimal rate call option with a strike of 1.3500. In essence, the investor believes that the foreign exchange rate will not reach the strike rate of $/sfr 1.3500 over this three-month period. The expectation is therefore that the highest spot foreign exchange rate reached will be below $/sfr 1.3500 and that the option will expire worthless.

Were the option to expire in-the-money, the investor would be required to pay the option holder the difference between the highest spot foreign exchange rate traded over the three-month period and the strike rate of $/sfr 1.3500. Against this, the investor would have received an upfront premium of, say, 3.35% of the dollar amount. This compares with, say, the 1.66% of the dollar amount the investor would have received had a European style call option been sold, with the same strike rate of 1.3500.

Optimal rate call option with payoff at expiry:

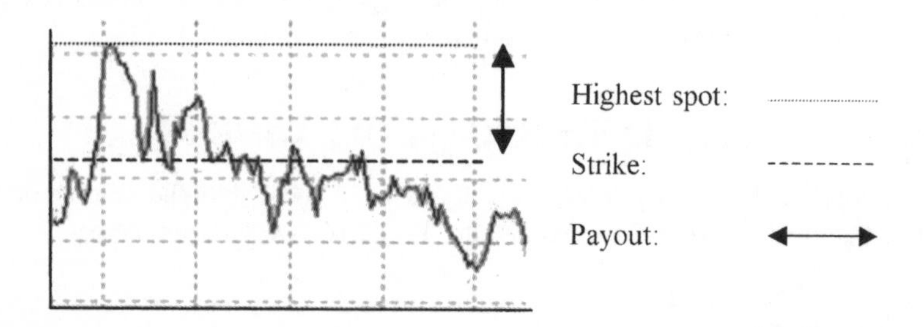

Figure 21.2

Optimal rate put option with payoff at expiry:

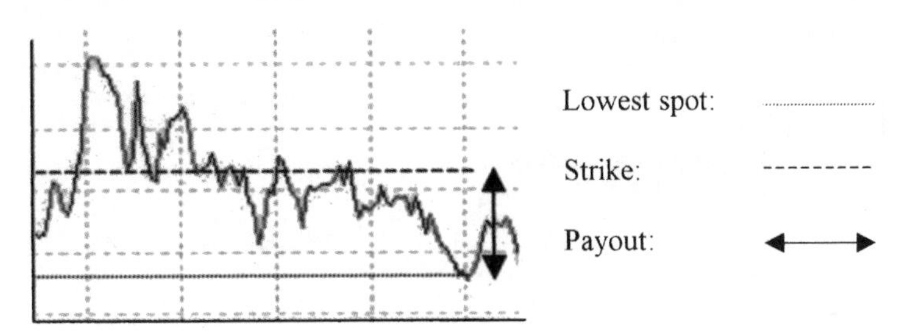

Figure 21.3

On the other hand, with an *optimal strike lookback*, the strike price of the option is not fixed until the expiry date of the option. The strike price is then fixed as the high (for a put) or low (for a call) of the spot foreign exchange rate over the lifetime of the option and then exercised against the spot foreign exchange rate prevailing on the expiry date for either cash or physical settlement. Again, the high (low) is typically determined using a fixing rate and appropriate reference source. Also, once again, the optimal rate option has greater potential for larger positive payouts than the standard vanilla European option of the same strike and will thus be more expensive.

Again, in essence, this option structure offers the option buyer the "benefit of hindsight" and gives the right to buy/sell the underlying at expiry at the "best price" traded over the life of the option. Thus, an optimal strike call option gives the option buyer the right to buy the underlying at the lowest price traded over the life of the option, while an optimal strike put option allows the option buyer to sell the underlying at the highest price traded over the option's lifetime.

For example, assume a dollar against the European euro spot foreign exchange reference rate of eur/$ 1.1525 and an expiry date of three months. The premium costs could be:

	European vanilla option	Lookback option
Dollar call/euro put	2.17% of dollar amount (strike at-the-money spot)	3.93% of dollar amount
Dollar put/euro call	1.51% of dollar amount (strike at-the-money spot)	3.38% of dollar amount

Both hedgers and investors again can make use of this option structure. A hedger would use this option to ensure that they obtain the best possible market rate over a given budget period, in return for a quantifiable upfront cost, while investors will take positions on actual market volatility. So if volatility increases over the option period, the payout on the option should more than offset the premium paid, although the upfront cost can be relatively high.

As an example, a Japanese company has a requirement to buy dollars in three months' time. The company wishes to ensure than it achieves the best possible rate. For this reason, the company decides to purchase a three-month dollar call/Japanese yen put optimal strike option. The payout on the option is equal to the difference between the spot dollar/yen foreign exchange rate at expiry of the option (the rate at which the company will actually be purchasing the dollars) and the lowest dollar/yen rate traded over the life of the option. Thus the net effect is that the company will be purchasing dollars at the lowest rate experienced over the three-month period.

Optimal strike call option with payoff at expiry:

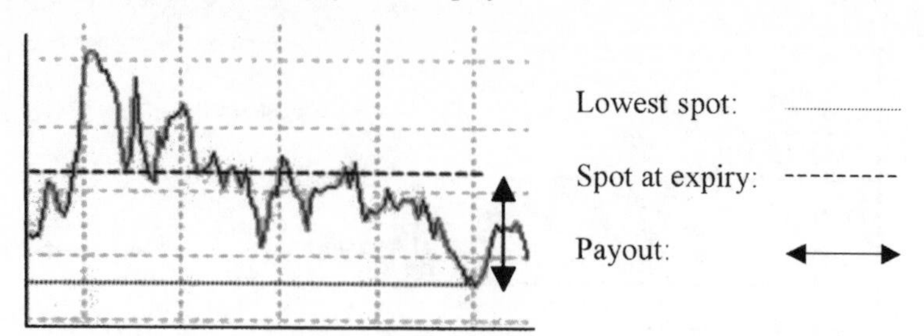

Figure 21.4

Optimal strike put option with payoff at expiry:

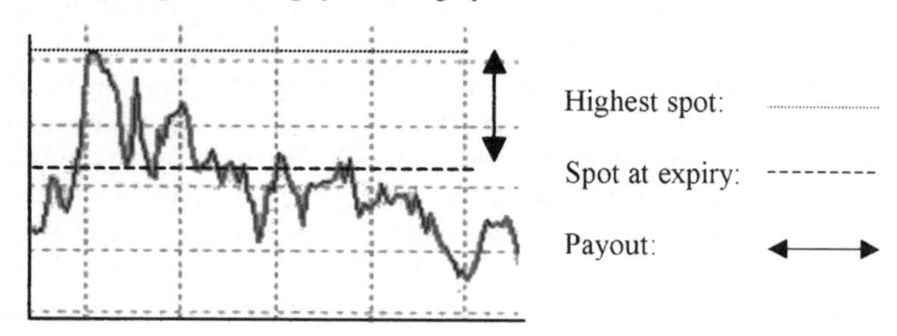

Figure 21.5

Ladder options were developed as the next generation of optimal rate options. Despite the added benefits of the lookback option, the substantially higher cost dissuaded many potential users and thus the product died a quick death. The best way to understand this option is by considering the following example.

A vanilla dollar call/Japanese yen put option with a strike of 118.00 would expire worthless on expiry if the spot foreign exchange price on that day was lower than $/jpy 118.00. If this same option had a lookback feature, and at anytime over the life of the option spot foreign exchange traded higher than $/jpy 118.00, then the option holder would exercise the option and cash settle against the highest level of spot observed during that period. It follows from the previous discussions, that this added benefit for the lookback feature makes this type of option more costly than a vanilla European style option.

However, it is possible with the ladder option to add "step" levels at spot foreign exchange rates above $/jpy 118.00. Therefore, if during the life of the option the spot foreign exchange rate touches one of the ladder levels, the option would then pay off at the highest step of the ladder achieved. From the example above, if a one-step level of $/jpy 122.00 is added, the ladder option price will ultimately fall somewhere between the price of the European style option and the lookback. It is also possible to set multiple step levels, for example at $/jpy 123.00 and $/jpy 124.00. Obviously, the more steps that are added, the more the price of the option will approach the price of a lookback.

21.4 CHOOSER

The chooser option has similarities to the purchase of a European style straddle; however, the purchaser must *choose* between a put and a call at some specified time before the expiry date of the option. This means that the chooser option will pay off in one direction only at expiry, unlike the straddle, which will pay off if the currency pair rises or falls. Thus, it allows the purchaser to benefit from market movements in either direction.

The chooser option has a premium reduction associated with it, which will give the strategy a better payoff than the equivalent European style straddle, provided that the "chosen" option expires in-the-money. However, in general, the chooser option will be more expensive than either of the individual options, put and call, between which the buyer of the chooser option has the choice.

The benefit from the chooser option is largely dependent on the option buyer's ability at the choice date to correctly identify which leg of the equivalent straddle will be in-the-money at expiry. For this reason, chooser options are often used around major events such as elections and referendums, where there is the expectation of a large market movement in either direction. The choice date will be set a few days after the major event, by which time it will be hoped that the direction of the market move will be clear. The option buyer thus hopes to generate the same return as a straddle at a lower cost by buying the chooser option.

Probably, this product is best explained by using an example:

Assume final expiry to be in three months' time.

(a) European style at-the-money forward straddle, strike 1.6260 for a premium cost of 840 Swiss franc pips. Therefore, the break-even foreign exchange rates at expiry are $/sfr 1.5420/1.7100 ($/sfr 1.6260 – 840 and $/sfr 1.6260 +840).
(b) Chooser at-the-money forward straddle, with a strike of 1.6260. Chooser expiry is one month and premium cost is 664 Swiss franc pips. After one month the purchaser needs to decide whether to own the dollar put or the dollar call. Therefore, the break-even foreign exchange rates at expiry are either $/sfr 1.5596 or $/sfr 1.6924 ($/sfr 1.6260 – 664 and $/sfr 1.6260 +664).

The chooser option gives the purchaser a period of time in which to decide whether they wish to own a put option or a call option. Once the put option or call option has been "chosen", the option becomes a simple European style option and can be exercised at maturity, if in-the-money, for either physical or cash settlement. It is important to remember that in exchange for a lower upfront premium cost, the option will ultimately pay off in only one direction, unlike the European style straddle.

The degree of the premium reduction will depend on the ratio of the chooser period to the ultimate expiry date of the option. As the length of the chooser period increases relative to the expiry date, the price of the chooser option becomes closer to that of the European style straddle.

21.5 DIGITAL (BINARY)

A binary option is an option that pays out a *fixed* amount of money, agreed on the initial deal date, provided that one or more conditions are satisfied before and/or at expiry. If these conditions are *not* satisfied then the option pays out nothing. Thus the binary option does not have the standard linear payoff at expiry of a European style option, but rather an " all or nothing" payout.

The exact structure of a particular binary option can vary greatly and hence it is hard to generalise the relative premium costs and payouts. Essentially, though, the pricing reflects the size of the fixed payout and the probability that this payout will be achieved. Therefore, the less likely it is that the option will pay off, the smaller the premium cost and/or the greater the payout amount.

Some examples of binary structures are:

- The option pays out a fixed amount if the spot foreign exchange rate is above (below) a certain level at expiry;
- The option pays out a fixed amount if the spot foreign exchange rate trades above (below) a certain level before expiry;
- The option pays out a fixed amount if, at expiry, the spot foreign exchange rate is above (below) a certain level and provided that some other level has already traded before expiry;
- If the trigger level trades before expiry, the fixed amount can be paid at that time or at expiry; and
- If the spot rate is within a certain range at expiry, a fixed amount of money is payable otherwise nothing is due.

Thus, digital options produce a fixed payout if the option is at- or in-the-money at expiry, which is if the underlying foreign exchange rate is above the option strike in the case of a call option, or below the foreign exchange rate in the case of a put option. Also, then, if the option is out-of-the-money at expiry, the option expires worthless and the option holder receives no payout.

The payout at maturity of the option is defined as a multiple of the upfront premium paid, referred to as the gearing factor. The further out-of-the-money the strike chosen, the greater will be the gearing factor and thus the potential payout relative to the upfront premium paid. Also, digital options produce the same payout no matter how far in-the-money the option is at expiry. For this reason, where the option expires only slightly in-the-money, a digital option will produce a higher payout than a vanilla option with the same strike and upfront premium. On the other hand, where the option expires deep in-the-money, the vanilla option would clearly produce the higher payout.

A variation on the theme is *one touch options* (also known as pay-if-touched options and are "American" style digital options), which are very closely related to digital options, except with the difference lying in the conditions under which they payout. One touch options pay out if they are at- or in-the-money at any time, while digital options pay out if the option is at- or in-the-money at expiry. Thus, a one touch option has a better chance of expiring in-the-money than does an otherwise identical digital option. For this reason, the one touch option will always offer a much lower gearing factor than will its digital counterpart. In other words, the payout on a one-touch option will be less than that on the equivalent digital option for the same upfront premium amount.

21.6 BASKETS

Of the generation of new products, one product that has drawn a great deal of interest is the basket option. It is a simple, inexpensive way to collect a series of identifiable foreign exchange risk positions and hedge them with a single transaction. Basically, the pricing model of a basket option creates an index that represents the dollar (or other home currency) value of a given portfolio of foreign exchange positions. The hedger can then buy a single option to ensure that the dollar value of the portfolio does not fall below a certain level. If the value of the portfolio rises, then the hedger will be able to capitalise on the increase.

The premium of such an option reflects the probability that the index will change in value, rather than the probability that the individual currencies will change. If the value of one portion of the portfolio increases, while the rest of it decreases by the same amount, the index itself will not change. Identification of the currencies involved and their propensities to move in the same direction are critical to the price of the basket option.

For example, assume a portfolio with just two currency positions of equal dollar value. If the two currencies are perfectly correlated, that is, they will rise and fall in lockstep with each other, the percentage change in the portfolio's value will be the same as the percentage change of the dollar against either currency. Its price volatility will be equal to that of the dollar against either currency. If the two currencies are perfectly negatively correlated, in that they move in perfectly opposite directions, the portfolio will never change value, as every move on the part of one currency will be neutralised by an offsetting move in the other. The price volatility of the portfolio will be zero. If the currencies are negatively correlated but the dollar values of the two currency positions are not equal, the price volatility of the portfolio will be a reflection of the weighted average of the two positions and their relative correlations. In this case, there will be a measurable price volatility to the portfolio, but it will be a fraction of that of the individual currency components.

Real-life experience is found between the extremes of perfect correlations. For example, some currencies are highly correlated. In the "old" days before the introduction of the euro, the Dutch guilder and the Deutschemark exhibited about 99% correlation. Others, such as the Australian dollar and the Deutschemark would only exhibit about 78% correlation. Clearly, the volatility of a given portfolio's value depends upon the currency make-up of the portfolio and the relative weightings of the currency components.

Thus, typically, the option will have a single call (or put) and a "basket" of put (or call) currencies. The proportions of these currencies will be specified in advance by a "weighting factor" in order that the product can be tailor-made to suit the individual requirements. At maturity, whether the option is in-the-money or not is determined by calculating the "basket spot rate" and comparing this with the strike price. The option may be cash or physically settled, depending on whether or not the option is being used as a hedge. Also, the degree of reduction in premium varies greatly, depending on the number of currencies and composition of the basket involved and the correlations between both the constituent currencies of the basket and the call (put) currency.

For example, looking at a basket of currencies pre-euro, then a basket of Deutschemarks, French francs and sterling against the dollar would show little price reduction from the sum of three individual premiums. However, a basket with 10 or more currencies would show a greater reduction in premium, provided that the individual currencies were not highly correlated. Thus, for a three-month dollar put option, with a strike rate of at-the-money spot and equal weightings of the call currencies, the average price of European style options for each of the 10 currency pairs might be 2.08%, while the price of the basket option might be 1.61% of dollars.

The advantages of covering a portfolio with a basket option are several:

1. It is administratively simple, in that there is only one option to execute rather than several options, which might have been bought in order to hedge the portfolio;
2. They are flexible, in that they can accommodate virtually any number of currencies (as long as liquid markets and enough data to establish correlations exist), in any position size. What is more, if the composition of the portfolio alters, the basket option can be rejigged to reflect the new weightings. However, this may entail an incremental payment of premium,

or receipt of premium, to reflect the change in portfolio values versus the basket strike price;
3. The cost, in that the premium of the basket option, depending on the composition of the portfolio, can be as much as 20% less than the combined premiums of the individual options.

It should be noted that the price advantage of a basket option increases notably when the basket is diversified to include currencies that are not highly correlated.

21.7 COMPOUND

The compound option is essentially an option on an option, giving the purchaser the right to buy (compound call) or the right to sell (compound put) an underlying option with fixed parameters, at a fixed premium on or before a specified date. In return for an additional upfront premium, the purchaser has a predetermined period of time (the compound period) over which to decide whether or not to purchase the underlying option. If the compound option is exercised then the secondary premium for the underlying option will be either payable (compound call) or receivable (compound put). The more favourable the premium level set on the underlying option, the greater will be the upfront premium paid for the compound option.

A compound call option will be exercised if, at expiry, the market value of the underlying option, whether put or call, is greater than the strike price on the compound option. This may result from movements in the underlying foreign exchange rate and/or, for example, an increase in option volatilities. Conversely, a compound put option will be exercised if, at expiry, the market value of the underlying option (put or call) is below the strike price on the compound option. Again, this may be due, for example, to movements in the underlying foreign exchange rate and/or a decrease on option volatilities.

Users of this option type are varied but in general hedgers may have a contingent exposure which would generally be hedged by buying a vanilla option and then selling this option if the contingent exposure did not materialise and the hedge was no longer required. Clearly, this would involve a relatively large upfront premium cost and there is no guarantee as to the market rate, which might be obtained at the time the hedge is sold. A compound call option would enable the hedger to protect the cost of buying a vanilla option should the contingent exposure materialise. If the compound option expires out-of-the-money, the vanilla option could be bought more cheaply in the market, if required. Conversely, if the compound option expires in-the-money but the underlying option is not required, the option can be sold for a windfall profit in the market.

For example, a British company is currently bidding for a three-month contract in America, to be awarded in three months' time. In the event the British company wins the contract, it will have dollar receivables, which it will need to convert back into sterling in six months' time. The British company decides to buy a three-month compound option of dollar put/sterling call, struck at 1.5475, with an expiry of six months from today.

The strike on the compound option (that is the premium the British company will pay if the compound option is exercised) is 1.90% of sterling. In three months' time, the compound option will expire and the British company will have the right to buy the underlying dollar put/sterling call for 1.90% of sterling.

The upfront premium on the compound option is 1.42% of sterling amount, resulting in a total cost of 3.32%(1.90% + 1.42%) of sterling in the event that the compound option is exercised. This compares with an upfront premium of 2.81% for a six-month vanilla dollar put/sterling call option with the same strike.

As another example, assume the following:

Compound option details:	Expiry three months Compound call Compound strike is 751 Swiss franc pips Premium cost is 259 Swiss franc pips
Underlying option details:	Dollar put/Swiss franc call Expiry nine months from compound expiry Strike price is at-the-money forward Premium price is 751 Swiss franc pips
For comparison purposes:	European style option Dollar put/Swiss franc call Expiry of one year Strike price is at-the-money forward Premium cost would be 852 Swiss franc pips

Therefore, the initial upfront cost is reduced to 259 Swiss franc pips. However, the overall cost of the compound option would be 1010 franc pips compared to 852 franc pips for the European style option.

Also, investors can use compound call and put options in order to take positions on the future level of option prices, as using compound option to speculate on options prices is much cheaper in terms of initial premium than buying the underling option itself.

Thus, the compound option allows the purchaser greater flexibility in the timing of the hedge and reduces the upfront premium cost, in return the overall cost is greater (or the premium receipt is smaller for a compound put). The compound option can be used for contingent foreign exchange exposures where the upfront cost needs to be minimised, or where extra flexibility is required in the timing and level of a hedge.

21.8 VARIABLE NOTIONAL

The variable notional option is similar to a European style currency option, having a fixed expiry date, fixed call and put currencies and a fixed strike price and may only be exercised on the expiry date. However, the variable notional option differs in that the principal amount of the option increases by a predetermined ratio as the option moves into the money. The ratio by which the principal increases is set on the initial deal date and can be varied to suit individual requirements. For example, the ratio might be set at a 5% increase in the principal for a 5% increase in the spot foreign exchange price.

The variable notional option clearly gives an advantage to the purchaser as the amount of the option increases as it moves into-the-money, and there is an associated increase in the price of the option relative to the equivalent European style currency option. The degree of the increase in price depends on the gearing of the option and will be *greater* for one where the principal amount increases *more* rapidly for the same movement in the spot price. Also, the gearing can be set as a step function, requiring the spot foreign exchange rate to reach a certain level before an increase in the principal amount is applied, or as a continuous function whereby the principal amount will increase continuously with the spot foreign exchange rate. The final principal amount of the option is determined on the expiry date.

For example, assume a dollar call/Swiss franc put with a strike price of at-the-money forward, for expiry in three months' time, then with:

	Gearing factor (spot increase:principal increase)	Price in % of dollar
(a)	European style option	2.46%
(b)	5%:5 %	2.61%
(c)	5%:10%	2.75%
(d)	10%:5%	2.50%
(e)	Continuous 1 for 1	2.66%

The variable notional option can be used as either a hedging or trading tool. As a hedge, it is an ideal product for a corporate whose exposure increases as the currency rises or falls. As for the trader, the leverage gained from the gearing factor would need to be balanced against market expectations and the increase in premium cost.

21.9 MULTI-FACTOR

The multi-factor option provides protection against two exposures, such as commodity prices and foreign exchange rates. Such an integrated strategy addresses a company's major risks in a coordinated way, at a lower cost relative to a traditional European option. In the multi-factor option, payoff of the option on one asset class is dependent upon the price behaviour in the other asset class.

For example, a steel producer has a liability in Swiss francs. The company is at risk if the dollar falls or the price of aluminium declines. The following matrix illustrates the point:

	Dollar/franc declines	**Dollar/franc rises**
Steel declines	Negative	Neutral
Steel rises	Neutral	Positive

The company can choose to hedge its Swiss franc risk by purchasing a standard franc call/dollar put option. Since the company benefits if the price of steel rises, a knock-out feature could be suggested if the price of steel rises beyond a certain level. In order to create the most effective hedge, the company should set the trigger level such that if the option gets knocked out, and if the value of the dollar should decline, the economic benefit to the company from the increase in steel prices more than offsets the negative aspects of the dollar decline. By analysing the company's production levels in steel and the size of the franc payable, it is possible to determine a "break-even" price in dollars/francs.

22

Structured Currency Options

Just like the chapter before with exotic currency options, there are many structured currency options on the market today. These products are combinations of vanilla and exotic options, and use "building blocks" to create payoffs to suit specific needs and views of the market, of both purchasers and sellers alike. Some of the most commonly used structures are listed below and it should be noted that these option structures are in fact *synthetic* structures.

22.1 TRIGGER FORWARD

The trigger forward option structure was primarily designed for trading purposes, although it can be used as an alternative hedge as well. Also, this option structure is essentially a zero-cost structure, whereby the purchaser enters into an outright forward at a rate significantly more attractive than the prevailing foreign exchange market rate, but whereby the whole structure knocks out if a predetermined trigger level is reached/traded at any time before the expiry date of the option structure.

For example, assume a spot foreign exchange reference rate of $/sfr 1.6300, with a maturity period of six months, a forward strike rate of $/sfr 1.5900 and a trigger level of $/sfr 1.7700. The purchaser of the structure enters into an outright forward foreign exchange contract to buy dollars and sell Swiss francs at $/sfr 1.5900 in six months' time unless $/sfr 1.7700 were to trade at any time during the life of the option structure, before expiry. However, if $/sfr 1.7700 were to trade, the whole synthetic forward structure knocks out.

Potential outcomes are:

- If the dollar depreciates against the Swiss franc, even beyond $/sfr 1.5900, the purchaser is obliged to buy dollars at $/sfr 1.5900;
- If the dollar appreciates against the Swiss franc and $/sfr 1.7700 *does not* trade at any time before expiry, the purchaser can buy dollars and sell Swiss francs at $/sfr 1.5900; and
- If the dollar appreciates against the Swiss franc and $/sfr 1.7700 *does* trade at any time during the life of the structure, the whole option structure knocks out.

This option structure could be of interest to a trader who is looking for a favourable limited move on the underlying and thinks that the knock-out level is unlikely to trade at any time during the life of the option structure. The potential to benefit is that the purchaser is able to buy/sell cash at a more favourable rate than the current forward foreign exchange rate in the market, but if the trigger level is reached, the whole forward structure ceases to exist. Also, it should be noted that the structure is a synthetic forward and therefore the purchaser is obliged to buy/sell the underlying also if the market moves unfavourably.

Thus, trigger forwards are higher risk strategies than the forward extra option structure, as there is a real need to accept the inherent risk that the purchaser may be left with no protection at a highly disadvantageous spot level.

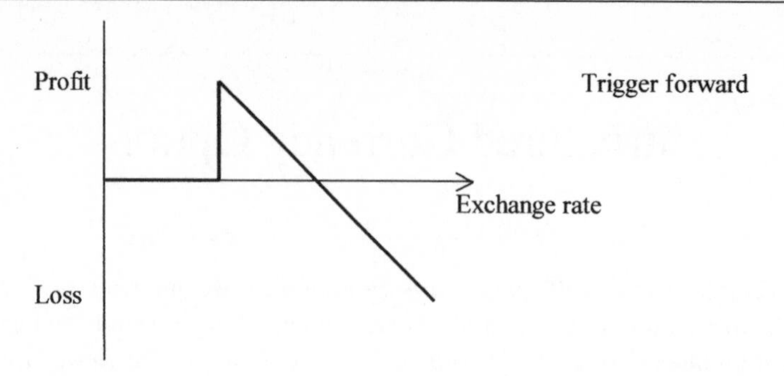

Figure 22.1

22.2 DOUBLE TRIGGER FORWARD

This option structure was primarily designed for trading purposes, although it can be used as an alternative hedge as well. Again, this is a zero-cost structure, whereby the purchaser enters into an outright forward foreign exchange at a rate significantly more attractive than the prevailing market foreign exchange rate, but whereby the whole forward structure knocks out if a predetermined trigger level is reached at any time before the expiry date of the structure. Also, there is an additional trigger level, whereby if it is traded, the purchaser is obliged to buy/sell the currency, but if not, some further benefit may be derived.

For example, assume a spot foreign exchange reference rate of $/sfr 1.6300, maturity of six months, forward strike rate of $/sfr 1.5750 and trigger levels of $/sfr 1.7700 and $/sfr 1.5100. The purchaser of the option structure can, therefore, enter into a synthetic outright foreign exchange forward contract to buy dollars against Swiss francs at $/sfr 1.5750 in six months' time unless $/sfr 1.7700 trades at any time before the expiry. If $/sfr 1.7700 does trade, however, the whole synthetic forward structure knocks out. The contract then becomes an obligation only if $/sfr 1.5100 trades.

Potential outcomes are:

- If spot remains between $/sfr 1.7700 and $/sfr 1.5750 for the whole lifetime of the option structure, the purchaser buys the dollars and sells Swiss francs at $/sfr 1.5750 on the expiry date;
- If spot trades at $/sfr 1.7700 at any time before expiry, the whole structure knocks out;
- If spot trades at $/sfr 1.5750 but not at $/sfr 1.5100 at any time before expiry, the purchaser buys dollars and sells Swiss francs at the prevailing foreign exchange market rate; and
- If spot trades at $/sfr 1.5100 at any time before expiry, the purchaser is obliged to buy dollars and sell Swiss francs at $/sfr 1.5750.

This option structure could be of interest to a trader who is looking for a favourable limited move on the underlying and the trader thinks that the knock-out level is unlikely to trade at any time during the life of the option structure. The potential benefit is that the purchaser is able to buy/sell cash at a more favourable rate than the current forward foreign exchange rate, but in case the trigger level is reached, the whole forward structure is lost. This structure is similar to the trigger forward, creating a potentially better synthetic forward foreign exchange rate, providing that the trigger level is not traded, but does introduce more potential risk due to the uncertainty of the additional trigger level to be reached.

22.3 AT MATURITY TRIGGER FORWARD

This option structure was also developed primarily for trading purposes, although it can also be used as an alternative hedge as well. Again, this option structure is essentially a zero-cost structure, whereby the purchaser enters into an outright forward foreign exchange contract at a rate significantly more attractive than the prevailing foreign exchange market rate, but whereby the whole structure ceases if the spot foreign exchange rate trades below/above a predetermined trigger level *at expiry*.

For example, assume a spot reference rate of $/sfr 1.6300, with expiry in six months' time and a forward strike rate of $/sfr 1.5900 with the trigger level set at $/sfr 1.7250. The purchaser of this option structure buys the dollars against the Swiss francs at $/sfr 1.5900 in six months' time unless the spot rate is above $/sfr 1.7250 on the expiry date. If the dollar trades above $/sfr 1.72500 at expiry, the whole structure expires worthless.

Potential outcomes are:

- If the dollar depreciates against the Swiss franc, even if beyond $/sfr 1.5900, the purchaser is obliged to buy dollars against the Swiss franc at $/sfr 1.5900;
- If the dollar appreciates against the Swiss franc and the spot foreign exchange rate is below $/sfr 1.7250 at maturity, the purchaser can buy dollars at $/sfr 1.5900; and
- If the dollar appreciates against the Swiss franc and spot is above $/sfr 1.7250 at maturity, the whole option structure ceases.

This option structure could be of interest to a trader expecting a favourable limited move on the underlying and who thinks the knock-out level is unlikely to trade at the expiry of the option. The potential benefit is that the purchaser is able to buy/sell cash at a more favourable foreign exchange rate than the current foreign exchange forward but in case the spot foreign exchange rate trades above/below the trigger level at expiry, the whole option structure is worthless. This option structure is similar to the trigger forward, but the trigger level is closer to the current spot foreign exchange rate due to the fact that this option structure has less chance of being terminated as the knock-out feature only functions on the expiry date of the option structure.

22.4 FORWARD EXTRA

The forward extra structure has been developed primarily for hedging purposes and is essentially a European option that turns into a forward foreign exchange contract if a trigger level is reached. For zero cost, the purchaser of the structure can acquire protection against an adverse foreign exchange rate move and can benefit from a favourable *limited* move on the underlying, provided that the trigger level has not traded during the life of the option.

For example, assume a dollar call/Swiss franc put forward extra option with a maturity period of six months, an option strike rate of 1.6300 and a trigger level of $/sfr 1.5100. Thus, the purchaser has the right to buy dollars and sell Swiss francs at 1.6300 in six months' time, unless $/sfr 1.5100 trades at any time during the life of the option, in which case the purchaser is locked into a synthetic forward foreign exchange obligation to buy dollars and sell francs at $/sfr 1.6300 (assume a spot reference rate of $/sfr 1.6200).

Potential outcomes are:

- If the dollar appreciates, the right to buy dollars at $/sfr 1.6300 protects the hedger;
- If the dollar depreciates, but $/sfr 1.5100 *does not* trade at any time during the life of the option, the dollars can be bought at the prevailing market foreign exchange rate; and

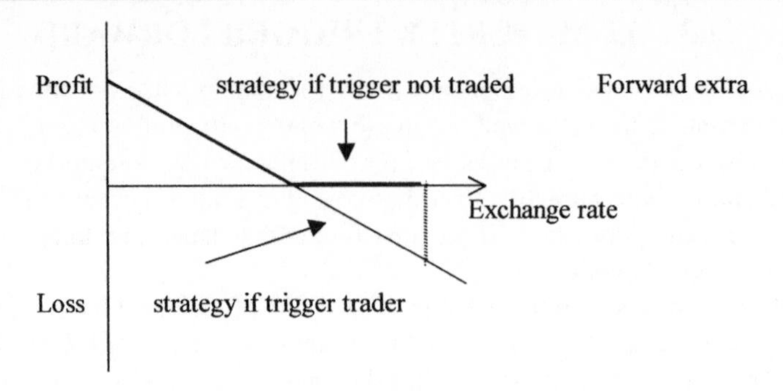

Figure 22.2

- If the dollar depreciates and $/sfr 1.5100 *does* trade at any time during the life of the option, the hedger is obligated to buy dollars at $/sfr 1.6300.

For example, a British company is due to pay its American supplier 2 million dollars in three months' time and has to set a budget rate for this transaction. Assume this rate to be set at gbp/$. 1.5000 Also, assume in the foreign exchange market, the actual foreign exchange spot rate is gbp/$ 1.5500, with the three months' forward outright foreign exchange rate being gbp/$ 1.5475.

In order to hedge this exposure, the British company could sell sterling outright forward for three months' time at gbp/$ 1.5475 or they could purchase a three-month sterling put/dollar call with a strike rate of 1.500. This option is likely to cost the British company, upfront, 65 sterling pips, which equates to 13 000 pounds (2 000 000 × 0.0065 = £13 000).

Alternatively, a three-month forward extra with a strike rate of 1.5200 would leave the potential to sell sterling at the market foreign exchange rate up to a maximum of gbp/$ 1.6580 (the trigger rate), so long as gbp/$ 1.6580 does not trade at any time over the life of the option contract. If gbp/$ 1.6580 does trade, the British company is locked into a forward foreign exchange rate of gbp/$ 1.5200. If this rate is not traded, then the British company is able to participate in any sterling appreciation up to the trigger level of gbp/$ 1.6580, while retaining the full downside protection at gbp/$ 1.5200.

Thus this product provides protection while giving potential to considerably out perform the outright forward rate.

22.5 WEEKLY RESET FORWARD

The weekly reset forward option structure was developed for both trading and hedging purposes and is essentially a synthetic forward, where each portion of the contract needs to be activated on a weekly basis. For each week where the pre-set "fixing" level is satisfied, a portion of the contract is locked in. If *none* of the weekly conditions are satisfied, then *none* of the contract is activated. However, if all the weekly conditions are satisfied, then the total amount of currency is bought (sold) at a more *favourable* outright foreign exchange rate than the prevailing market foreign exchange rate.

For example, assume a spot reference rate of $/sfr 1.6300, with a maturity period of six months and a forward strike rate of 1.6050 with a trigger level of 1.6900. The purchaser can buy a portion of the total dollar amount at $/sfr 1.6050, for each week that satisfies the condition to remain below $/sfr 1.6900 at the fixing. Hence, for example, if the purchaser has 1 million

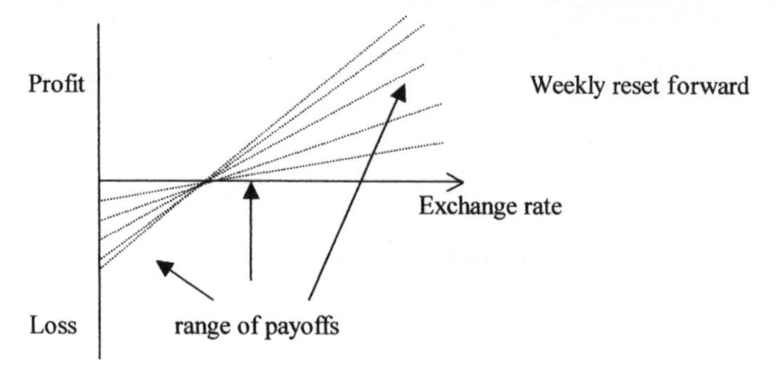

Figure 22.3

dollars to buy each week for 52 weeks and the spot foreign exchange rate fixes below \$/sfr 1.6900 for 40 of those weeks, the purchaser buys 40 million dollars at \$/sfr 1.6050 on the six-month expiry date.

Potential outcomes for each weekly reset date are:

- If spot fixes *above* \$/sfr 1.6900, the contract will *not* be activated for that portion; and
- If spot fixes *below* \$/sfr 1.6900, the purchaser is *obliged* to buy dollars against Swiss francs at \$/sfr 1.6050 for that week, even if spot is below \$/sfr 1.6050 at maturity.

Please note that the number of weeks that the spot foreign exchange rate fixes below \$/sfr 1.6900 determines the size of the trade ($x/52$nd of the total amount) to buy dollars against Swiss francs for value two working days after the final expiry date.

This product is an interesting alternative to those hedgers who have their cash flows spread over a period of time and for balance sheet hedgers. The structure provides an opportunity to deal at a rate significantly better than the outright forward foreign exchange rate, but *only* for the portion of the amount that the foreign exchange spot rate fixes above/below the trigger level. It should be remembered that if the trigger level *has* traded, that portion of the exposure would *not* be hedged.

22.6 RANGE BINARY

The range binary structure was developed primarily for trading purposes and the trader will benefit if a spot foreign exchange rate stays within a range, whereby the trader specifies a currency range over a fixed period. A premium will be paid upfront and provided the spot foreign exchange rate stays within the range, then a multiple of the premium invested will be payable. If, however, either limit of the range has traded before the expiry of the structure, then no payout will occur and the premium will be forfeited. This structure can be used on its own as a currency play for range trading foreign exchange markets or it can be combined with a deposit as a yield enhancement structure. See Figure 22.4.

22.7 CONTINGENT PREMIUM

The contingent premium structure was primarily developed for hedging purposes and is essentially a currency option whereby the premium is only paid if the option is in-the-money at expiry.

For example, assume the underlying currency option is a dollar call/Swiss franc put, with a spot reference of \$/sfr 1.6300, with an expiry of six months and a strike rate of 1.6300 with

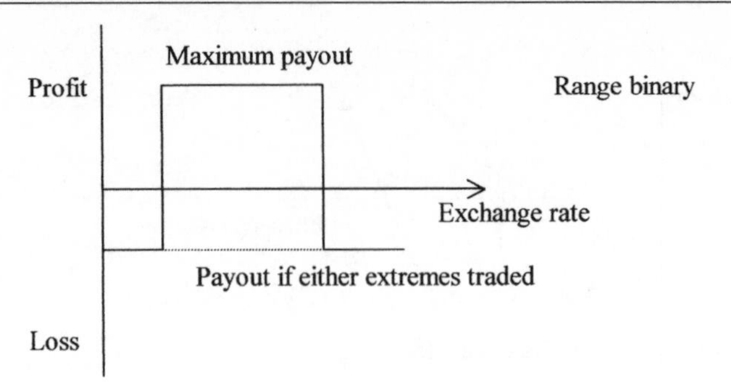

Figure 22.4

an upfront premium of zero. The purchaser buys a dollar call/Swiss franc put with a strike of \$/sfr 1.6300 for six months. No upfront premium is paid, but if the foreign exchange spot rate is above \$/sfr 1.6300 at expiry, the purchaser is obliged to pay 6.88% of dollars, against the cost of a European strike 1.6300 dollar call/Swiss franc put of 2.75% of dollars.

Potential outcomes are:

- If spot is below \$/sfr 1.6300 at expiry, the purchaser pays no premium for the option, which will then be allowed to expire worthless; and
- If spot is above \$/sfr 1.6300 at expiry, the purchaser pays 6.88% of dollars for the in-the-money option.

This option structure represents a potentially zero-cost strategy if spot is below \$/sfr 1.6300, in which case the underlying is in-the-money. However, if spot is above \$/sfr 1.6300, then the break-even would be \$/sfr 1.7373. The worst-case scenario is therefore that the spot foreign exchange rate is just above \$/sfr 1.6300 at expiry, so the higher premium has to be paid for the option, which is only slightly in-the-money.

22.8 WALL

The wall option structure was developed primarily for trading purposes and is essentially a bet on a spot foreign exchange rate staying below/above a certain predetermined level. This strategy, like a range binary, is often linked with a deposit for yield enhancement purposes.

The purchaser specifies a currency rate over a fixed period. A premium is paid upfront and the purchaser accrues interest every day that spot foreign exchange fixes above/below the predetermined spot foreign exchange rate.

For example, assuming a spot foreign exchange reference rate of \$/sfr 1.6300, with a maturity period of six months and a predetermined rate of \$/sfr 1.6700 with a fixed multiple for potential payout of 3.6 times the premium invested.

Potential outcomes are:

- The more days that spot foreign exchange rate fixes above \$/sfr 1.6700, the higher will be the purchaser's payoff;
- If spot stays above \$/sfr 1.6700 for the *whole period*, maximum payoff, that is, 3.6 times the original premium invested is payable to the purchaser; and
- If spot *never* fixes above \$/sfr 1.6700, then the premium invested will be forfeited and no payout will be due.

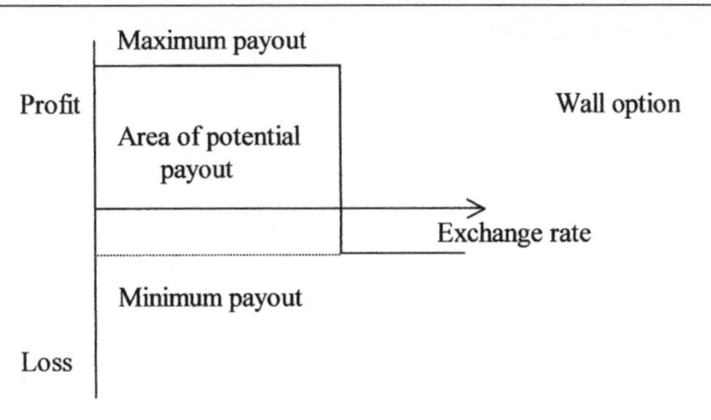

Figure 22.5

This particular product can be used on its own as a currency play for a purchaser with a view on the market's direction, or with corridor and range binary options, combined with a deposit for a potential yield enhancement structure.

22.9 CORRIDOR

The corridor option structure was designed principally again for trading purposes. The structure profits to the extent that spot foreign exchange stays within a range and is often linked with a deposit for yield enhancement purposes. The purchaser specifies a currency range and pays a premium upfront. For every day during a set period that the spot foreign exchange rate fixes within the specified range, a portion of the payout is locked in. If the spot foreign exchange rate fixes within the range every day, then the maximum payout will be due. However, if no days fix within the range, then the payout will be zero. The actual payout is calculated on a pro-rata basis.

This product is similar to the range binary option in that both options will profit if a spot foreign exchange rate stays within a range. The difference is that, whereas the range binary structure is terminated if either of the boundaries trade at any time during the life of the option, the corridor option structure exists for the whole maturity period, with only the payout for that day forfeited should the spot foreign exchange rate trade outside the range. As the corridor option has a less aggressive risk profile, its maximum payout will be smaller than for the range binary equivalent.

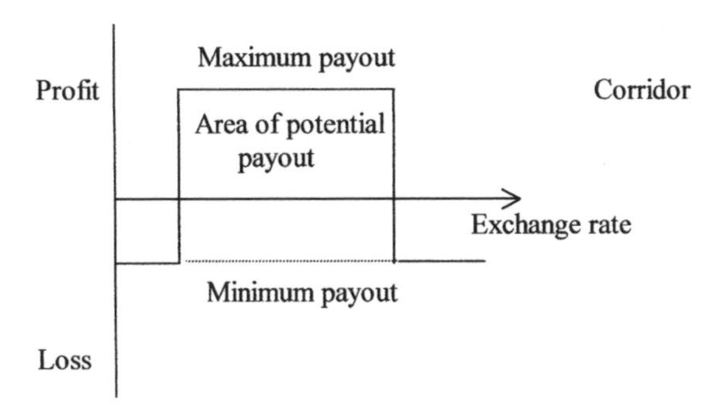

Figure 22.6

23 Case Studies

The following examples show a few of the most commonly used vanilla, exotic and structured currency option strategies for hedging, trading and investment purposes. In all cases, figures and assumptions have been made for the convenience of showing how the examples can be used and do not relate to any actual rates in the market.

Currency:	dollar/Swiss franc
Expiry:	3 months
Spot reference:	1.5700
Forward reference:	1.5673
Volatility:	9.8%

23.1 HEDGING

The following strategies demonstrate ways of using options to hedge a transactional exposure, assumed to be short dollars and long Swiss francs, booked at a rate of \$/sfr 1.5700.

A vanilla European currency option is the most straightforward option hedge. The hedger buys the option and has the right to buy dollars at a foreign exchange rate of \$/sfr 1.5700, if the spot foreign exchange rate trades above \$/sfr 1.5700 at expiry. Should the option be exercised, the effective foreign exchange rate for this hedger will be \$/sfr 1.5700 + 0.0287 = \$/sfr 1.5987. On the downside, gains on the underlying cash position begin to offset the cost of the option breaking even at a foreign exchange rate of \$/sfr 1.5413. The maximum profit of the combined structure is unlimited below this level.

Thus, buy a dollar call/franc put option with a strike of 1.5700, for a cost of 1.83% of dollar amount (or 287 franc pips). Scenarios at expiry are:

- Spot above \$/sfr 1.5700 at expiry – underlying hedged at effective rate of \$/sfr 1.5987;
- Spot below \$/sfr 1.5700 at expiry – underlying benefits below break-even of \$/sfr 1.5413.

A range forward (risk reversal, collar or cylinder) strategy provides the hedger with the right to buy dollars at a foreign exchange rate of \$/sfr 1.6000, if the spot foreign exchange rate trades above \$/sfr 1.6000 at expiry, or with an obligation to buy dollars at \$/sfr 1.5365, if the spot foreign exchange rate trades below that level at expiry. The strike prices in this example are set so that the premium received from the sold option equals the premium paid for the purchased option. This makes the transaction premium free (zero cost). When combined with the short cash position, the exposure is locked into a range, whereby in this example, the maximum cost at expiry would be 300 franc pips and the maximum profit 335 franc pips.

Hence, buy a dollar call/franc put option with a strike of 1.6000 and sell a dollar put/franc call option with a strike of 1.5365. Net cost is zero. Scenarios at expiry are:

- Spot above \$/sfr 1.6000 – underlying hedged by purchased option;
- Spot below \$/sfr 1.5365 – profits on underlying capped by sold option;

- Spot between $/sfr 1.5365 and $/sfr 1.6600 – underlying exchanged at prevailing spot foreign exchange market rate.

An *average rate* currency option provides the holder with the right to receive the difference between the strike price and the average rate at maturity. For example, if the average rate of the 12 weeks is fixed at $/sfr 1.6200, the holder of the average rate option will receive the difference, that is 500 franc pips as a cash settlement. This currency option is particularly suited to a hedger who wishes to cover the exposure for a series of cash flows. Please note this is a cash settled instrument and not a deliverable one.

Thus, buy a dollar call/franc put average rate currency option, with a strike of 1.5700. The fixing frequency is weekly for 12 weeks, every Friday for a premium cost of 1.15% or 180.5 franc pips. Scenarios at expiry are:

- Average above $/sfr 1.5700 – underlying hedged at effective average rate of $/sfr 1.58805;
- Average below $/sfr 1.5700 – underlying benefits below average rate of $/sfr 1.55195.

A mini-premium currency option is initially where no premium is paid. However, if any of the premium trigger levels trade at any time before expiry, the hedger would have to pay 235.5 franc pips at each level. Therefore, if all three levels trade at any time before the option expires, a total of 706.5 franc pips would have to be paid to the currency option seller at maturity. This would be larger than the normal European currency option, but in order for the trigger levels to be reached, the cash would have moved in favour of the hedger's underlying position. If none of the trigger levels trade at any time before expiry, then the currency option will have been bought for zero cost. Scenarios at expiry could be are:

	Mini-premium levels traded	Premium spent and effective exchange rate
> $/sfr 1.5700	None	Zero – 1.5700
	1.5300	235.5 franc pips – 1.59355
	1.5300 and 1.5100	471 franc pips – 1.6171
	1.5300, 1.5100 and 1.4900	706.5 franc pips – 1.64065
< $/sfr 1.5700	None	Zero – spot
	1.5300	235.5 franc pips – spot + 235.5
	1.5300 and 1.5000	471 franc pips – spot +471
	1.5300, 1.5000 and 1.4900	706.5 franc pips – spot + 706.5

The *forward extra* option structure provides the holder with the right to purchase dollars at $/sfr 1.5700 if the spot foreign exchange rate is above this level, but to take benefit from a limited favourable spot foreign exchange rate move, for zero cost in six months' time unless $/sfr 1.5150 trade at any time before the expiry of the option structure. If $/sfr 1.5150 does trade at any time before the currency option expiry, then the option purchaser is locked into a synthetic forward contract to buy dollars against the franc at 1.5700. This structure provides full protection while giving some potential to outperform the initial prevailing forward outright rate.

For example, buy a European dollar call/franc put with a strike of 1.5700 and sell a dollar put/franc call with a strike of 1.5700, but with a knock-in at $/sfr 1.51500 for net zero cost.

Scenarios at expiry are:

Spot above 1.5700	1.5150 has not traded	Underlying hedged at 1.5700
	1.5150 has traded	Underlying hedged at 1.5700
Spot below 1.5700	1.5150 has not traded	Underlying benefits below 1.5700
	1.5150 has traded	Obligation to buy dollars and sell francs at 1.5700

23.2 TRADING

The following strategies show how traders might profit from foreign exchange moves.

A *call spread* currency option strategy is mainly used for trading purposes and allows the holder the right to purchase dollars at 1.5700, if spot trades above $/sfr 1.5700 at expiry. However, there is an obligation to sell dollars at 1.6000, if spot is trading above $/sfr 1.6000 at expiry. The maximum profit for this strategy is 181 franc pips (1.6100 – 1.5700 – 119 franc pips), whereas the maximum loss is the premium paid for the strategy, that is, 119 franc pips. The upfront premium cost of the 1.5700 dollar call is reduced by the sale of the 1.6000 dollar call, thereby improving the break-even point but capping the upside gains. The strategy would therefore suit those looking for limited dollar gains and who are looking to reduce the premium outlay.

An example would be to buy a dollar call/franc put option, with a strike of 1.5700 and sell a dollar call/franc put option, with a strike of 1.6000 for a net cost of 0.76% of the dollar amount or 119 franc pips. Scenarios at expiry are:

- Spot above $/sfr 1.6000 – maximum profit 181 franc pips;
- Spot below $/sfr 1.5700 – maximum loss 119 franc pips.

A seagull currency option strategy provides the purchaser with the right to buy dollars at 1.5700, if spot is trading above $/sfr 1.5700 at expiry and with the obligation to sell dollars at 1.6025, if spot is trading above $/sfr 1.6025. Also, the purchaser has the obligation to buy dollars at 1.5325 if spot is trading below this level at expiry. This is due to the short dollar put currency option. Although this strategy is mainly used for trading purposes, a hedger with the conviction that the up move will be limited can also use it. As the strategy is net zero cost, the strikes act as break-even rates, with the maximum profit for the option strategy limited to 325 franc pips above an exchange rate of $/sfr 1.6025 and potentially unlimited loss below $/sfr 1.5325.

Thus, as an example, buy a dollar call/franc put option with a strike of 1.5700 and sell a dollar call/franc put option with a strike of 1.6025. At the same time, sell a dollar put/franc call option with a strike of 1.5325 for net zero cost. Scenarios at expiry could be:

- Spot above $/sfr 1.6025 – maximum profit 325 franc pips;
- Spot below $/sfr 1.5325 – unlimited potential loss;
- Spot above $/sfr 1.5325 but below $/sfr 1.5700 – zero.

With a *barrier* strategy, the purchased currency option ceases to exist if the spot foreign exchange rate trades at the knock-out level of $/sfr 1.5400 at any time before expiry. However, the premium cost of the option is reduced compared with the European option due to the knock-out feature. The break-even rate for the option is $/sfr 1.5904 as opposed to a break-even of $/sfr 1.5987 for the European option. The maximum profit on the option is unlimited above $/sfr 1.5904, provided that the knock-out level has not traded and the maximum loss is the premium of 204 franc pips. As an example, buy a dollar call/franc put option, with a strike of 1.5700 and with a knock-out at $/sfr 1.5400. Premium cost is 1.30% of dollars or 204 franc pips (the European comparable option cost would be 1.83% of dollars). Scenarios at expiry are:

- Spot above 1.5700, 1.5400 not traded, profit above break-even of 1.5904;
- Spot below 1.5700, 1.5400 not traded, option lapses and premium lost;
- Any closing spot, 1.5400 has traded, option terminated and premium lost.

23.3 INVESTMENT

The following strategies show some examples of how options may be utilised by investors looking for potential yield enhancement structures.

Dollar deposit combined with a purchased option – with this structure, the investor takes a view on the currency move. If the view is correct, the yield on the original deposit will be significantly enhanced. However, if the view is incorrect, the principal is preserved and a lower yield only is achieved. It should be noted that the principal amount deposited is not at risk.

For example, consider a dollar-based investor with a one-year deposit, using a deposit rate of 7.65% could buy a dollar put/franc call option with a strike of 1.5700. Again, expiry is one year and pays an option premium of 4.85% of the dollar amount. It is assumed that a portion of the interest that would be earned on the deposit is used to pay for the option purchase. Therefore:

Minimum return	2.80%
Maximum return	2.80% plus foreign exchange gains below $/sfr 1.5700

Thus, return at $/sfr 1.4500 finishing spot foreign exchange rate will be 11.08% of dollars, as defined by the following formula:

If spot is less than 1.5700, return will be:

$$2.80\% + \frac{((1.5700 - \text{spot at expiry}) \times 100)}{\text{spot at expiry}}$$

However, if the spot foreign exchange rate at expiry is greater than $/sfr 1.5700, the return will be just 2.80%.

Dollar deposit combined with a range binary option – in this case, the premium is invested in the range binary with limits at $/sfr 1.4500 and $/sfr 1.6500. Provided that the spot foreign exchange rate stays within the prescribed range and does not trade at either of the range limits at any time during the life of the option, then a fixed multiple of the premium amount invested will be payable at maturity. If, however, either of the limits trade at any time before the maturity date, then the range binary will be terminated and the premium invested will be lost. The investor would then receive the full principal invested plus a deposit yield. Of course, this yield will be lower than the standard yield due to the deduction of the premium needed to finance the purchase of the range binary option. Also, the principal amount deposited will not be at risk.

For example, consider a one-year dollar deposit rate of 7.65%, with a range binary option, with limits of $/sfr 1.4500 and $/sfr 1.6500. The payout ratio is 1:12 and the premium invested is 2.00% of the dollar amount. Here, once again, a portion of the interest that would be earned on the deposit is used to pay for the purchase of the option. Therefore:

Minimum return on investment	5.65%
Maximum return on investment	29.65%

(provided that \$/sfr 1.4500/\$/sfr 1.6500 range is not broken)

Dollar deposit combined with corridor option – in this structure, the premium is invested into a corridor currency option with limits set at \$/sfr 1.4500 and \$/sfr 1.6500. For each day that the spot foreign exchange rate stays within the prescribed range, a portion of the payout is locked in and this payout is a multiple of the total premium invested. Therefore, if the spot foreign exchange rate stays within the range for every day of the period, the maximum payout will be due, but if the spot foreign exchange rate never fixes within the range, no payout will be due. The actual payout is calculated on a pro-rata basis for the number of days that the spot foreign exchange rate stays within the prescribed levels. The principal of the deposit is preserved with a minimum payout (in this case 2.65%) also assured. Again, the principal amount deposited is not at risk. The return on the investment is defined by the following formula:

$$\text{Return}\ (\%) = 2.65\%\$ + \frac{(\text{days} \times \text{multiple})}{\text{total days}}$$

where:

- Days = number of days spot fixes in the range;
- Multiple = fixed multiple of premium invested; and
- Total days = total number of business days.

For example, a one-year dollar deposit at a rate of 7.65%, with a corridor range of \$/sfr 1.4500 to \$/sfr 1.6500. The payout ratio is 1:2.75 and the premium invested is 5% of the dollar amount.

Once again, a proportion of the interest that would be earned on the deposit is used to pay for the option purchase, therefore:

Minimum return on investment	2.65%
Maximum return on investment	16.40%

23.4 BID TO OFFER EXPOSURE

Bid to offer is the term used to describe the potential foreign exchange exposure arising out of a bid for a contract priced in a currency other than the company's home currency. As the actual foreign exchange exposure is dependent/contingent upon winning the contract, this type of exposure is also often referred to as "contingent exposure".

Bid to offer exposure is one of the most difficult foreign exchange exposures to hedge, as the exposure depends upon some event outside of the foreign exchange markets occurring, that is, for example, whether or not the contract is awarded to the bidder. The foreign exchange exposure can therefore be thought of as a secondary one, as the success of a contract bid is not usually dependent upon foreign exchange market moves. However, the foreign exchange exposure arising out of an awarded contract can be substantial. The problem is further compounded by the fact that in the types of business where bids for contracts are used, companies often have multiple quotes out at any one time, but their success rates may be low, for example one in 10.

Due to the contingent nature of the potential exposure, any hedging strategy that involves an obligation to transact is not appropriate, as with no underlying foreign exchange to offset against the hedge, unlimited foreign exchange losses (or profits) might ensue. This rules out the use of foreign exchange forwards, sold vanilla currency option contracts and any zero-cost currency option structures, for example range forwards or participating forwards.

Thus, unfortunately, there is no easy answer to what are the alternatives, especially as bidders are usually constrained by cost. Some kind of purchased currency option strategy would seem the most appropriate, due to the asymmetrical option payoff, whereby the downside is covered and benefit can be taken in any upside moves. However, the outlay of currency option premiums for each individual bid may be prohibitive.

A *Purchased European* currency option can provide an efficient hedge. The right but not the obligation of the long currency option to transact allows the potential foreign exchange exposure to be hedged should the contract be awarded, but the currency option can be allowed to lapse if no foreign exchange exposure arises, that is, the contract has not won. A premium obviously has to be paid upfront to buy the currency option, which could prove expensive if multiple bids are being offered. However, as the table shows, there are four potential outcomes for the currency option hedge plus the bid to offer exposure and in only one out of the four outcomes will the worst case be achieved. Also, it should be noted that sometimes the premium could be built into the cost of the tender.

	Option in-the-money	**Option out-of-the-money**
Contract awarded	Foreign exchange exposure hedged by the currency option	Foreign exchange exposure free to benefit from favourable moves
Contract not awarded	No foreign exchange exposure but value can be recouped for some or all of the cost	No foreign exchange exposure but option premium forfeited

The *compound* currency option differs from a standard currency option in that the product allows the purchaser the right, over a specified period of time, to buy (or sell) an underlying European style currency option, with specified parameters, at a fixed premium. The extra flexibility of this product gives a further potential hedge for bid to offer exposure. The compound period (the time in which one can decide whether or not to buy the underlying option) would be set to correspond to the bidding period and the underlying currency option would be set to match the duration of the potential underlying cash flow. An additional upfront premium is payable by the purchaser of the compound currency option, but the secondary premium for the underlying currency option is only payable should the owner decide to exercise the compound option. Typically, the upfront cost of the compound currency option is smaller than the premium for a standard European currency option, decreasing the worst-case cost should the contract be unsuccessful. However, if the compound currency option were used, then the overall cost would be greater than the purchase of the equivalent standard European currency option originally. The increased cost is related to the extra flexibility gained from the product and so the relationship between the initial premium and secondary premiums and the overall cost will vary depending on the structure.

A similar table of outcomes can be constructed for the compound option.

	Compound option in-the-money	**Compound option out-of-the-money**
Contract awarded	Foreign exchange exposure hedged by underlying option	Foreign exchange exposure can be hedged at more favourable rate
Contract not awarded	No foreign exchange exposure but value can be recouped for some or all of the cost	No foreign exchange exposure but compound option premium forfeited

The use of a compound currency option, over a standard European option, reduces the potential worst-case loss. However, the overall cost of the strategy, if used, would be greater, but the extra flexibility of the product allows a different risk/reward profile.

With the *portfolio approach*, either of the above strategies could be successfully employed to hedge either an individual bid to offer or a small number of bid to offers. For those businesses where a large number of bids are submitted, the upfront premium cost may inhibit the hedging of each individual contract. In these circumstances, it may be more efficient to analyse the portfolio of bids in terms of the overall, and individual probabilities of winning and the associated foreign exchange exposure. The bidding company is in the best position to assess the probability of winning an individual bid, thus allowing a more or less aggressive hedging stance. On bids where it is felt that it is very likely that the contract will be awarded, a more aggressive hedging strategy could be taken. On those where it is considered that there is a very low probability of winning, a less aggressive hedge could be put into place.

Where possible, one approach might be to group together bids with similar characteristics, for example bidding in the same currency or for contracts and underlying periods of similar lengths. The overall probability of winning one or more contracts and the subsequent foreign exchange exposure arising from these could then be estimated. With this estimated figure and maturity in mind, a standard European currency option or a compound option could then be employed as a portfolio hedge. However, with this approach, some slippage in terms of timing and amounts may well occur, but if a hedge can be gained for the bulk of the exposure, at a reduced cost, the strategy might be appealing to those with multiple bid to offers.

23.5 CONCLUDING REMARKS

As is evidenced by the above, the hedging of bid to offer exposure is complicated but the contingency factor. Exposures can be fully hedged by buying options, but for multiple contracts with low hit rates, the premium cost can be prohibitive. Analysis of the probability of winning contracts can therefore be key to the hedging strategy. This approach may allow a lower cost hedging strategy, but there could well be some slippage in the cover, if probability estimates prove to be unrealistic.

24

Option Hedge Matrix

Refer to the strategies on the following pages

Underlying position – exposure →	*Long above market*	*Long at market*	*Long below market*	*Short above market*	*Short at market*	*Short below market*	*No position – spec.*
Market view of ↓							
Convinced of move up:	5–1	1–1	3–1	3–4	1–4	5–4	8–1
Afraid of move up:	6–1	2–1	4–1	4–4	2–4	6–4	
Convinced of move down:	5–3	1–3	3–3	3–2	1–2	5–2	8–2
Afraid of move down:	6–3	2–3	4–3	4–2	2–2	6–2	
Convinced market does not move:	7–1	7–2	7–3	7–4	7–5	7–6	8–3
No idea – convinced of move:	11–3	9–3	11–1	11–2	9–4	11–4	8–4
No idea – afraid of move:	10–1	9–1	10–3	10–4	9–2	10–2	

	1–1	1–2	1–3	1–4
Customer exposure	***Long at market***	***Short at market***	***Long at market***	***Short at market***
Market view	***Convinced market higher***	***Convinced market lower***	***Convinced market lower***	***Convinced market higher***
Forex hedge and Risk profile	Do nothing and full market risk if market declines	Do nothing and full market risk if market rises	Sell 100% forward and low risk but missed profit potential if market later rises	Buy 100% forward and low risk but missed profit potential if market later falls
Option purchase and Risk profile	OTM put (disaster insurance) improved. If market declines, p/l protected by long put. If market rises, earn all upside profit less option cost	OTM call (disaster insurance) improved. If market rises, p/l protected by long call. If market falls, earn all downside profit less option cost	ATM put improved. If market declines, p/l protected by long put. If market rises, earn all upside profit less option cost	ATM call improved. If market rises, p/l protected by long call. If market falls, earn all downside profit less option cost
Option sale and Risk profile	ATM or slightly OTM call Earn good extra income, but major risk if market starts dropping against expectations	ATM or slightly OTM put Earn good extra income, but major risk if market starts rising against expectations	ATM call Earn good extra income, but if ever market rises against expectations, potential upside profit is missed	ATM put Earn good extra income, but if ever market moves against expectations potential downside profit is missed

	2–1	2–2	2–3	2–4
Customer exposure	*Long at market*	*Short at market*	*Long at market*	*Short at market*
Market view	*Afraid market higher*	*Afraid market lower*	*Afraid market lower*	*Afraid market higher*
Forex hedge and Risk profile	Do partial cover to reduce risk Market risk on uncovered portion	Do partial cover to reduce risk Market risk on uncovered portion	Sell 100% forward Low risk but missed profit potential if market later rises	Buy 100% forward Low risk but missed profit potential if market later falls
Option purchase and Risk profile	ATM put (insurance) Improved. If market declines, p/l protected by long put. If market rises, earn all upside profit less option cost	ATM call (insurance) Improved. If market rises, p/l protected by long call. If market falls, earn all downside profit less option cost	OTM put (disaster insurance) Protection at lower levels, but at relatively moderate cost. Gives the staying power to fish for better levels to sell	OTM call (disaster insurance) Protection at lower levels, but at relatively moderate cost. Gives the staying power to fish for better levels to buy
Option sale and Risk profile	OTM call at target rate Earn extra upfront premium income but downside risk not protected	OTM put at target rate Earn extra upfront premium income but upside risk not protected	OTM call Earn some extra income while leaving room to profit from an upward movement if it ever happens	OTM put Earn some extra income while leaving room to profit from a downward movement if it ever happens

	3–1	3–2	3–3	3–4
Customer exposure	***Long below market***	***Short above market***	***Long below market***	***Short above market***
Market view	***Convinced market higher***	***Convinced market lower***	***Convinced market lower***	***Convinced market higher***
Forex hedge and Risk profile	Do nothing and pray Full upside potential. If market falls, loss may surpass profit margin	Do nothing and pray Full downside potential. If market rises, loss may surpass profit margin	Sell forward to lock in profit Low risk but possible missed profits if market later rises	Buy forward to lock in profit Low risk but possible missed profits if market later falls
Option purchase and Risk profile	OTM put (disaster insurance) Protects against possible market fall. Allows full upside profit less option cost	OTM call (disaster insurance) Protects against possible market rise. Allows full downside profit less option cost	ATM put Locks in minimum selling price but allows full participation in further market rise less option cost	ATM call Locks in minimum purchase price but allows full participation in any further market fall less option cost
Option sale and Risk profile	OTM call at target rate Earn extra upfront income but downside risk not protected if market rises	OTM put at target rate Earn extra upfront income but upside risk not protected if market drops	OTM call Limits upside potential but generates immediate income that helps protect against loss	OTM put Limits downside potential but generates immediate income that helps protect against loss

	4–1	4–2	4–3	4–4
Customer exposure	***Long below market***	***Short above market***	***Long below market***	***Short above market***
Market view	***Afraid market higher***	***Afraid market lower***	***Afraid market lower***	***Afraid market higher***
Forex hedge and Risk profile	Do nothing and pray Full market risk if market declines and wipes out profit	Do nothing and pray Full market risk if market rises and wipes out profit	Sell forward to lock in profit Low risk but possible missed profits if market later rises	Buy forward to lock in profit Low risk but possible missed profits if market later falls
Option purchase and	OTM put (disaster insurance)	OTM call (disaster insurance)	OTM put at break-even or slightly higher	OTM call at break-even or slightly lower
Risk profile	Protects against possible market fall. Allows full upside profit less option cost	Protects against possible market rise. Allows full downside profit less option cost	Protects break-even rate while minimising option cost. Provides the staying power	Protects break-even rate while minimising option cost. Provides the staying power
Option sale and Risk profile	OTM call Earn premium, which helps to protect against possible market fall	OTM put Earn premium, which helps to protect against possible market rise	ATM call Locks in profit at current level. Provides extra income but further upside profit potential is lost	ATM put Locks in profit at current level. Provides extra income but further downside profit potential is lost

	5–1	5–2	5–3	5–4
Customer exposure	***Long above market***	***Short below market***	***Long above market***	***Short below market***
Market view	***Convinced market higher***	***Convinced market lower***	***Convinced market lower***	***Convinced market higher***
Forex hedge and	Trust yourself. Do nothing and pray.	Trust yourself. Do nothing and pray.	Close out and take loss	Close out and take loss
Risk profile	High risk. Cannot sell forward as this would lock in loss	High risk. Cannot buy forward as this would lock in loss	Locked in loss	Locked in loss
Option purchase and	OTM put	OTM call	ATM put	ATM call
Risk profile	Risk reduced. Known downside maximum risk gives staying power	Risk reduced. Known downside maximum risk gives staying power	Risk locked at current levels. No further loss will be seen	Risk locked at current levels. No further loss will be seen
Option sale and	OTM call	OTM put	ATM call	ATM put
Risk profile	No increased risk but profit potential limited to target level	No increased risk but profit potential limited to target level	Earn good income but must forego any profit potential. Risk increases if market recovers against expectations	Earn good income but must forego any profit potential. Risk increases if market recovers against expectations

	6–1	6–2	6–3	6–4
Customer exposure	***Long above market***	***Short below market***	***Long above market***	***Short below market***
Market view	***Afraid market higher***	***Afraid market lower***	***Afraid market lower***	***Afraid market higher***
Forex hedge and Risk profile	Do nothing and pray High risk. Cannot sell forward as this would lock in loss	Do nothing and pray High risk. Cannot buy forward as this would lock in loss	Close out and take loss Locked in loss	Close out and take loss Locked in loss
Option purchase and Risk profile	ATM put Risk reduced. Protects against further market decline. Allows full participation in expected market rise less option cost	ATM call Risk reduced. Protects against further market rise. Allows full participation in market fall less option cost	Put at the holding price Risk reduced. Protects against realising losses. Allows full participation in possible market rise less option cost	Call at the holding price Risk reduced. Protects against realising losses. Allows full participation in possible market fall less option cost
Option sale and Risk profile	OTM call (at target level) Limits upside profit but premium gained will help offset market loss	OTM put (at target level) Less risk. Limits profit but premium earned helps offset market loss	OTM call Limits upside profit but premium earned will help offset market loss	OTM put Less risk. Limits downside profit but premium earned helps offset market loss

	7–1	7–2	7–3	7–4	7–5	7–6
Customer exposure	***Long above market***	***Long at market***	***Long below market***	***Short above market***	***Short at market***	***Short below market***
Market view	***Convinced market does not move***	***Convinced market does not move***	***Convinced market does not move***	***Convinced market does not move***	***Convinced market does not move***	***Convinced market does not move***
Forex hedge and	Stay long the higher yield currency	Stay long the higher yield currency	Stay long the higher yield currency	Stay long the higher yield currency	Stay long the higher yield currency	Stay long the higher yield currency
Risk profile	Try to capture the interest rate differential while market is quiet	Try to capture the interest rate differential while market is quiet	Try to capture the interest rate differential while market is quiet	Try to capture the interest rate differential while market is quiet	Try to capture the interest rate differential while market is quiet	Try to capture the interest rate differential while market is quiet
Option purchase and Risk profile	Not advised	Not advised	Not advised	Not advised	Not advised	Not advised
Option sale and	Call at holding price	ATM call	Call at holding price	Put at holding price	ATM put	Put at holding price
Risk profile	Avoid locking in loss. Not protected if market falls	Earn premium. Not protected if market declines	Lock in current profit, but still exposed to market decline	Lock in current profit, but still exposed to risk of rise	Earn premium. Not protected if market rises	Avoid locking in current loss. Not protected if market rises

	8–1	8–2	8–3	8–4
Customer exposure	***None***	***None***	***None***	***None***
Market view	***Convinced market higher***	***Convinced market lower***	***Convinced market does not move***	***No idea of direction but convinced of violent move***
Forex hedge and Risk profile	Buy foreign exchange Full downside risk	Sell foreign exchange Full upward risk	Not advised	Not advised
Option purchase and Risk profile	ATM call Expensive but has maximum profit potential if view is right and market rises	ATM put Expensive but has maximum profit potential if view is right and market declines	Not advised	ATM call and put Very expensive but has guaranteed profit potential if view is right and market moves substantially either way (beware of time decay)
Option sale and Risk profile	ATM put Nice upfront income but risky if ever view is wrong and market declines	ATM call Nice upfront income but risky if ever view is wrong and market rises	Both ATM call and put Very nice upfront income but very risky if ever view is wrong and market becomes volatile	Not advised

	9–1	9–2	9–3	9–4
Customer exposure	***Long at market***	***Short at market***	***Long at market***	***Short at market***
Market view	***No idea – afraid of move***	***No idea – afraid of move***	***No idea – but convinced of a move***	***No idea – but convinced of a move***
Forex hedge and Risk profile	Sell forward partially Market risk on unhedged portion	Buy forward partially Market risk on unhedged portion	Sell forward partially Possible large market risk on unhedged portion	Buy forward partially Possible large market risk on unhedged portion
Option purchase and Risk profile	Slightly OTM put Low risk, protects against market falls. Profit from market rise less cost of option	Slightly OTM call Low risk, protects against market rise. Profit from market fall less cost of option	ATM put Low risk, protects against market falls. Profit from market rise less cost of option	ATM call Low risk, protects against market rise. Profit from market fall less cost of option
Option sale and Risk profile	OTM call If market rises, profit potential limited to strike. If market drops, upfront premium helps to offset losses if market declines	OTM put If market falls, profit potential limited to strike. If market rises, upfront premium helps to offset losses if market drops	Not advised	Not advised

	10–1	10–2	10–3	10–4
Customer exposure	***Long above market***	***Short below market***	***Long below market***	***Short above market***
Market view	***No idea – afraid of move***	***No idea – afraid of move***	***No idea – afraid of move***	***No idea – afraid of move***
Forex hedge and Risk profile	None High risk	None High risk	Sell forward partially Market risk on unhedged portion	Buy forward partially Market risk on unhedged portion
Option purchase and Risk profile	ATM put Protects against market fall but allows upside profit potential less option cost	ATM call Protects against market rise but allows downside profit potential less option cost	ATM put Locks in minimum selling price/profit but allows full participation in further market rise less option cost	ATM call Locks in minimum buying price/profit but allows full participation in later market fall less option cost
Option sale and Risk profile	OTM call Limits upside profit potential but premium earned helps to offset market loss	OTM put Limits downside profit but premium earned helps to offset market loss	OTM call Limits upside profit but premium earned helps to offset any market declines	OTM put Limits downside profit but premium earned helps to offset any losses if market rises

	11–1	11–2	11–3	11–4
Customer exposure	***Long below market***	***Short above market***	***Long above market***	***Short below market***
Market view	***No idea – but convinced of a move***	***No idea – but convinced of a move***	***No idea – but convinced of a move***	***No idea – but convinced of a move***
Forex hedge and Risk profile	Sell forward partially Lock in some profit, but exposed to risk for residual position	Buy forward partially Lock in some profit, but exposed to risk for residual position	Sell forward partially Lock in some loss and still exposed to risk for residual position	Buy forward partially Lock in some loss and still exposed to risk for residual position
Option purchase and Risk profile	ATM put Locks in profits and gives peace of mind to profit from any up or down swing in market less option cost	ATM call Locks in profits and gives peace of mind to profit from any up or down swing in market less option cost	ITM put at holding price Locks in losses but gives staying power to look for an opportunity if ever market moves favourably	ATM call Locks in losses but gives staying power to look for an opportunity if ever market moves favourably
Option sale and Risk profile	Not advised	Not advised	Not advised	Not advised

Exotic Currency Option Glossary

Listed below are "exotic" currency options and terms. Please note that not all of the below have been mentioned in this primer but have been included here to try to increase the market awareness/knowledge of the reader. This is by no means a complete list.

Average rate option A cash-settled currency option that pays the difference between the average rate of the underlying (calculated on predetermined fixings of an agreed reference rate) compared with a predetermined strike rate. The volatility on this currency option is lower than the constituent rates and is thus cheaper than standard European style currency options.

Average strike option A currency option whose strike price is set at the expiration date to be the average rate of the underlying compared with its final value at expiration (calculated on predetermined fixings of an agreed reference rate). The currency option can be exercised for physical delivery or be cash-settled against the underlying price prevailing at maturity. The volatility on this currency option is lower than the constituent rates and is thus cheaper than standard European style currency options.

Barrier option A **path-dependent** currency option that is either cancelled or activated if the underlying instrument reaches a set level. Also, known as a **knock-out**, **knock-in** or **trigger** currency option. It is usually a straightforward European style currency option until or from the time the underlying reaches the barrier price. There are four major types:

1. **Up-and-outs** are cancelled if the underlying rises above a certain point;
2. **Up-and-ins** will have no value at maturity unless the underlying rises in the interim above a set price, at which point it becomes a standard European style put or call currency option;
3. **Down-and-outs** are cancelled if the underlying falls below a certain price;
4. **Down-and-ins** are activated when the underling's price falls to a set level, at which point the currency option becomes a standard European style put or call currency option.

Because of these extinguishing or activating features, these currency options are usually cheaper than ordinary currency options and are therefore more attractive to purchasers who are unwilling to paying a premium.

Basket options Enables a purchaser to buy or sell a basket of currencies.

Bear spread A currency option strategy that combines a bearish view of the market with a view on volatility. Each strategy has limited risk but also limited potential gain. There are two choices. The first is the purchase of a **put spread**, whereby the purchaser believes implied volatility is underpriced. The second is the sale of a **call spread**, whereby the seller believes implied volatility to be overpriced.

Binary option Unlike vanilla currency options, which have continuous payout profiles, this currency option is discontinuous and pays out a fixed amount if the underlying reaches a predetermined level (the strike price). The two main forms are **all-or-nothing**, which pays out a set amount if the underlying is above/below a certain point at expiry, and **one-touch**, which pays out a fixed amount if, at any time during the life of the option, the underlying reaches a certain point. Binary currency options are frequently combined with other currency options or cash positions to create a structured product, for example **contingent** currency options.

Box options Used to buy/sell mispriced currency options and to hedge the market risk, using only currency options. For example, if a certain strike put is underpriced, the trader buys the put and sells a call at the same strike, creating a synthetic short futures position. To get rid of the market risk, the trader sells another put and buys another call, but at different strike prices.

Break forward A strategy that involves buying a synthetic off-market currency forward (buying and selling a put and a call at the same strike price) and the simultaneous purchase of another currency option, allowing the purchaser to benefit from favourable exchange rate movements. The transaction is usually constructed for zero cost because the premium from the off-market forward pays for the currency option.

Bull spread A currency option strategy that combines a bullish view of a market with a view on volatility. Each strategy has limited risk but also limited potential gain. The two potential choices are the purchase of a **call spread**, whereby the purchaser believes the implied volatility is underpriced, and a **put spread**, whereby the seller believes it is overpriced.

Butterfly spread The simultaneous sale of an at-the-money straddle and the purchase of an out-of-the-money strangle. The structure profits if the underlying remains stable and has limited risk in the event of a large move in either direction.

Calendar spread A strategy that involves buying and selling currency options with the same strike price but with different maturities. This strategy is used to play expected changes in the shape of the volatility term curve. For example, if one-month volatility is high and six-month volatility is low, arbitrageurs might buy the six-month currency option and sell the one-month currency option, thereby selling short-term volatility and buying long-term volatility. If short-term volatility declines relative to long-term volatility, the strategy will make money.

Call spread A strategy that reduces the cost of buying a call currency option by selling another call currency option at a higher level. This limits potential gain if the underlying moves higher, but the premium received from selling the out-of-the-money call partly finances the at-the-money call currency option. This strategy may also be advantageous if the purchaser thinks there is only limited upside in the underlying.

Caption A currency option on a cap. It is a type of **compound option** in which the purchaser has the right, but not the obligation, to enter into a cap at a predetermined rate on a predetermined date. Captions can be a cheap way of leveraging into the more expensive option.

Chooser option Offers the purchaser the choice, after a predetermined period, between a put and a call currency option. The payouts are similar to those of a straddle but chooser options are cheaper than straddles because purchasers must choose before expiry whether they want the put or the call currency option.

Collar The simultaneous purchaser of an out-of-the-money call option and the sale of an out-of-the-money put option. The premium from selling the put option reduces the cost of purchasing the call option. The amount saved depends on the strike rate of the two currency options. If the premium raised by the sale of the put option exactly matches the cost of the call option, the strategy is known as a zero-cost collar.

Compound option An option on an option, permitting the purchaser to buy (or sell) an option on an underlying at a fixed price over a predetermined period. The upfront premium is less than for a normal European style currency option but if the option is exercised, the overall cost will be greater. Due to their greater flexibility the cost, if both options are exercised, is greater than a conventional currency option.

Condor The simultaneous purchase (sale) of an out-of-the-money strangle and sale (purchase) of an even further out-of-the-money strangle. The strategy gives a limited profit/limited loss payoff and is directionally neutral.

Contingent option An option for which the purchaser pays no premium unless the option is exercised. As a rule of thumb, the premium cost is equal to the premium payable on a normal currency option divided by the currency option delta. Hence, the price increases dramatically for out-of-the-money options. This strategy is zero cost (unless exercised) and can be broken down into a **binary option** plus a conventional currency option.

Covered call A technique is used to sell a call currency option while owning the underlying on which the currency option is written. Generally, covered call writers would undertake the strategy only if they thought volatility was overpriced in the market. The lower the volatility, the less the covered call writer gains in return for giving up upside in the underlying. Basically, this technique provides downside protection only to the extent that the currency option premium offsets a market downturn.

Covered put Used to sell a put currency option while holding cash. This technique is used to increase income by receiving option premium. If the market moves lower and the currency option is exercised, the cash can be used to buy the underlying to cover.

Cylinder, also known as range forward The simultaneous purchase of an out-of-the-money put currency option and the sale of an out-of-the-money call currency option at different strike prices. This strategy enables purchasers to hedge their downside at reduced cost and is at the expense of foregoing upside beyond a certain level, since the purchase of the put currency option is financed by the sale of the call currency option.

Digital option (binary option) Provides the purchaser with a fixed payout profile. This means that the purchaser receives the same payout irrespective of how far in-the-money the option closes. Digitals are therefore very simple to understand and are cheaper to buy than standard options. They can also be currency protected.

Exotic option Any option with a more complicated payoff than standard put or call currency options.

Floortion An option on a floor. The purchaser has the right, but not the obligation, to enter into a floor at a predetermined rate and date.

Forward start option An option that gives the purchaser the right to receive, after a specified time, a standard put or call currency option. The currency options strike price is at-the-money at the time the currency option is activated, rather than when it is granted.

High-low option A combination of two lookback options. A high-low currency option pays the difference between the high and low of an underlying.

Knock-in option (barrier option) A currency option that comes alive, that is, knocks in, when a certain barrier is reached. If the barrier is never reached, the currency option will automatically expire worthless, as without reaching the barrier, it never exists. If the barrier is reached, the currency option knocks in and its final value will depend on where the spot foreign exchange rate settles in relation to the strike. They are therefore substantially cheaper than ordinary standard currency options. Where the barrier on a knock-in call currency option is above the spot foreign exchange rate, it is called an "up and in call". Where the barrier is below the spot foreign exchange rate, it is a "down and in call".

Knock-out options (barrier options) The reverse of knock-in options and provides the purchaser with an unlimited upside and a known downside, i.e. the premium. The knock-out feature limits the upside given to the buyer and therefore makes the currency option considerably cheaper. When an investor purchases a standard currency option, the payout depends on where the spot foreign exchange rate closes on a particular day. With the knock-out feature, if at any time up to and including the maturity, the knock-out level is reached, the option will expire worthless. Where the barrier on a call currency option is above the spot foreign exchange rate, the currency option is known as an "up and out call", and where the barrier on call is below the spot foreign exchange rate, the currency option is known as a "down and out call".

Ladder option Has the strike periodically reset when the underlying trades through specified trigger levels, at the same time locking in the profit between the old and the new strike. The trigger strikes appear as rungs on a ladder. Ladder options can be structured to reset the strike in either one or both directions. This option is also known as a **ratchet option** and **lock-in option**.

Lookback option Gives the purchaser the right to exercise the option at the lowest (in the case of a call currency option) or the highest price (in the case of a put currency option) reached by the underlying over the life of the currency option, compared with a set strike price. Such options' potential benefits tend to be outweighed by their cost.

Lookback strike option Permits the purchaser to purchase or sell the underlying at the low or high than the underlying reaches over a predetermined period.

Money-back option Will repay at least the original option premium at expiry. However, the leverage of the currency option is greatly reduced compared with a standard currency option, effectively the premium is simply the coupon foregone on the original principal.

Naked option An option, which is sold (purchased) without an offsetting position in the underlying.

One-touch option (binary option) Provides the purchaser with a fixed payout profile. The purchaser receives the same payout irrespective of how far in-the-money the currency option closes. Unlike ordinary digitals, one-touch options payout if the underlying reaches the strike at any time from start to maturity. They can therefore be considered as an American style digital currency option and the straight digital as European style, that is, exercise only at maturity.

Option combination strategies Currency options that may be combined so that their payouts produce a desired risk profile. Some combinations are primarily trading strategies, but currency option combinations can be useful in, for example, allowing investors to construct a strategy to take advantage of a particular view they have on the market. Other strategies allow purchasers to reduce their premiums by giving up some of the benefits they may have received from market movements. Such strategies are **bear/bull spread**, **calendar spread**, **call/put spread**, **condor**, **cylinder**, **ratio spread**, **straddle** and **strangle**.

Participating forward The simultaneous purchase of a call currency option (or put currency option) and sale of a put currency option (or call currency option) at the same strike price, usually for zero cost. The currency option purchased must be out-of-the-money and the currency option sold, in order to finance the currency option purchase, is for a smaller amount but must be in-the-money.

Path-dependent option Has a payout directly related to movements in the price of the underlying during the option's life. By contrast, the payout of a standard European style currency option is determined solely by the price at expiry.

Put spread Reduces the cost of buying a put currency option by selling another put at a lower level. This limits the amount the purchaser can gain if the underlying goes down, but the premium received from selling an out-of-the-money put partly finances the at-the-money put. A put spread my also be useful if the purchaser thinks there is only limited downside in the market.

Range forward (cylinder) The simultaneous purchase of an out-of-the-money put currency option and the sale of an out-of-the-money call currency option at different strike prices. This strategy enables purchasers to hedge their downside at reduced cost and is at the expense of foregoing upside beyond a certain level, since the purchase of the put is financed by the sale of the call.

Ratio spread Involves buying different amounts of similar currency options with differing strike prices. The selling of more out-of-the-money currency options finances the purchase of an in-the-money currency option. Conversely, selling less of an in-the-money currency option finances the out-of-the-money currency options.

Shout option An option that allows a purchaser to lock in a minimum return if the purchaser thinks the market is at its high (low). If, for example, the purchaser buys a shout option at 100 and the market moves up to 110, the purchaser can, if the thought is that this level is the highs, "shout" and lock in 10 points. If the market declines, the purchaser still receives 10 points. If, on the other hand, the market finishes higher, the holder receives the extra payout. With a lookback option, the holder is guaranteed to sell at the highest price the market reaches, even if the market then moves lower again. The holder of the shout option is able to sell only at the level shouted, even if the market rises before moving lower.

Straddle The sale or purchase of a put currency option and a call currency option, with the same strike price, on the same underlying and with the same expiry. The purchaser benefits, in return for paying two premiums, if the underlying moves enough either way. It is a way of taking advantage of an expected upturn in volatility. Sellers of straddles assume unlimited risk but benefit if the underlying does not move. Straddles are primarily trading instruments.

Strangle As with a straddle, the sale or purchase of a put currency option and a call currency option on the same instrument, with the same expiry, but at strike prices equally out-of-the-money. The strangle costs less than the straddle because both currency options are out-of-the-money, but profits are only generated if the underlying moves dramatically, and the break-even is worse than for a straddle. Sellers of strangles make money in the range between the two strike prices, but lose if the price moves outside the break-even range.

Synthetic option A technique for replicating an option payout by buying and selling the underlying in proportion to movements in the theoretical currency option's delta. Essentially, it is delta hedging with nothing to hedge. Those trying to replicate a long currency option position lay themselves open to increases in market volatility. Conversely, they benefit if volatility declines. Synthetic replication is generally used if implied volatility of options, and therefore their price, is thought to be too high.

Trigger options (barrier option) A family of options that either come alive or die when predetermined trigger points (barriers) are reached. There are two major types – knock-ins and knock-outs. Knock-in options come alive when the barrier is reached and knock-out options die when the barrier is reached. The barrier can be any tradable variable and may or may not be directly related to the underlying of the original option. Most available currency options can be adapted to be barrier options.

Vertical spread Any currency option strategy that relies on the difference in premium between two currency options on the same underlying with the same maturity, but different strike prices. Thus, put spreads and call spreads would both be vertical spread.

Volatility trading A strategy based on a view that future volatility in the underlying will be more or less than the implied volatility in the currency option price. Currency option market makers are volatility traders. The most common way to buy/sell volatility is to buy/sell currency options, hedging the directional risk with the underlying. Volatility buyers make money if the underlying is more volatile than the implied volatility predicted. Sellers of volatility benefit if the opposite holds. Other methods of buying/selling volatility are to buy/sell combinations of currency options, the most usual being to buy/sell straddles and strangles. Other strategies take advantage of the difference between implied volatilities of differing maturity currency options, not between implied and actual volatility. For example, if implied volatility in short-term currency options is high and in longer options low, a trader can sell short-term currency options and buy longer ones.

Zero-cost option Any strategy that involves financing a currency option purchase by the simultaneous sale of another currency option of equal value.

25
Concluding Remarks

The currency turmoil seen in recent years, together with increasingly global and competitive markets, has added to the difficulties faced by most participants of the foreign exchange markets in managing foreign exchange risk. Thus, demand for effective risk management instruments has grown dramatically.

Market participants have found that currency options allow them opportunities to capitalise on favourable exchange rate movements while providing protection from adverse movements. With competitors within the market equally able to neutralise risk without sacrificing the opportunities to be found in favourable markets, today's risk managers are finding that the advantages of currency options cannot be ignored.

Market participants who hedge with currency options range from the simplest one-person treasury to the "ultra-sophisticated" profit-orientated dealing room. All realise that the foreign exchange market can be too volatile to remain exposed and yet business may be too competitive to sacrifice opportunity. Thus, many financial organisations have responded to this need and have been extremely active in designing currency option strategies and products to meet various client needs. New and exotic currency option products are constantly being developed, enabling market providers to tailor currency option strategies to individual business or investment requirements.

The key advantage of using currency options for hedging, trading or investment purposes is the flexibility that they provide. Currency options allow their users to put a value on risk, which is an important aid in the process of making decisions on risk portfolio management. Flexibility is also a feature in terms of the number of currency pairs and the maturities available in the market today.

The basic principle of a currency option is a simple one. The holder has the right (but not the obligation) to transact and the writer has an obligation to transact should the holder wish to exercise. More complex currency option combinations and exotic currency options are based on these fundamental principles. The risk/reward implications of different currency option strategies are clearly definable.

In today's environment, individual risk appetites, market views and hedging objectives differ greatly. At the same time, there is a vast array of currency option structures and exotic currency option products available, which could be applied to any risk portfolio situation. In order for currency options to be integrated effectively, expectations, cost and risk mitigation priorities have to be kept in mind.

As the global market expands, so does the demand for currency options, not only in the major currency pairs of the world, but also in the more exotic currencies, especially as liquidity comes into those currencies in the spot and forward markets.

Index